Valuing Ecosystem Services

The Case of Multi-functional Wetlands

R. Kerry Turner, Stavros Georgiou and Brendan Fisher

publishing for a sustainable future
London • Sterling, VA

First published by Earthscan in the UK and USA in 2008

ISBN: 978-1-84407-615-4

Typeset by Domex e-data Pvt Ltd
Printed and bound in the UK by Cromwell Press, Trowbridge
Cover design by Yvonne Booth

For a full list of publications please contact:

Earthscan
Dunstan House
14a St Cross Street
London, EC1N 8XA, UK
Tel: +44 (0)20 7841 1930
Fax: +44 (0)20 7242 1474
Email: earthinfo@earthscan.co.uk
Web: **www.earthscan.co.uk**

22883 Quicksilver Drive, Sterling, VA 20166-2012, USA

Earthscan publishes in association with the International Institute for Environment and
Development

A catalogue record for this book is available from the British Library

Library of Congress Cataloging-in-Publication Data

Turner, R. Kerry (Robert Kerry)
  Valuing ecosystem services : the case of multi-functional wetlands / R. Kerry Turner,
Stavros Georgiou, and Brendan Fisher.
       p. cm.
  Includes bibliographical references.
  ISBN 978-1-84407-615-4 (hardback)
  1.   Wetland management–Economic aspects. 2.   Ecosystem management–Economic
aspects.   I. Georgiou, Stavros G. II. Fisher, Brendan. III. Title.
QH75.T874 2008
333.91'8–dc22

                                                        2008015717

The paper used for this book is FSC-certified and
totally chlorine-free. FSC (the Forest Stewardship
Council) is an international network to promote
responsible management of the world's forests.

Mixed Sources
Product group from well-managed
forests and other controlled sources
www.fsc.org Cert no. TT-COC-2082
© 1996 Forest Stewardship Council

Contents

List of Figures, Tables and Boxes

FIGURES

TABLES

BOX

Acknowledgements

The origins of this volume are linked to research sponsored by DEFRA, RSPB, ESRC and Leverhulme Trust in the UK, and the European Commission. Many colleagues have commented on the manuscript in its various forms or have allowed us to use some of their results. Particular thanks are due to Ian Bateman, David Hadley, Diane Burgess, Tom Crowards, Brett Day, Roy Brouwer, Matthew Zylstra, Rudolf DeGroot, Andrew Balmford, Rhys Green and Paul Morling. Karen Crockett has turned our amateur drafts into a professional manuscript with her usual patience and good humour.

List of Acronyms and Abbreviations

CBA	cost–benefit analysis
CDB	Convention on Biological Diversity
CITES	Convention on International Trade in Endangered Species
CM	choice modelling
CV	contingent valuation
CVM	Contingent Valuation Method
DEFRA	Department for Environment, Food and Rural Affairs
EMAP	Environmental Monitoring Assessment Programme
ESApp	Ecosystem Services Approach
ESRC	Economic and Social Research Council
GIS	geographical information systems
HGM	hydrogeomorphic method
HPM	Hedonic Price Method
IPCC	Intergovernmental Panel on Climate Change
MA	Millennium Assessment
MCA	multi-criteria analysis
NPV	net present value
NRM	natural resource management
OECD	Organisation for Economic Co-operation and Development
PES	payments for ecosystem services
RSPB	Royal Society for the Protection of Birds
SAC	Special Area of Conservation
SMS	safe minimum standards
SOC	social opportunity cost of capital
SPA	Special Protection Area
SRES	Special Report on Emissions Scenarios
SRTP	social rate of time preference
SSSI	Site of Special Scientific Interest
TCM	Travel Cost Method
TEV	total economic value
WET	Wetland Evaluation Technique
WTA	willingness to accept
WTP	willingness to pay

1
Introduction

Although natural ecosystems perform many services and are potentially very valuable, these values have often been ignored, with the result that degradation of ecosystems has occurred. The debate over what is the value of ecosystems, or of the environment and nature more generally, has highlighted the fact that the concept is complex and multidimensional. An economic perspective on ecosystems portrays them as natural assets providing a flow of goods and services, physical as well as aesthetic, intrinsic and moral. While it can be argued that biodiversity has intrinsic value in and of itself (either assigned by humans, or, more controversially, possessed regardless of human recognition), we do not accept as a consequence that allocation decisions involving environmental assets should be decided solely by non-economic means (O'Neil, 1997; Sagoff, 2004). Deliberative processes need not be seen as substitutes for economic cost–benefit analysis. The latter can better inform the former in a complementary relationship. We will set out what we call an Ecosystem Services Approach (ESApp) to the full appraisal of the role of ecosystem services in the economy and society.

The main problem when including the full range of ecosystem goods and services in economic choices is that many of these goods and services are not valued on markets. There is a gap between market valuation and the economic value of many ecosystem services. The non-marketed gaps must first be identified and then where possible monetized. In the case of many of the services, the identification of economically relevant services is of special importance, since over time those services not allocated by the market have continuously gained in significance as society has evolved.

The main objective of this book is to provide guidance on ESApp and the valuation of ecosystem services, using the case of multi-functional wetlands to illustrate and make recommendations regarding the methods and techniques that can be applied to appraise ecosystem management options. To this aim the book offers: a review of ESApp and ecosystem service valuation rationale, including their importance from both a policy and a project appraisal perspective; a useful reference when considering policy and appraisal of ecosystem management options; and ways in which legal obligations and other high-level management targets should be taken into account in valuation exercises, thus giving important policy context to the management options. Although concentrating on wetlands, the approaches suggested provide an assessment framework for other types of ecosystem assets.

The book is structured in the following way. Chapter 2 presents the relevant *conceptual background.* This covers the ecosystem services approach that provides the framework and linkages between ecosystems, their healthy functioning and the outcomes in terms of goods and services of benefit to human society. Chapter 3 then sets the valuation procedure within a range of possible policy contexts, and explores the correct procedures to adopt given the prevailing circumstances, that is, ecosystem conversion, ecosystem creation and ecosystem trade-offs. It also sets out the basis of socio-economic project, policy and programme appraisal and distinguishes between cost-effectiveness analysis, cost–benefit analysis and multi-criteria analysis. Chapters 4 and 5 provide guidelines on the *practical application* of the ecosystem services approach to the case of multi-functional wetlands. Chapter 6 describes a number of selective wetland case studies that outline the approach and the valuation techniques used in the previous sections. Finally we provide conclusions and an assessment of future prospects for the further deployment of the ecosystem services approach and its policy impact.

REFERENCES

O'Neil, J. (1997) 'Managing without prices: The monetary valuation of biodiversity'. *Ambio* 26: 546–550

Sagoff, M. (2004) *Price, Principle and the Environment.* Cambridge University Press: Cambridge

The Ecosystem Services Approach to Natural Resource Management

Historically, conservation rationales have been centred on scientific and/or ethical grounds. The founding of the world's first legislated national park, Yellowstone, was a function of preserving the 'wonders within'. Likewise, international agreements such as the Convention on International Trade in Endangered Species (CITES) and the Convention on Biological Diversity (CBD) invoke ethical arguments for saving the 'last of', as well as biological variation. Biodiversity and ecosystem conservation has more recently incorporated utilitarian arguments, such as biodiversity as an insurance policy against undesirable changes in ecosystem services. Moving from purely scientific and ethical conservation motivations, a whole range of utilitarian arguments have sprung up under the concept of ecosystem services. A massive undertaking in this realm was the UN's Millennium Ecosystem Assessment (MEA, 2005). This was the product of over 1300 scientists' input and was explicitly structured around the concept of ecosystem services as an attempt to fully integrate ecological sustainability, conservation and human welfare. But how did we get to ecosystem services?

Humanity is completely reliant upon nature for our welfare and survival. The history of civilization is, at its most basic, a story of people trying to find places where natural resources are abundant and protection from the elements is available. Around 10,000 years ago when we began to domesticate nature the story changed a bit as we were now harnessing nature's services more directly through husbandry and agriculture. Humankind has always recognized the importance of what we now call ecosystem services. The ancient Greeks saw how important soil retention was when deforestation led to thinning soils resulting in their eventual reliance on olive trees for income since these can persist in poor soils. The classic example is of the society on Easter Island where cultural beliefs led to complete deforestation precluding soil retention, water regulation and raw material provision for sea vessels (see Ponting, 1993). Jared Diamond's *Collapse: How Societies Choose or Fail to Succeed* (2005) painstakingly documents the collapse of several societies throughout history, and points to loss of habitat and the services supplied by ecosystems (including fish stocking, soil retention, biomass production and water regulation) as the key factors in their demise.

In the 20th century, key issues like deforestation, ozone depletion, fisheries collapses and climate change have galvanized scientific investigation and political movements on the role that well-functioning ecosystems have in supplying or improving human welfare. Two such examples are the collapse of cod stocks in the North Atlantic Ocean in the early 1990s and stratospheric depletion of ozone. The marine ecosystems responsible for continually providing cod to the US and western Europe since the 10th century could no longer function at the level of extraction and completely collapsed less than two decades ago. We consider this a loss of ecosystem functioning. Since humanity derived welfare benefits from this ecological process (i.e. fish), the provision of fish stocks from this area is considered an ecosystem service. In the other example, the release of chlorofluorocarbons, which were at one time considered to be a wonderful invention for their benign effect on environmental systems, caused a breakdown in the ecosystem service we could call atmospheric regulation. One human *disservice* caused by the breakdown of functioning would be the rise in skin cancer incidents in the southern hemisphere.

This strong and positive relationship between well-functioning ecosystems and human welfare is unquestioned. The two endpoints are connected by what we are now calling ecosystem services. In this book we take a systematic look at

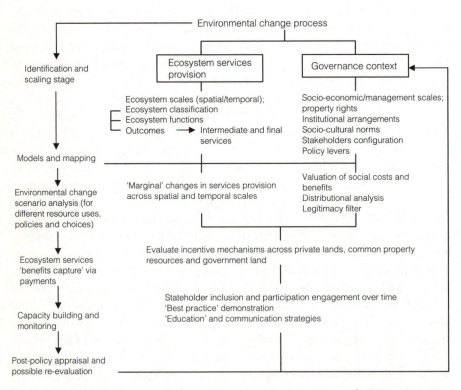

Figure 2.1 *Framework for an Ecosystem Services Approach (ESApp)*

what ecosystem services are; the roles of biodiversity and human agents in providing and appropriating them; how mapping can aid effective management decisions; and the importance of integrating policy-oriented science into a common methodology for ecosystem service evaluation. All these investigations can be integrated under a common approach that we are calling an Ecosystem Services Approach (ESApp). We argue that investigations of ecosystem services will require a systems approach from concept definition through compensation mechanisms to post-policy appraisal (Figure 2.1). A key aspect is a 'closed loop' structure, starting with biophysical research and closing with policy appraisal. Using Figure 2.1 as a guide, illustrating the ESApp is the purpose of this chapter.

Ecosystem services defined

Before we can talk about an ecosystem services approach we need to understand precisely what ecosystem services are. In the literature, there seems to be a consensus on a *general* meaning of ecosystem services. A few definitions in the literature are repeatedly cited (Costanza et al, 1997; Daily, 1997; MEA, 2005). The Millennium Assessment (MA) (MEA, 2005) defines ecosystem services as 'the benefits people obtain from ecosystems and divides ecosystem services into supporting, regulating, provisioning and cultural services'. This definition is general by design and, while it provides a context for discussion, it falls short as an operative definition. Despite the proliferation of interest in ecosystem services there have been relatively few attempts to define the concept clearly to make it operational (de Groot et al, 2002; Boyd and Banzhaf, 2007). Our position is that there is no single classification system for ecosystem services that is appropriate for use in all cases. In fact, a classification system should be informed by (1) the characteristics of the ecosystem or phenomena under investigation; and (2) the decision making context for which ecosystem services are being considered. We believe that there needs to be a clear and consistent definition of what ecosystem services are. This is because a functional definition, widely agreed upon, would allow for meaningful comparisons across different projects, policy contexts, time and space. Such a definition would also provide us with boundaries for the characteristics we are interested in. For example, if we use the MA definition, that is, benefits to humans, then the characteristics in focus include things outside ecological systems, such as imputed cultural and/or symbolic meanings. However, if ecosystem services are defined as ecological phenomena, as we propose in this book, then the characteristics we are interested in are characteristics of ecological systems only. Some of the identified characteristics, along with the decision context for mobilizing ecosystem services, will inform an appropriate classification system for use.

Drawing on Boyd and Banzhaf, we propose that *ecosystem services are the aspects of ecosystems consumed and/or utilized to produce human well-being*. Defined this way, ecosystem services include ecosystem organization (structure), operation (process) and outflows, as all are consumed or utilized by humanity either directly or indirectly.

The study of ecosystems has always demanded a systems approach or holistic view in order to truly understand operation and process (Allen and Starr, 1982). Investigating ecosystem services will require the same level of systemic insight, and whether they are consumed directly (raw materials) or indirectly (nutrient cycling) the key points of the definition (i.e. ecological components and connection to human welfare) are satisfied. Despite calling for this encompassing definition, it is also important to delineate between direct consumption and indirect utilization of ecosystem services. This will be important for valuation as well as for any natural capital accounting systems. In the ESApp we designate services to be either *intermediate* or *final* with human welfare benefits flowing from these final services. Figure 2.2 illustrates this delineation. For example, when considering the human benefit (i.e. product) of wild fruits, food provision is the final service and pollination an intermediate service.

This delineation is not strict as services are often a function of the beneficiary's perspective (Boyd, 2007). For example, water regulation services provided by vegetated landscape might be valued as a final service to someone interested in steady water supply, but valued as an intermediate service to someone interested in a final service of clean water for the benefit of drinking water. In this way the ESApp differs from the MA and its typology of supporting, regulating, provisioning and cultural services. While these categories undoubtedly offer strong heuristic value they can lead to confusion when trying to operationalize (either through accounting systems or for valuation purposes) ecosystem services. For example, nutrient cycling is a supporting service in the MA, water regulation is a regulating service, and recreation is a cultural service. However, all three could be referring to the same benefit that humans are concerned with, such as clean water. In accounting systems, valuation exercises

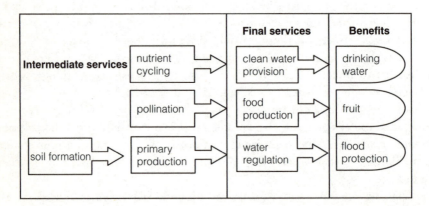

Figure 2.2 *Relationships among intermediate services, final services and benefits*

and policy decisions we are most often concerned with benefits, and therefore a more transparent method for evaluation is simply to consider the system in terms of intermediate services, final services and benefits. Given this schema we know only to add up, value or weigh the benefits for comparison.

Additionally, just as discrete ecosystems can deliver several ecosystem services, ecosystem processes can provide multiple benefits for human welfare. These are considered 'joint products'. Figure 2.3 is a simplified linear schematic of this situation. Water regulation is an ecosystem process (intermediate service) – simply an automatic operation of an ecosystem. As an ecosystem process, water regulation provides for final ecosystem services such as storm protection, improving water quality and extending water provision as a time delay, that is providing a regulated hydrologic flow. This third final service is similar to municipal water systems where the user pays for the water used, as well as a premium to guarantee that service continues reliably, where both are beneficial services.

As we argued earlier, the decision context for utilizing ecosystem service research is also crucial for mobilizing the ecosystem services concept. Our primary focus in this volume is the valuation of ecosystem services and our classification approach has been formulated with this context in mind. But other contexts may be the focus of attention and require other classification schemes.

One decision context for utilizing the concept of ecosystem services might be to promote understanding and to educate a larger public about the services and benefits that well-functioning ecosystems provide to humans. This was a major focus of the MA and its classification scheme was fit for purpose. The MA divided ecosystem services into a few very understandable categories – supporting services, regulating services, provisioning services and cultural services. This classification utilized the complexity characteristic of ecosystems and the public–private good dynamic to draw distinct boundaries of different ecosystem services. For example, by acknowledging the many interconnections among ecosystem components and processes, the MA classification placed supporting service as an underpinning to

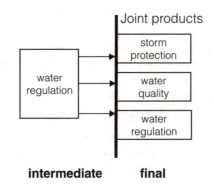

Figure 2.3 *An example of joint products stemming from a single ecosystem process*

the other service categories. This in turn makes their classification readily accessible as a heuristic – one of the key goals of the MA.

Another way to classify ecosystem services would be to use their spatial characteristics. This might be appropriate if the decision context was how to manage a given landscape for the provision of ecosystem services. In this case, it is important for the manager to know what services are provided on the landscape and how these services flow across that landscape. The European Union's Habitats and Water Framework Directive is taking such a tack by incorporating spatio-temporal characteristics of natural system into policy solutions. Utilizing the spatial characteristics a classification scheme might involve categories that describe relationships between service production and where the benefits are realized. Such a classification might include categories such as:

- *in situ* – where the services are provided and the benefits are realized in the same location;
- *omnidirectional* – where the services are provided in one location, but benefit the surrounding landscape without directional bias;
- *directional* – where the service provision benefits a specific location due to the flow direction.

A classification scheme as such could also use scale qualifiers, such as local omnidirectional (e.g. pollination), and regional direction (flood protection). Understanding the distribution of services and benefits as well as the landscape (or seascape) where the services are provided informs where management interventions should be concentrated. Classifying ecosystem services in this way recognizes such characteristics as the spatio-temporal dynamics of ecosystems and benefit dependence of services. This distributional classification can also highlight the possibility of cases where beneficiaries might have to compensate providers, such as in *payments for environmental services* schemes.

Through the economic concept of an externality – where the action of one agent brings about an inadvertent gain or loss to another without payment or compensation – economists have long been interested in the effects that changes in environmental quality can have on welfare. The work of Alfred Marshall and A.C. Pigou in the late 19th and early 20th centuries on externalities and common property problems laid early foundations for the future of environmental economics. With regard to ecosystem services, one person's harvesting of timber may preclude another person's benefit of bush meat due to declining habitat. The linked effect that the human economy has on the environment and that the environment has on the human economy is difficult to assess since the externalities reverberate throughout complex social and ecological systems (Crocker and Tschirhart, 1992). Dynamic modelling of complex systems can help to identify unintended consequences of these linked systems (Finnoff and Tschirhart, 2003).

In light of externalities and distribution issues, one possibly important classification scheme considers the decision context of how ecosystem services relate to equity in the provision of human welfare. This is important as it is now well accepted that failing environmental quality disproportionately affects people more marginalized by the market economy (Dasgupta, 2002). The decision context might be a government interested in measuring how the natural environment distributes and provides services and consequent benefits across their constituents. This is made complex by the fact that stakeholders at different spatial scales have different interests in ecosystem services (Hein et al, 2006). For example, the benefits people receive from existence values of biodiversity might conflict with benefits impoverished people receive from converting biologically diverse habitats, where poverty and species diversity have been shown to be highly correlated (Fisher and Christopher, 2007). In this decision context several characteristics are important for consideration – including the public–private goods aspect, spatio-temporal dynamic and how services are benefit-specific. Linking these characteristics to the decision context, that is fulfilling human needs and wants to a somewhat hierarchical classification, is found in Wallace (2007). Here an ecosystem service classification starts with basic needs – which Wallace labels adequate resources. Other categories include protection from predators, disease, parasites; benign physical and chemical environment; and socio-cultural fulfilment. Dividing services in this way across a landscape can provide decision makers with information about at what level people's needs are being met by ecosystems and their services.

THE ECOSYSTEM SERVICES APPROACH

Identification and scaling stage

Understanding the concept of ecosystem services, and how intermediate services, final services and benefits all interrelate, lays the building blocks for a systematic investigation of the link between ecosystems and human welfare. The ESApp requires a range of scientific experts, social scientists, stakeholders and decision-makers (Figure 2.1). In broad strokes the ESApp requires biophysical understanding of how and where services are generated; where and in what terms the benefits are realized; what level of value the services provide; how ecosystems are governed; what options there are for compensating providers of public goods and in what ways services flows and values are likely to change under different management and utilization scenarios. In addition to these aspects, the ESApp also inherently incorporates stakeholder involvement and capacity building. Policy recommendation and post-policy appraisal are further vital elements of the ESApp.

The first step in the ESApp is really a scoping stage. Researchers must identify the ecosystem services of interest and understand a range of characteristics about these services including:

- the spatial and temporal scales at which they operate;
- the different services of the ecosystem(s) in question;
- the outcomes in terms of intermediate and final services and benefits;
- the social and economic aspects involved in managing and governing the system;
- socio-cultural norms, stakeholder identities and existent policy mechanisms.

Once this 'identification and scaling stage' is complete then the ESApp necessitates an in-depth mapping and modelling phase.

Models and mapping

Despite our knowledge gaps on the functional roles of biodiversity, our ability to model ecosystem organization and operation is growing appreciably. This understanding provides the foundational insight for the ESApp. Basic scoping models can help to understand the patterns of ecosystem processes as well as identify the nesting and overlapping of systems and processes. Detailed data-driven process models yield quantitative insights into the functioning of the system and can highlight system drivers and sensitivities.

These biophysical characteristics determine the spatial distribution of ecosystem services. The location for services creation and where the benefits are received are not always identical. In fact there is a variety of ways in which provision units and benefit units vary in space. In some cases both the service provision and benefit occur at the same location (e.g. soil formation, provision of raw materials). Some services are provided omnidirectionally, that is the service provision unit provides benefits to the surrounding landscape (e.g. pollination, carbon sequestration). In some cases services are provided with a specific directional flow. For example, down slope areas benefit from services provided in uphill areas for services like water regulation services provided by forested slopes. Another example of this is the service provision of coastal wetlands providing storm and flood protection to the coastline and interior.

By mapping ecosystem services we can gain insight on where scarce funds can be used to optimize biodiversity or ecosystem service conservation or human welfare. Previous mapping exercises have demonstrated several insights such as where cost–benefit outcomes can be optimized (Balmford et al, 2003; Naidoo and Ricketts, 2006) where different taxa overlap; and correlations between alternative conservation assessments (Brooks et al, 2006). Also, by understanding the biophysical aspects of ecosystem service provision and how the benefits are realized we can use economic valuation techniques to apply an economic value to the services provided. Economic valuation techniques are discussed throughout this volume, and also in Appendix A. For conceptualizing the ESApp it is important to know that these values can be mapped across a landscape depending on where and how the benefits from ecosystem services are distributed and realized spatially.

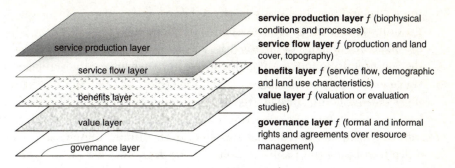

Figure 2.4 *Mapping layers integral to the ESApp*

In addition to the biophysical modelling, service mapping and valuation, governance systems must also be identified spatially. The various spatial and temporal scales at which governance operates means that understanding overlaps and gaps is crucial for successful ecosystem management. Governance represents both formal and informal systems of rights, regulations and arrangements. These can range from informal stakeholder agreements to international institutional arrangements. Additionally, a spatial understanding of governance and ecosystem service provision is an essential step for developing effective and fair compensation mechanisms (discussed below).

The governance dimension gives rise to several practical challenges. First of all there is typically a mismatch of the spatial and temporal scales at which ecosystems and political systems operate (Carpenter et al, 2006). The processes that are responsible for the provision of ecosystem services operate on scales from microscopic (nutrient exchange) to global (climate regulation). Picture any political boundary and you can imagine ecosystem services where either their provision or their use migrates over that boundary. Ecosystems such as the Amazon River Basin contribute services to not only the six countries that it encompasses, but globally. Governing for efficient and equitable allocation of these services would require an incredible amount of international cooperation and compensation. Temporally, governance systems vary from ancient community management norms to brief formal government terms lasting only a few years. The temporary nature of political tenure creates another hurdle to sustainable management.

Figure 2.4 shows how the mapping and modelling stage provides researchers with a series of maps that can be overlaid to get a holistic view of the system under investigation.

Environmental change scenario analysis

Once we understand how the system works in its current state we need to be able to identify changes in the system in terms of services, benefits and operation under different possible futures. By comparing the current system outcomes with alternative futures the ESApp can provide valuable input to policy decisions. This can be done using *scenario analysis*. Scenarios are plausible and consistent descriptions of the future that aid in forecasting and predictive analysis. Scenarios are not state predictions themselves, but rather they are typically qualitative storylines bolstered with some degree of quantitative data (Turner, 2005). The fundamental underpinning of scenarios is that the future is uncertain, so the goal is to develop plausible but distinct storylines of the future. By creating these storylines (*a priori*) it is possible to follow them logically through the system under investigation so that analyses of trade-offs among alternative futures and different policies are possible. Scenario analysis typically starts with broadscale or global drivers and suggests how these impact local drivers and the system state, and suggests policy responses. The scenarios of the Intergovernmental Panel on Climate Change's (IPCC) Special Report on Emissions Scenarios (SRES) and the MA's scenarios (Global Orchestration, Order from Strength, Adapting Mosaic, TechnoGarden) are two such examples.

Under the ESApp, scenario building would move from the qualitative storyline at the global scale and drive more quantitative regional and local situations. Depending on the scale of interest the scenarios provide information to test for a range of policy options. Figure 2.5 shows how scenario analysis is integrated into the ESApp, as the system of interest is analysed under the different scenarios. For each scenario (Future I and Future II) the landscape changes in regard to its service provision, flow, beneficiaries, valuation and perhaps its governance. For example, imagine that the current state of an agro-forestry landscape mosaic is represented by the series of maps labelled 'Current'. Imagine 'Future I' to be a scenario developed to look at how these maps change if we increase the amount of land under large-scale monocropping and 'Future II' to represent a sustainable forestry focused future. In these two scenarios the Current provision, distribution and value of ecosystem services will change in very different ways. Considering these changes can help decision makers formulate policies that suit the needs of their constituents.

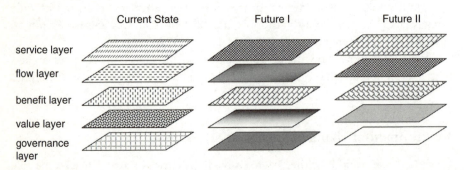

Figure 2.5 *The integration of mapping exercises and scenario analysis*

Ecosystem services 'benefits capture'

After the modelling and mapping stages, the valuation exercises and scenario analysis can provide additional spatially explicit layers to give further insight into which stakeholders gain or lose under different ecosystem states and forecasts. For fair allocation of benefits, 'users' will have to compensate 'providers' and because of the public goods aspect of ecosystem services this will have to be activated through some institutional (formal or informal) structure. This is where research on governance associated with ecosystems and natural resources becomes integral to the ESApp. When we understand the governance structures, or their absence, we can design successful compensation mechanisms to ensure sustainable ecosystem service provision and fair allocation of the benefits. This fair allocation of benefits – ecosystem services for users and compensation for providers – is what we consider *benefits capture*.

There are several currently operational mechanisms for benefits capture. Market-based mechanisms are becoming increasingly popular to achieve conservation goals and are already being used to compensate providers of ecosystem services. Instruments currently being used include taxes and user fees on undesirable behaviours, as well as payment and subsidies for desirable behaviours. Examples of the former include licensing for logging, fishing and hunting; harvesting taxes; and user fees on public lands.

A currently popular price-based instrument is the so-called *payments for ecosystem services* (PES). This approach has been recommended particularly for use in non-OECD countries, where regulatory and taxation systems are likely to be weak. In these schemes landowners are compensated for providing services that previously were uncompensated. The Mexican government has such a system to pay landowners for conserving forest in catchments important for hydrologic flows (Pagiola et al, 2005). The best-known payment scheme is Costa Rica's, which was established in 1995 and compensates landowners for carbon sequestration, water regulation services, biodiversity and scenic beauty provision. The measurement proxy is area of land forested and payments are around US$45/ha/yr.

The other general approach for compensating ecosystem service provision, or conservation in general, utilizes quantity-based instruments. These mechanisms are predicated upon an institution that sets a target quantity. Setting this quantity or scale creates a scarcity and therefore encourages more efficient allocation. Quantity-based instruments include marketable permits, such as tradable fishing quotas, and market credits, such as carbon credits and wetland banks. The quantity-based approach is quite a common policy prescription, from use in the United States to ensure no net loss of wetlands (Whigham, 1999) to fishing quotas in Canada and New Zealand (Dewees, 1998) to carbon markets considered in the Clean Development Mechanisms under Kyoto.

Despite the popularity and increasing theoretical and empirical investigation of compensation mechanisms for ecosystem service provision, a number of not so trivial obstacles exist for successful implementation. These include the difficulty of establishing property rights when necessary; being able to observe actual behaviour and measure and verify outcomes; linking payments directly to desired outcomes and not some proxy outcome; getting prices correct; overcoming cultural disjoints and equity concerns; mitigating externalizing behaviour and 'hotspots'; and financing the mechanisms. (See Box 2.1 for further description of these limitations.)

Another obstacle to implementing a benefits capture mechanism is the difficulty of moving from the current state (i.e. with extant welfare reducing behaviour) to the desired state envisioned as the goal of the mechanism. For example, how does the global community go from a world of high deforestation rates to a world without deforestation? We can imagine a payment system where the global community compensates tropical countries for reducing their deforestation rate. However, this penalizes countries who have had historically low deforestation rates, or encourages them to increase deforestation until the mechanism becomes operational, so that they can gain from future deforestation rate decreases. The example points to the mismatch between the mechanism incentives and the long-term goal. To satisfy some long-term goals we can imagine encountering incredible inertia in the present system, and therefore mechanisms will have to consider both short- and long-term components. Once again, stemming global deforestation rates will require a mechanism that allows incremental changes in behaviour (short-term) towards some more stringent long-term objective. In this way it should be practical, in the short term, for countries with historically high deforestation rates to be included in any such mechanism, and for countries with historically low deforestation rates, if they choose some moderate level of ecosystem conversion for national welfare improvements, to avoid penalization.

BOX 2.1 OBSTACLES TO MARKET-BASED CONSERVATION MECHANISMS

Property rights

The establishment of property or assignment rights over the good or service being provided is often necessary, but seldom easy. Designating who 'owns' resources such as wetlands, or who has the 'rights' to utilize the waste absorption capacity of the atmosphere is fraught with governance and equity issues. Without property rights, incentives to invest (divest) in sustainable (unsustainable) actions often do not exist, and free-riding is likely.

Measuring and monitoring

The ability to measure and monitor service provision is not straightforward with public or common pool resources. Individual behaviour might not be observable as it might take place in hinterlands, or the service might not lend itself to measuring, such as with pollination services.

Directly linking behaviour and compensation

In connection with the difficulties of measuring and monitoring ecosystem service provision direct links between service provision and compensation might not be possible and therefore allow defection. If we are interested in biodiversity provision, it might be impossible to measure and monitor the service directly and therefore we might use forested area as a proxy. In this case, we might easily achieve the proxy goal without the associated biodiversity goal (e.g. pressures from hunting could hinder the latter, but not affect the proxy).

Correct pricing

For price-based mechanisms, finding the correct price level to incentivize ecosystem service provision is not likely to be straightforward. For payment schemes, the payments would need to cover an agent's opportunity cost, but this is not always easy to elicit and the incentive exists for agents to overstate their opportunity cost. In Costa Rica the lands under payment contracts are more likely to be on steep slopes and inaccessible, suggesting that the buyer is overpaying. Information costs may be prohibitive.

Cultural hurdles

Price and quantity-based mechanisms assume to some degree that a market institutional set-up is common. In some places, assigning property rights to individuals or offering payments for expected behaviours may not be common practice or even acceptable (Adams et al, 2003). In several cases it has been shown that the price incentive is not always effective in changing behaviour (Gowdy and Erickson, 2005).

Externalizing

Conservation is often in danger of pushing deleterious activities to peripheries or at times to particular 'hot spots'. Additionally, the translocation of services, such as wetlands banking, is unlikely to guarantee the same quality of services (Salzman and Ruhl, 2006).

Monitoring, capacity building and post-policy appraisal

Effective, fair and sustainable ecosystem service provision will require scale-appropriate governance capacity and frequent monitoring. For some services local and regional knowledge of ecosystem processes will be high. In these cases the ability to design and implement solutions may already exist, such as with some pasture lands in Mongolia or Nepalese irrigation systems (Ostrom et al, 1999). However, in many cases education and capacity building from local to national and international scales will be necessary. Such is the current case with managing the climate regulation services of the earth's atmosphere. Cases like this will require coordination of science, policy, institutions and all concerned stakeholders. Several challenges exist including transboundary service provision and use, difficulty in measuring services, and difficulties in creating effective governance and compensation mechanisms (see Box 2.1). Any ESApp will recognize the importance of stakeholder inclusion, capacity building, and monitoring for outcomes throughout the research or project programme. These are not steps to be tacked on at the end, but must be integrated throughout for successful and sustainable outcomes. An example is the conservation of cloud forest for hydrologic flows in Loma Alta, Ecuador by incorporating stakeholder knowledge and concerns and providing scientific capacity (Becker, 2003).

Post-policy appraisal and re-evaluation

Finally, in addition to the challenges posed by monitoring, capacity building, and coordination, there is little guarantee that even well-informed and cooperative policy solutions will produce the desired outcomes. Post-policy and post-project appraisal is seldom undertaken in conservation spheres, and conservation initiatives have historically lacked robust quantitative evaluations of their performance despite their importance for informing future policy and funding decisions (Ferraro and Pattanayak, 2006). Information, institutional and market failures will all affect ecosystem service provision, and without post-policy appraisal we could follow costly prescriptions without the assumed associated benefits. The importance of monitoring and post-project appraisal deems that the policy role of the scientist (or integration to the policy process) is essential for an ESApp. In the next section we take a closer look at different policy contexts involving ecosystem services valuation and management.

REFERENCES

Adams, W.M., Brockington, D., Dyson, J. and Vira, B. (2003) 'Managing tragedies: Understanding conflict over common pool resources'. *Science* 302(5652): 1915–1916

Allen, T. and Starr, T.B. (1982) *Hierarchy: Perspectives for Ecological Complexity*. University of Chicago Press: Chicago

Balmford, A., Gaston, K.J., Blyth, S., James, A. and Kapos, V. (2003) 'Global variation in terrestrial conservation costs, conservation benefits, and unmet conservation needs'. *Proceedings of the National Academy of Sciences of the United States of America* 100(3): 1046–1050

Becker, C.D. (2003) 'Grassroots to grassroots: Why forest preservation was rapid at Loma Alta, Ecuador'. *World Development* 31(1): 163–176

Boyd, J. (2007) 'Nonmarket benefits of nature: What should be counted in green GDP?' *Ecological Economics* 61(4): 716–723

Boyd, J. and Banzhaf, S. (2007) 'What are ecosystem services? The need for standardized environmental accounting units'. *Ecological Economics* 63(2–3): 616–626

Brooks, T.M., Mittermeier, R.A., da Fonseca, G.A.B., Gerlach, J., Hoffmann, M., Lamoreux, J.F., Mittermeier, C.G., Pilgrim, J.D. and Rodrigues, A.S.L. (2006) 'Global biodiversity conservation priorities'. *Science* 313(5783): 58–61

Carpenter, S.R., Defries, R., Dietz, T., Mooney, H.A., Polasky, S., Reid, W.V. and Scholes, R.J. (2006) 'Millennium ecosystem assessment: Research needs'. *Science* 31, 4(5797): 257–258

Costanza, R., d'Arge, R., de Groot, R., Farber, S., Grasso, M., Hannon, B., Limburg, K., Naeem, S., O'Neill, R.V., Paruelo, J., Raskin, R.G., Sutton, P. and van den Belt, M. (1997) 'The value of the world's ecosystem services and natural capital'. *Nature* 387: 253–260

Crocker, T.D. and Tschirhart, J. (1992) 'Ecosystems, externalities and economics'. *Environment and Resource Economics* 2: 551–567

Daily, G.C. (1997) *Nature's Services: Societal Dependence on Natural Ecosystems*. Island Press: Washington DC

Dasgupta, P. (2002) *Economic Development, Environmental Degradation and the Persistence of Deprivation in Poor Countries*. World Summit on Sustainable Development: Johannesburg

Dewees, C.M. (1998) 'Effects of individual quota systems on New Zealand and British Columbia fisheries'. *Ecological Applications* 8(1): S133–S138

Diamond, J. (2005) *Collapse: How Societies Choose to Fail or Succeed*. Viking: New York, p592

Ferraro, P.J. and Pattanayak, S.K. (2006) 'Money for nothing? A call for empirical evaluation of biodiversity conservation investments'. *PLoS Biology* 4(4): 482–488

Finnoff, D. and Tschirhart, J. (2003) 'Harvesting in an eight-species ecosystem'. *Journal of Environmental Economics and Management* 45: 589–611

Fisher, B. and Christopher, T. (2007) 'Poverty and Biodiversity: Measuring the overlap of human poverty and biodiversity hotspots'. *Ecological Economics* 62: 93–101

Gowdy, J. and Erickson, J. (2005) 'Ecological economics at a crossroads'. *Ecological Economics* 53(1): 17–20

Groot, R.S. de, Wilson, M.A. and Boumans, R.M.J. (2002) 'A typology for the classification, description and valuation of ecosystem functions, goods and services'. *Ecological Economics* 41: 393–408

Hein, L., Van Koppen, K., de Groot, R.S. and van Ierland, E.C. (2006) 'Spatial scales, stakeholders and the valuation of ecosystem services'. *Ecological Economics* 57(2): 209–228

MEA (UN Millennium Ecosystem Assessment) (2005) *Millennium Ecosystem Assessment*. Washington DC: Island Press

Naidoo, R. and Ricketts, T.H. (2006) 'Mapping the economic costs and benefits of conservation'. *PLoS Biology* 4(11): 2153–2164

Ostrom, E., Burger, J., Field, C.B., Norgaard, R.B. and Policansky, D. (1999) 'Sustainability – revisiting the commons: Local lessons, global challenges'. *Science*, 284(5412): 278–282

Pagiola, S., Arcenas, A. and Platais, G. (2005) 'Can payments for environmental services help reduce poverty? An exploration of the issues and the evidence to date from Latin America'. *World Development* 33(2): 237–253

Ponting, C. (1993) *A Green History of the World*. Penguin Books: London

Salzman, J. and Ruhl, J. (2006) 'No net loss – instrument choice in wetlands protection'. In Freeman, J. and Kolstad, C. (eds) *Moving to Markets in Environmental Regulation: Twenty Years of Experience*. Oxford University Press: Oxford

Turner, R.K. (2005) 'Integrated environmental assessment and coastal futures'. In Vermaat, J., Bouwer, L., Turner, R.K. and Salomons, W. (eds) *Managing European Coasts: Past, Present and Future*. Springer: Berlin

Wallace, K.J. (2007) 'Classification of ecosystem services: Problems and solutions'. *Biological Conservation* 139: 235–246

Whigham, D.F. (1999) 'Ecological issues related to wetland preservation, restoration, creation and assessment'. *Science of the Total Environment* 240(1–3): 31–40

3

Policy Appraisal Perspectives and Socio-economic Appraisal Approaches

POLICY CONTEXTS

In this section we first highlight the complications generated by the precise policy context in which ecosystem services valuation is taking place and the implications for the level of detail subsequently required in the assessment process. We then outline the main approaches that can be used to undertake socio-economic appraisal within the overall ESApp. The UK, for example, has adopted a broad minimum standard of 'no net loss' of biodiversity within the context of its international commitment to conserve biological diversity, its own nature conservation measures and relevant EU Directives.

It is therefore important, before embarking on the actual appraisal exercise, to set out a range of possible policy contexts (with an increasing data and expert knowledge cost burden) within which ecosystem valuation may be required, for example:

- Contexts in which ecosystems maybe destroyed and all services are lost – this presents a relatively straightforward valuation problem in which the ecosystem's conservation benefits are compared with the benefits (or forgone opportunity costs) of the development option.
- Contexts in which ecosystems are degraded, such that partial service loss is incurred – a more complex valuation problem involving more scientific data and economic value interdependencies; valuation is complicated by the fact that ecosystems are characterized by multiple, interdependent services that possibly exhibit complex dynamics and discontinuities around critical thresholds (Limburg et al, 2002; Holmes et al, 2004). So a decision is needed about whether to value a *set* of ecosystem services holistically, via a contingent valuation study for example, or whether to focus valuation on trade-offs between specific services, via attribute-based stated preference or other methods (Holmes and Adamowicz, 2003).
- Contexts in which new ecosystems are created – the difficulty over valuation will depend on how simple or complex, in terms of services provided, the new ecosystem is supposed to be.

- Contexts in which ecosystems are converted and replaced with 'functionally equivalent' created ecosystems – a more complex valuation problem that requires cost estimates for ecosystem construction/restoration and estimates of time lag costs, that is the social benefits forgone in the time taken for a newly created ecosystem to gain functional equivalency with the established site.
- Contexts in which existing ecosystems need to be prioritized in order to allow trade-off decisions – requires full evaluation procedure.
- Contexts in which one or more ecosystem services need to be prioritized or traded-off, both within individual ecosystems or across ecosystems – requires full evaluation procedure.

The type of economic valuation method that needs to be applied will depend first and foremost on the type of environmental change that is the focus of attention. Figure 3.1 sets out a simple schema which categorizes damage impacts under two main headings – damage to replaceable and irreplaceable ecosystems. It is then necessary to distinguish between marginal damage, which affects part of an ecosystem or one or more services, and non-marginal damage, which removes an entire ecosystem. Finally, the damage impact needs to be split into temporary and permanent types. The figure then shows which type of valuation method, market-based or surrogate/shadow pricing, needs to be deployed; or whether a standards and regulations approach is more appropriate. In the latter case such standards still need to be 'costed' in terms of opportunity costs forgone when ecosystem conservation is the *a priori* chosen option. We discuss the various valuation techniques and the economic valuation of particular services and corresponding outputs later.

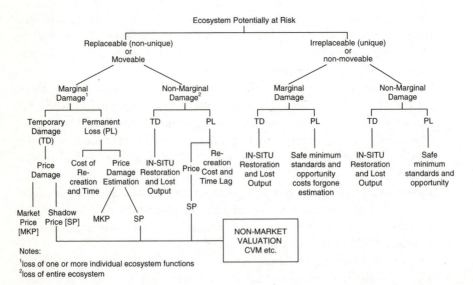

Figure 3.1 *Ecosystem damages and valuation*

Clearly the level of complexity is related to how the prevailing regulations and legislation are interpreted, for example, how a 'no net loss' or 'net gain' ecosystem policy objective is actually pursued in practice. It has been assumed here that the ecosystem assessment that could be adopted would represent an initial incremental step forward from existing appraisal practice and not a full blown ESApp 'expert assessment' system. Another complication, which is related to the institutional arrangements operating at any given time or place (designations on nature conservation or other grounds, environmental regulations, legislation and custom and practice), centres around the problem of reflecting rarity/endangered habitats or cultural/symbolic significance and so on in any ecosystem assessment system. For present purposes it is assumed that the existing nature designations process adequately reflects rarity and other characteristics of ecosystems.

Finally, from an economic efficiency perspective, it is unclear whether any decision to rely on mitigation ecosystem procedures (if established ecosystems are converted) incurs less social cost than conserving the established site. Ecosystem creation costs and time lag costs will tend to increase in line with the complexities and difficulties posed by the substitution of one or more ecosystem services. On economic grounds, it is clear that ecosystem conservation should be chosen if the substitution costs exceed the forgone opportunity costs of development (Gutrich and Hitzhusen, 2004).

Where an ecosystem is under pressure from human activity that provides measurable economic benefits to society, it will be necessary to illustrate the economic value of the final services provided by the ecosystem. The provision of such economic information is essential if an efficient level of ecosystem resource conservation, restoration or re-creation is to be determined. Maintaining an ecosystem will rarely be entirely costless. There will be costs associated with forgoing other uses of the land or with limiting activities which might impinge upon the ability of the ecosystem to continue functioning. Hence the importance of making explicit the value of the multiple services that ecosystems perform, and of assessing this value within a framework that allows comparison with the gains to be made from activities that might threaten ecosystems. This should serve not only to better protect these threatened ecosystems but also to improve decision making for the benefit of society. Economic valuation is therefore a logical extension to any assessment of the services performed by ecosystems for the purpose of public decision making.

EXISTING SOCIO-ECONOMIC APPRAISAL APPROACHES

The main approaches, which can form the methodological basis for strategic socio-economic option appraisal, are (see Figure 3.2):

- cost-effectiveness analysis;

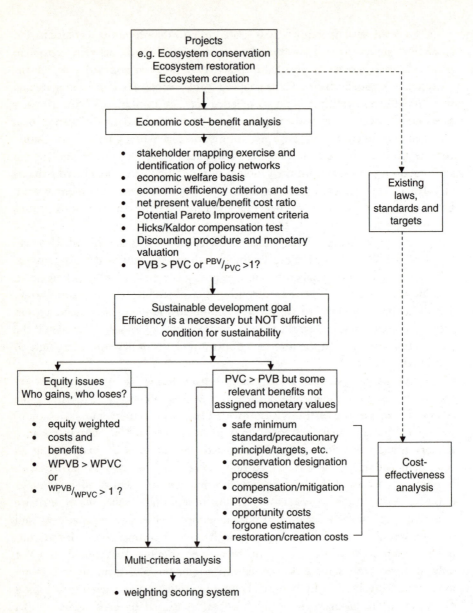

Figure 3.2 *Project appraisal framework CBA+MCA*

- cost–benefit analysis;
- multi-criteria analysis.

Figure 3.2 (which should be read vertically from top to bottom) summarizes the thinking behind the 'cost–benefit' approach to ecosystem conservation versus development wetlands policy appraisal. The analysis begins with an economic efficiency analysis of the gains and losses involved and a time horizon over which these costs and benefits will be incurred. An adjustment is made (discounting) to account for the assumption that future costs and benefits are valued less highly than more immediate costs and benefits. This analysis is then subjected to a sustainability filter, which introduces other decisions criteria such as equity (i.e. who gains or loses in society or environmental significance, rarity, etc.). The former criterion (efficiency) requires that the costs and benefits are assigned weights and the latter (sustainability) that standards or regulations could be imposed to enforce conservation status and maintain ecosystem diversity. The imposition of such environmental standards should itself be subject to a cost-effectiveness exercise to determine 'value for money' outcomes. Finally, in complex ecosystem/policy contexts a formal multi-criteria analysis (MCA) might be deployed to assess options on the basis of a number of criteria. MCAs all require some forms of weighting and scoring systems to be applied to the different impacts that are involved in the ecosystem change context. The key point here is that CBA as a generic framework and economic efficiency analysis, cost-effectiveness analysis and MCA need not be substitutes for each other. They are complementary and should be deployed as necessary (given precise policy circumstances) within the overall strategy set out in Figure 3.2.

Usually all the analytical approaches will involve some form of *stakeholder analysis* – in that they can involve stakeholders at a number of different points within the appraisal process. Stakeholders could for example be involved in the setting of management objectives, or in the determination of values. Deciding how stakeholders should be involved is thus a key issue, together with the identification of the linkages between stakeholders, government and other official agencies (i.e. the prevailing policy networks).

Suggested changes in management practices of the resource, arising within national and international environmental regulation, may reduce or reinforce conflicts between the various interests involved. Trying to satisfy all interest groups will often be difficult. From a policy point of view how these interests can be balanced in the best possible way is important. In order to be able to do that, insight is needed into what the various interests in the resource are, who the stakeholders are and what the distribution of the positive and negative effects of changes in management regimes will be.

The economic component of assessment consists of the identification and economic valuation of these positive and negative effects, that is the costs and benefits, that will arise with the proposed management option and their comparison with the situation as it would be without the option. The difference is the incremental net benefit arising from the project investment. CBA is one of the evaluation tools used by economists to determine whether a policy, project or action is economically efficient. Its principle feature is that all the pros and cons of a project, if technically possible, including social, socio-cultural and historical contexts that surround a particular value gain/loss, are translated into monetary terms. As a rule, a project is efficient if total benefits exceed total costs.

An important element of any assessment should be to consider the validity and reliability of economic indicators of the values people hold for environmental changes as a result of suggested management options. In those cases where a valid and reliable measure of these values (benefits) cannot be estimated, an efficient allocation of resources cannot be determined by this type of analysis. Therefore, the policy or management objective must be determined on some other basis. Once that objective is specified, the analysis tells us what the consequences are in terms of costs of choosing between different means of achieving that objective. This is called cost-effectiveness or least cost analysis.

Both cost–benefit analysis and cost-effectiveness analysis consider the implications of adopting an option in terms of the impacts on individuals or groups of people. They may therefore fail to take into account a range of indirect and secondary effects, which may be important in certain circumstances. Additional assessments may be required such as those provided within an MCA. This covers a range of techniques for assessing decision problems characterized by a large number of diverse attributes. MCA aims at providing a means for aggregating information into a single indicator of relative performance based on the full range of performance attributes. Compared to CBA, the fundamental difference lies in the recognition that economic efficiency is often not the sole objective of policy. MCA offers one way of combining expert and non-expert scientific understanding, knowledge and values in order to illuminate policy trade-offs and to aid decision making. In the following chapters we concentrate on wetland ecosystems and the valuation of the final service benefits they provide to society.

REFERENCES

Gutrich, J.J. and Hitzhusen, F.J. (2004) 'Assessing the substitutability of mitigation wetlands for natural sites: Estimating restoration lag costs of wetland mitigation'. *Ecological Economics* 28(4): 409–424

Holmes, T.P. and Adamowicz, W.L. (2003) 'Attribute-based methods'. In Champ, P.A., Boyle, K.J. and Brown, T.C. (eds) *A Primer on Non-market Valuation*. Kluwer Academic Publishing: Dordrecht, The Netherlands

Holmes, T.P., Bergstrom, J.C., Huszar, E., Kask, S.B. and Orr III, F. (2004) 'Contingent valuation, net marginal benefits, and the scale of riparian ecosystem restoration'. *Ecological Economics* 49(1): 19–20

Limburg, K.E., O'Neill, R.V. and Costanza, R. (2002) 'Complex systems and valuation'. *Ecological Economics* 41(3): 409–420

4

The Ecosystem Services Approach: Valuation of Multi-functional Wetlands

OVERVIEW OF APPROACH AND ANALYTICAL STAGES

The conceptual framework and the methods and techniques detailed in this book are based on the ecosystem services approach to natural resource management. As we shall see, this interdisciplinary approach can be used to examine the value of wetland ecosystems and resources via the linkage between wetland structures and processes and the outcomes of the functioning of such systems in terms of intermediate and final services provided as benefits to society. It is compatible with the Convention on Biological Diversity (CBD) and its ecosystem approach, which has been adopted as a fundamental delivery mechanism for progress towards sustainable development.

Given the generic policy goal of sustainable development, management agencies should seek to maintain the resilience of wetland ecosystems, in terms of the ability to cope with stress and shock. Maintenance and/or enhancement of system resilience is, as will be discussed in the following sections, linked to the ecological concept of functional diversity and the social science analogue, functional (services provision) value diversity.

Wetlands provide a wide range of services with benefits of significant value to society, such as flood alleviation, recreation and aesthetic services. We can conceive of 'valuing' wetlands as essentially valuing the benefit characteristics of the system, and can capture these values in an economic value framework. Figure 4.1 presents a framework for an ecological-economic analysis and evaluation of the services and values of wetlands that underlies such a management strategy. At the core of the interdisciplinary analytical framework is a conceptual model, based on the concept of *functional diversity*, which links ecosystem characteristics, processes and structure via intermediate and final services to benefit outputs, which can then be assigned monetary, economic and/or other values.

In order to assess any wetland it is necessary to compile a complete list of all the *boundary conditions* for the wetland catchment. These are the characteristic properties that describe the wetland area in the simplest and most objective terms possible. They are a combination of generic and site-specific features. A general list would include the biological, chemical and physical features that describe

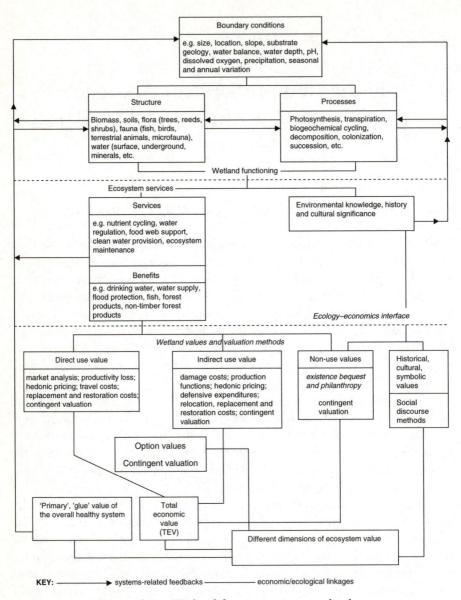

Figure 4.1   *Wetland functioning, uses and values*

a wetland, such as species present, substrate properties, hydrology, size and shape (see Table 4.1). However in principle this list is endless and site-specific.

Wetland structure is then defined as the biotic and abiotic webs whose characteristics are elements, such as vegetation type and soil type. By contrast *wetland processes* refer to the dynamics of transformation of matter or energy. The interactions among wetland hydrology and geomorphology, saturated soil and

Table 4.1 *Examples of wetland characteristics*

- Size
- Shape
- Species presence/abundance/rarity
- Vegetation structure
- Patterns of vegetation distribution
- Soils
- Geology
- Geomorphology
- Processes (biological, chemical and physical)
- Nature and location of water entry and water exit
- Climate
- Location in respect of human settlement and activities
- Location in respect of other elements in the environment
- Water flow/turnover rates
- Water depth
- Water quality
- Altitude
- Slope
- Fertility
- Nutrient cycles
- Biomass production/export
- Habitat type
- Area of open water
- Recent evidence of human usage
- Historic or prehistoric evidence of human usage
- Tidal range/regime
- Characteristics of the catchment

Source: Claridge, 1991.

vegetation more or less determine the general characteristics and the significance of the processes that occur in any given wetland. These processes also enable the development and maintenance of the wetland structure, which in turn is key to the continuing provision of services. These ecological concepts constitute the upper part of Figure 4.1. The economic benefit worth of ecosystem structure (the plants, animals, soil, air and water stocks and flows of which it is composed) is generally more easily appreciated than that of ecosystem processes. To evaluate processes for any given ecosystem pushes scientific knowledge to its limits and also requires careful separation of intermediate and final service categories. A precautionary approach may therefore be required in any wetland management strategy.

Ecosystem services are the result of interactions among characteristics, structures and processes. They include such services as water regulation, nutrient cycling and food web support. The concept of ecosystem services and ecosystem functioning is essential in linking ecology and economy (i.e. the step between wetland functioning and wetland values that is labelled 'wetland uses' in Figure 4.1). Although multiple definitions of (environmental) services exist in the literature, they have in common that they all reflect an anthropocentric perspective on ecosystem functioning, where ecosystem characteristics, structure and processes contribute to human welfare and well-being (Hueting, 1980; de Groot, 1992).

The conceptual model we advocate is not reductionist in the sense that it neglects the overall systems perspective that is key to the understanding of the environmental change process. Rather it is narrowly drawn in foundational terms (at the level of individual ecosystem services) in order to provide analytical rigour, as well as practical regulatory/policy relevance. At no time is sight lost of the overall value of a healthy evolving set of environmental systems. In this respect, integrated wetland management can be interpreted as follows (Mitchell, 1990):

- in *systems ecology terms*, that is how each component of the wetland system (at the catchment scale) influences other components;
- in *wider biogeochemical and physical systems terms*, that is where water interacts with other biophysical elements (one of the most characteristic features of a wetland);
- in *socio-economic, socio-cultural and political terms*, that is the linkage of wetland management to relevant policy networks and economic and social systems (with attendant culture and history) so that chances of achieving a cooperative solution or mitigation strategy are maximized.

Management of wetlands is therefore intimately connected with an appreciation of the full functioning of the hydrological, ecological and other systems and the total range of structures, processes, services and outputs of benefits that are provided. Wetland management and pricing must therefore be based on a relatively wide (at least catchment scale) appreciation of the landscape ecological processes present, together with the relevant environmental and socio-economic driving forces.

In order to manage wetlands holistically, one of the primary issues is whether the scale of administrative structures and appropriately refined scientific support equate with the scale of catchment processes. Management of wetlands and water resources more generally is all too often focused on a sectoral basis, and constrained by political and institutional considerations. The proprietorial interests shown by communities towards their localities in catchments are extremely powerful forces, which democratic systems often find difficult to accommodate. Yet wetland ecosystems are driven by hydrological and ecological processes that transcend the local scale and the short term. These linked hydrological-ecological systems provide a wide range of benefits and services that are often ignored or undervalued in water use planning, leading to their long-term loss.

Under a catchment wide perspective, interrelationships are made explicit and provide an important basis for decision making involving multiple wetland users. For instance, water abstraction or water pollution upstream may have severe consequences downstream. The human recipients of the wetland benefits will also be distributed across different spatial and temporal scales. The important issue of the distribution of costs and benefits of (changes in) wetland use only becomes visible if considered at the appropriate scale in time and space. For wetland ecosystems this is the catchment level, without which it will be difficult to trace the impact of any upstream user's decision on the downstream beneficiaries of the service. Thus it is difficult to allocate the value of the service and include it in the decision making process. Furthermore, many wetland values can only be realized if a minimum of upstream users take the catchment perspective into account in their decisions. For example, in a given area, a minimum number of land users may have to agree to maintain riparian buffer strips to guarantee a certain water quality for domestic use for a downstream city, which makes negotiations complex. In such cases where land uses have a noticeable impact on downstream water values, the land property rights will be just as important to take into account in valuation exercises as the water property rights. Furthermore, economic analysis is not limited to areas with functional linkages to the wetland, but is generally more concerned with the economic region of influence and the range of relevant stakeholder interests and positions. This may roughly conform to patterns of the local physical environment but is by no means determined by it.

The extent or degree to which different benefits (goods/services) are deemed 'valuable' is thus conditioned by a diversity of catchment level contextual factors. These will include human populations and access and demographic factors such as proximity, size and characteristics of human settlements; adjacent land uses within the wetland's catchment (topographic and habitat characteristics); the configuration of downstream resources; and scarcity/rarity issues at the regional scale and beyond (substitution possibilities). Wetlands should therefore be seen within a catchment scale context and should be managed as part of an integrated set of resources in line with the EC's Water Framework Directive and its provisions.

A management strategy based on the principle of sustainable wetland resource utilization should have at its core the objective of catchment ecosystem integrity maintenance, that is the maintenance of ecosystem components, interactions among them and the resultant behaviour or dynamic of the system. Integrity is best protected when efforts are made to secure a diverse range of wetland services and their asset values, that is *functional value diversity*. The diversity of the services provided by wetlands is dependent on the complexity and diversity of their structures and processes. These provide stability, resistance and recovery from disturbance and change. Functional diversity provides capacity for environmental-economic systems to maintain services provision under stresses and shocks, building on concepts of ecosystem integrity and resilience. In this context, integrity can be defined as the maintenance of system components, the interactions between them and the resultant behaviour of the system (King, 1993).

Resilience is the system's capability to maintain stability in the presence of disturbances (often human induced), determined by the system's stability and adaptability. The maintenance of functional diversity secures a range of wetland structures and processes, which best protects the integrity of the wetland and is therefore consistent with sustainable management. From a social science perspective, a policy objective of maximum diversity maintenance also serves to ensure the maximum functional capacity and associated functional value in terms of goods and services provision. Use of the concept of functional diversity highlights the importance of the deterministic relationship between the structures and processes of a wetland and the services that it provides. From an ecological stance, functional diversity creates variety in response to environmental change, in particular variety in the spatial and temporal scales over which organisms react to each other and to the environment (Steele, 1991). The onus is then on analysts and managers to take a wider perspective and examine changes in large-scale hydrological and ecological processes, together with the relevant environmental and socio-economic driving forces. Such a management strategy requires the practical coupling of economic, hydrological and ecological models.

The use of an ecosystem services approach is advocated for a number of reasons (Maltby et al, 1999):

- It should allow more efficient use of scarce resources by determining relationships such as the compatibility and intensity of land use activities with functioning, the capacity of ecosystems to tolerate impacts, and their resilience to human disturbance.
- Being ecosystem- rather than habitat-led the approach recognizes a wide range of both ecological and environmental interactions and is not restricted to a narrow view of conservation.
- Ecosystem dynamics are more easily translated into economic terms, which are usually readily understandable to the public and politicians.
- The implications of an ecosystem services approach are more appealing to the political agenda, since they extend to better use of water and land resources, improvement of environmental quality and human health and welfare.
- It allows scope for policy innovation.
- Assessment of ecosystem functioning should lead to more effective environmental protection. Two dimensions are relevant: optimizing the use of limited financial resources; and identifying priority areas for protection, rehabilitation or restoration.

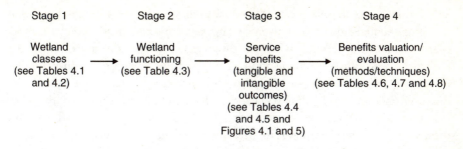

Figure 4.2   *Ecosystem service approach*

The ecosystem service perspective proposed here sets out a number of stages through which the analysis proceeds – see Figure 4.2. The initial stage requires a working classification of all relevant wetland types. We recommend a simplified version of the hydrogeomorphic method (HGM) (see section on wetland classification). Once this classification is established the set of services provided by particular wetland ecosystems needs to be identified (see section on wetland ecosystem functioning).

The third stage involves the matching of services and/or combinations of services with tangible and intangible benefit outcomes utilized or appreciated (i.e. affecting welfare) by human society (see section on wetland functioning service benefits). The final stage is concerned with the valuation of the final outcome benefits provided by the wetlands (see section on wetlands valuation/evaluation). To fit in with current UK appraisal practice, economic valuations are emphasized, but this overall method can be adapted to a broader evaluation framework with multiple criteria, not just economic efficiency benefits, as discussed in Chapter 3.

Following the schema as set out in Figure 4.2, we now discuss each of the stages in turn.

STAGE 1: WETLAND CLASSIFICATION: THE SIMPLIFIED HYDROGEOMORPHIC METHOD (HGM)

Wetland classification research has a relatively long history across a number of countries, but in the past two decades scientists and government agencies in the US have been developing a number of very detailed wetland classification systems for the functional assessment of wetlands (Cowardin et al, 1979). This therefore seems the most appropriate knowledge base to work with. There are currently three assessment methods used within the US which are representative of the methods available or being used by wetland managers and planners. These are the Wetland Evaluation Technique (WET), the Environmental Monitoring Assessment Programme (EMAP-Wetlands) and the Hydrogeomorphic (HGM) approach.

WET assigns specific services of individual wetlands a value, a probability rating reflecting the likelihood that a given wetland performs a service on the basis of its characteristics. The EMAP-Wetlands programme focuses on determining the ecological condition of a population of wetlands in a region. It does this by comparing a statistical sample of wetland to a reference wetland in a region. The final assessment method – the HGM approach – combines the features of the other two methods: the services of individual wetlands are measured and are also compared to the services performed by other wetlands. It is this final approach, while not directly applicable to wetland valuation, which could be used as a basis for the development of a practical way forward (King et al, 2000). A characteristic of the HGM method is that wetland ecosystems are the unit of assessment, *not* individual services, so that overall ecosystem health/integrity is appraised.

The HGM approach is itself in part a reaction to these earlier approaches in that it is meant to be a simpler and more practical procedure. The US HGM approach to wetlands assessment is based on *reference wetlands*, that is, fully functional examples of a wetland class/sub-class that have been relatively unaffected by human attention and therefore continue to function at a high level across a suite of identified services. The reference wetland concept is then used to distinguish between wetland classes and within classes in terms of fully or partially functioning wetland sites. The HGM approach is a very data-intensive procedure and it also requires a specialist interdisciplinary team of experts to keep it operational. This level of detail is necessary because of the type of wetland assessments that are required under US legislation and in particular to help in making trade-off decisions among wetlands or wetland services, often in mitigation banking/compensation cases.

The HGM classification is based on three fundamental factors that condition wetland functioning: the position in the landscape (geomorphic setting), the water source (hydrology) and the flow and fluctuation of the water once in the wetland (hydrodynamics). In the USA, seven major classes have been identified – see Table 4.2.

Adapting this classification to UK conditions and simplifying the approach further results in a 'reduced form' generic typology – see Table 4.3.

The next stage is to link different categories of wetlands to a set of typical services that are routinely provided by a healthy ecosystem.

STAGE 2: WETLAND ECOSYSTEM FUNCTIONING AND THE SERVICES OF WETLANDS

The structures and processes of a healthy ecosystem determine a variety of typical services that are categorized according to whether they are hydrological, biogeochemical or ecological services.

Table 4.2   *HGM wetland classification*[a]

HGM class	Dominant water source	Dominant hydrodynamics
Riverine (flood plains/riparian corridors)	Overbank flow from channel	Unidirectional, horizontal
Depressional	Return flow from groundwater and interflow	Vertical
Slope (fens)	Return flow from groundwater	Unidirectional, horizontal Vertical
Mineral soil flats	Precipitation	Vertical
Organic soil flats (peat bogs)	Precipitation	–
Estuarine fringe (bays/estuaries, inc. saltmarshes and intertidal areas)	Overbank flow from estuary	Bidirectional, horizontal
Lacustrine fringe (lakesides)	Overbank flow from lake	Bidirectional, horizontal

Note: [a]Excludes man-made wetlands.
Source: King et al, 2000.

Table 4.3   *Simplified wetlands classification*

Wetland classes[a]	
Saltwater dominant	Freshwater dominant
• Estuarine and coastal dominant (bays, estuaries and intertidal areas)	• Riverine (floodplains/riparian corridors, marshes)
	• Depressional (e.g. Norfolk and Suffolk Broads)
	• Slope (fens)
	• Organic soil flats (peat bogs)
	• Lacustrine fringe (lakesides)

Note: [a]Excluding man-made wetlands: aquaculture ponds, farm-based water bodies, settling ponds, reservoirs and so on.

Hydrological services refer to the wetland's ability to store flood waters, the interactions between ground and surface waters and the storage of sediments:

- Flood water detention: the short- and long-term detention and storage of waters from overbank flooding and/or slope run-off.
- Groundwater recharge: the recharge of groundwater by infiltration and percolation of detained flood water into an aquifer.
- Groundwater discharge: the upward seepage of groundwater to the wetland surface.
- Sediment retention: the net retention of sediments carried in suspension by waters inundating the wetland from river overbank flooding and run-off from a contributory area.

Biogeochemical services of a wetland refer to the export and storage of naturally occurring chemical compounds that can have significant effects on the quality of the environment:

- Nutrient retention: the storage of excess nutrients (nitrogen and phosphorus) via biological, biochemical and geochemical processes in biomass (living and dead) and soil mineral compounds of a wetland.
- Nutrient export: the removal of excess nutrients (nitrogen and phosphorus) from a wetland via biological, biochemical, physical and land management processes.
- In-situ carbon retention: the retention of carbon in the form of partially decomposed organic matter or peat in the soil profile due to environmental conditions that reduce rates of decomposition.
- Trace element storage and export: the storage and removal of trace elements from a wetland via biological, biochemical and physical processes in the mineral compounds of wetland soils.

Ecological services relate primarily to the maintenance of habitats within which organisms live:

- Ecosystem maintenance: the provision of habitat for animals and plants through the interaction of physical, chemical and biological wetland processes (including habitat and biological diversity). Nursery for plants, animals, micro-organisms.
- Food web support: the support of food webs within and outside a wetland through the production of biomass and its subsequent accumulation and export.

A review of the literature has highlighted a convenient overlap of all these services provided by most of the different wetland classes – see Table 4.4.

Table 4.4   *Wetland classes and representative services and benefits sets*

Wetland classes	Typical services benefits provision (potentially available)
Saltwater:	
Estuarine and coastal fringe	Flood control/storm protection
	Shoreline stabilization/erosion control
	Sediment, nutrients, contaminants
	Retention/storage → water quality
	Biomass export
	Carbon sequestration
	Fish nurseries and other services
	Recreation/tourism
	Culture/heritage
Freshwater:	
Riverine	Water storage/groundwater recharge/discharge Flood control
Depressional	Sediment etc. Retention/storage → water quality Recreation/tourism
Slope	Biodiversity maintenance (inc. fisheries)
Organic soil flats	Culture/heritage
Lacustrine fringe	Carbon sequestration

The relationships between services are both hierarchical and often complex.

e.g.   element cycling   habitat provision
                         ↓   ↓
        nutrient cycling   or   group of species
                         ↓   ↓
        nitrogen cycling   or   single species
                         ↓
        denitrification

There may be close linkages between services within wetland classes but also to a lesser extent between classes. For example, the detention of surface water in a wetland affects particulate retention and nutrient cycling, while also providing feeding opportunities for fish and aquatic organisms. The outcomes of their functioning over time in an integrated ecosystem can be manifested both on site and off site, as human welfare is impacted (positively or negatively) in direct or indirect ways.

STAGE 3: WETLAND FUNCTIONING SERVICE BENEFITS

What counts at this stage of the assessment process is whether human welfare is increased or decreased due to the provision of, or changes in the provision of wetland derived services. While the interrelationships between wetland services can be complex, some of this complexity can be reduced where more aggregative impact/welfare effects are determined and then valued. It is often the case that a combination of services within a wetland will combine to produce an intermediate and a final service, the benefit of which humans value. The strength of the HGM approach is evident because it focuses the analysis on the importance of ecosystem integrity rather than individual services. From the economic valuation perspective, complementarity or substitutability relationships between services and the danger of double counting of the benefits provided by services are key issues (see section on wetland valuation/evaluation).

Some of the wetland service benefit outcomes are generated within the wetland itself, on site, while a much wider range are provided off site (see Figure 4.3).

Table 4.5 brings together the wetland ecosystem characteristics and processes in terms of intermediate and final services and matches them to typical environmental

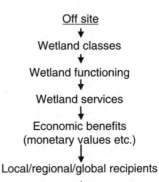

On site	Off site
↓	↓
Wetland classes	Wetland classes
↓	↓
Wetland functioning	Wetland functioning
↓	↓
Wetland services	Wetland services
↓	↓
Economic benefits (monetary values etc.)	Economic benefits (monetary values etc.)
↓	↓
Local/regional/global recipients	Local/regional/global recipients

On site:

Active use values:
e.g. harvesting
reed/sedge/hay
grazing
wildfowling
fish nurseries

Non-use values:
existence
bequest
option

Off site:

Active use values:
e.g. water storage
flood alleviation
biodiversity protection
recreation/tourism
carbon sequestration
nutrient/contaminants
storage/retention →
water quality

Non-use values:
existence
bequest
option
cultural/historical/
symbolic

Figure 4.3   *On-site and off-site wetland service benefits*

Table 4.5 *Wetland services and associated socio-economic service outcomes*

Biophysical structure or process maintaining service	→ Services	→ Socio-economic service outcomes (benefits)	Threats
	Hydrological Services		
Short- and long-term storage of overbank flood water and detention of surface water run-off from surrounding slopes	Flood water detention	Natural flood protection alternative, reduced damage to infrastructure (road network etc.), property and crops	Conversion, drainage, filling and reduction of storage capacity, removal of vegetation
Infiltration of flood water in wetland surface followed by percolation to aquifer	Groundwater recharge	Water supply, habitat maintenance	Reduction of recharge rates, overpumping, pollution
Upward seepage of groundwater through wetland surface	Groundwater discharge	Effluent dilution	Drainage, filling
Net storage of fine sediments carried in suspension by river water during overbank flooding or by surface run-off from other wetland units or contributory area	Sediment retention and deposition	Improved water quality downstream, soil fertility	Channelization, excess reduction of sediment throughput
	Biogeochemical Services		
Uptake of nutrients by plants (N and P), storage in soil organic matter, absorption of N as ammonium, absorption of P in soil	Nutrient retention	Improved water quality	Drainage, water abstraction, removal of vegetation, pollution, dredging

Table 4.5 *Wetland services and associated socio-economic service outcomes.* (cont'd)

Biophysical structure or process maintaining service	→ Services	→ Socio-economic service outcomes (benefits)	Threats
Flushing through water system and gaseous export of N	Nutrient export	Improved water quality, waste disposal	Drainage, water abstraction, removal of vegetation, pollution, flow barriers
Organic matter accumulation	In-situ retention of C	Preventing acceleration of greenhouse effect, fuel, Paleo-environmental data source	Overexploitation, drainage
Storage and removal of trace elements via biological, biochemical and physical processes in the mineral compounds of wetland soils	Trace element storage and export	Improved water quality	Drainage, water abstraction, removal of vegetation, pollution, dredging
	Ecological Services		
Provision of microsites for macro-invertebrates, fish, reptiles, birds, mammals and landscape structural diversity	Habitat for (migratory) species (biodiversity)	Fishing, wildfowl hunting, recreational amenities, tourism	Overexploitation, overcrowding and congestion, wildlife disturbance, pollution, interruption of migration routes, management neglect
Provision of microsites for macro-invertebrates, fish, reptiles, birds, mammals	Nursery for plants, animals, micro-organisms	Fishing, reed harvest	Overexploitation, overcrowding and wildlife disturbance, management neglect
Biomass production, biomass import and export via physical and biological processes	Food web support	Farming	Conversion, extensive use of inputs (pollution)

Source: Modified from Turner et al, 1997 and Burbridge, 1994.

change drivers and pressures. It offers a practical way to set out the relevant contexts and wetland services that require assessment. It also emphasizes the importance of at least a catchment wide perspective in the assessment process.

Finally Table 4.6 makes more explicit the link between any given wetland ecosystem service (left-hand column), or combination of services, and the service outcomes in terms of selective benefits that impinge on human welfare. The last stage in this assessment process is the evaluation exercise itself. If an economic stance is taken then the valuation of the outcomes provided by wetlands is undertaken through the common medium of money values.

In the next section we bring together the ecological and economic dimensions in order to make explicit the links between wetland services provision and their reflected value in society.

STAGE 4: WETLAND VALUATION/EVALUATION

The final stage of the ecosystem service approach is concerned with the monetary valuation of the benefits provided by wetlands. As we shall see the economic valuation of a range of wetland benefits is a practicable and meaningful exercise. Nevertheless, the limits to this monetizing approach should also be borne in mind, especially in terms of transferring economic value data across time and geographical space; and the existence of intangible natural values of cultural, historical and even ethical significance.

Total economic value and total system value

Given the multifaceted nature of benefits associated with wetlands there is a need for a useable typology of the associated social, economic and cultural values. In this book, we mainly focus on socio-economic values. These values depend on human preferences, that is what people perceive as the impact wetlands have on their welfare. In general, the economic value of an increased (or a preserved) amount of wetland benefit is defined as the amount of other resources that individuals are willing to forgo in order to obtain the increase (or maintain the status quo). Economic values are thus relative in the sense that they are expressed in terms of something else that is given up (the opportunity cost), and they are associated with the type of incremental changes to the status quo that public policy decisions are often about in practice. Furthermore, who gains or loses as the result of decisions about wetlands will also be a significant element in actual decision making and from a sustainability perspective equity issues are as important as economic efficiency issues. Before considering how to evaluate the economic value of the services performed by a wetland in practice, it will be useful to consider how and to what extent the concept of economic value captures the variety of wetland values.

Table 4.6 *Wetland services and service outcomes (benefits)*

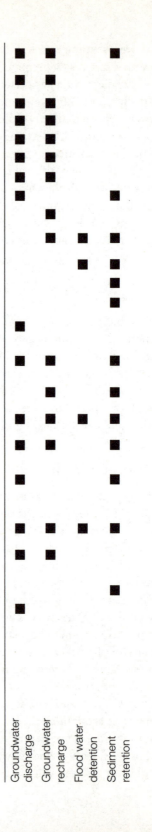

Service outcomes (benefits)	Groundwater discharge	Groundwater recharge	Flood water detention	Sediment retention
Potable water for household use	■	■		■
Water for landscape maintenance and peat soil	■	■		
Water for crop irrigation	■	■		
Water for livestock consumption	■	■		
Water for food processing	■	■		
Water for other manufacturing processes	■	■		
Water for power plants	■	■		
Water transport	■			■
Prevention of saline intrusion		■		
Water/soil support for prevention of land subsidence		■	■	■
Natural erosion, flood and storm protection			■	■
Shoreline stabilization				■
Sediment removal				■
Transport, treatment and medium for wastes and other by-products of human activities	■			
Improved air quality through the support of living organisms	■	■		■
Improved water quality through the support of living organisms		■		■
Biological diversity provision	■	■	■	■
Recreational swimming, boating, fishing, hunting, trapping and plant gathering	■	■		■
Commercial fishing, hunting, trapping and plant gathering	■			■
Energy production				
On- and off-site observation and study for leisure, education and scientific purposes	■	■	■	■
Micro-climate regulation	■	■		
Macro-climate regulation				
Toxicant removal				■
Toxicant export	■			
Cultural value provision				
Historical value provision				
Aesthetic value provision				
Wilderness value provision				

Service outcomes (benefits)	Nutrient retention	Nutrient export	Trace element storage	Trace element export	Carbon sequestration	Biodiversity maintenance	Culture/heritage
Potable water for household use							
Water for landscape maintenance and peat soil							
Water for crop irrigation							
Water for livestock consumption							
Water for food processing							
Water for other manufacturing processes							
Water for power plants							
Water transport							
Prevention of saline intrusion							
Water/soil support for prevention of land subsidence							
Natural erosion, flood and storm protection							
Shoreline stabilization							
Sediment removal							
Transport, treatment and medium for wastes and other by-products of human activities	■						
Improved air quality through the support of living organisms	■					■	
Improved water quality through the support of living organisms	■	■				■	
Biological diversity provision	■	■			■	■	
Recreational swimming, boating, fishing, hunting, trapping and plant gathering	■				■	■	■
Commercial fishing, hunting, trapping and plant gathering	■					■	
Energy production					■	■	
On- and off-site observation and study for leisure, education and scientific purposes	■	■			■	■	■
Micro-climate regulation						■	
Macro-climate regulation					■		
Toxicant removal							
Toxicant export		■					
Cultural value provision							■
Historical value provision							■
Aesthetic value provision	■					■	■
Wilderness value provision						■	

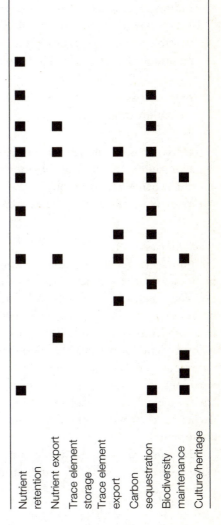

When considering environmental values, economists have generally settled for a taxonomy (see Figure 4.4), the components of which add up to total economic value (TEV). The key distinction made is between use values and a remainder called non-use value.

Use values

- Direct use values arise from direct interaction with wetland ecosystem services. They may be consumptive, such as use of water for irrigation, the harvesting of fish, or they may be non-consumptive such as recreational swimming, or the aesthetic value of enjoying a view. It is also possible that 'distant use' value can be derived through the media (e.g. television and magazines), although the extent to which this can be attributed to a specific site and the extent to which it is actually a use value, are unclear.
- Indirect use values are associated with services that are provided by wetland ecosystems that do not entail direct interaction. They are derived, for example, from flood protection provided by wetland ecosystems or the removal of pollutants by aquifer recharge.

There is a further type of value that is related to *future* direct and indirect uses. This is option value:

- Option value is the satisfaction that an individual derives from ensuring that a wetland service is available for the future given that the future availability of the benefit is uncertain. It can be regarded as insurance for possible future demand for the resource rather than a distinct component of TEV.

Non-use values

Non-use value reflects value in addition to that which arises from usage. Thus individuals may have little or no use for a given environmental asset or attribute but would nevertheless feel a 'loss' if such things were to disappear. However the boundaries of the non-use category are not clear-cut and some human motivations that may underlie the position that the asset should be conserved 'in its own right', and labelled existence value, are arguably outside the scope of conventional economic thought. In practice, what is at issue here is whether it is meaningful to say that individuals can assign a quantified value to the environmental asset, reflecting what they consider to be intrinsic value; or at a deeper level whether such intrinsic value exists, regardless of any human appreciation.

Non-use values can be divided into three types of value (which may overlap): existence value, bequest value and altruistic value:

- Existence value is the satisfaction derived from wetland ecosystems and their services continuing to exist, regardless of whether or not they might be of benefit to others. Motivations here could vary and might include having a feeling of concern for the asset itself (e.g. a threatened species) or a 'stewardship' motive whereby the 'valuer' feels some responsibility for the asset.
- Bequest value is the satisfaction derived from ensuring that wetland ecosystems and their services will be passed on to future generations so that they will have the opportunity to enjoy them in the future.
- Altruistic value is the satisfaction derived from ensuring that wetland ecosystems and their services are available to contemporaries in the current generation.

Economic values can now be combined with the ecosystem service (and related benefits) approach to provide a comprehensive economic assessment framework for wetland valuation (as shown in Figure 4.1). It is important to note that what is therefore being valued is not the wetland per se, but rather independent elements of ecosystem services provided by wetlands. The aggregation of the main service-based values provided by a given environmental ecosystem has been labelled total economic value (TEV).

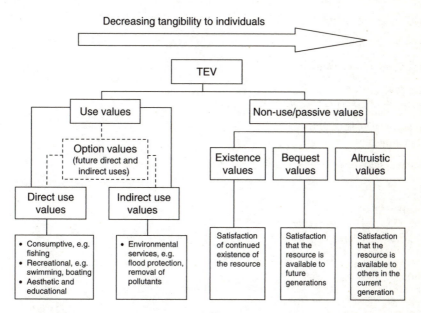

Figure 4.4   *Components of the total economic value of wetlands*

Table 4.7 shows the comprehensive list of wetland ecosystem service outcomes (benefits) and links them to their respective TEV components. As such it provides the final stage in integrating the physical components of a wetland ecosystem and the TEV of the services provided by the wetland ecosystem.

Table 4.7 *Wetland ecosystem service outcomes, TEV and accounting values*

Service outcomes (benefits) terminology	Total economic value terminology		Accounting terminology	
	Use values	Non-use values	Stocks	Flows
Water for household use	*			*
Water for landscape maintenance and peat soil	*			*
Water for crop irrigation	*			*
Water for livestock consumption	*			*
Water for food product processing	*			*
Water for other manufacturing processes	*			*
Water for power plants	*			*
Water transport	*			*
Prevention of saline intrusion	*		*	*
Water/soil support for prevention of land subsidence	*		*	*
Natural erosion, flood and storm protection	*		*	*
Shoreline stabilization	*		*	*
Sediment removal	*		*	*
Transport, treatment and medium for wastes and other by-products of human activities	*		*	*
Improved air quality through the support of living organisms	*		*	*
Improved water quality through the support of living organisms	*		*	*

Biological diversity provision (incl. habitat and nursery provision)	*	*	*	*
Recreational swimming, boating, fishing, hunting, trapping and plant gathering	*			*
Commercial fishing, hunting, trapping and plant gathering	*			*
Bioenergy production	*		*	*
On- and off-site observation and study for leisure, education and scientific purposes	*		*	*
Micro-climate regulation	*		*	*
Macro-climate regulation	*		*	*
Toxicant removal	*		*	*
Toxicant export	*		*	*
Cultural value provision		*		*
Historical value provision		*		*
Aesthetic value provision	*			*
Wilderness value provision		*		*
Other non-use service provision		*		

Table 4.7 also indicates whether the various categories of benefits and TEV components are commonly expressed as either stock (asset) values or flow values, or as both. It is important to distinguish between stocks and flows if one is to avoid the problem of double counting or other errors. Flows of value, such as those from extractive uses, are those that recur over time, as opposed to stock values, which are the values of assets that yield flows of services (and hence values) over time. Flow values and stock values are linked because a stream of values can be converted into an asset value by calculating the present discounted value of the flow. In instances where values are commonly expressed as either stocks or flows, it is important to specify whether the value is a flow or a stock.

In practical terms the assessment of TEV is limited to those components that it is feasible to quantify. Use of total economic value in the analysis of alternative allocations ensures that the full social benefits provided by wetlands are taken into account. This is necessary to indicate to decision makers the welfare improvement that is offered by alternative allocations. Total economic value does not, however, provide an exhaustive assessment of the value of wetlands to society. It measures the extent to which the services provided by wetlands touch on the welfare of society, as direct determinants of individuals' well-being or via production processes. It represents two fundamental sets of values: individual values and production values. Individual values include recreational and amenity values, as well as non-use values (existence, bequest and philanthropic values) of benefits provided by wetlands. Production values occur through the influence of wetlands on the production and cost functions of other marketed goods and services (such as use of water as an intermediate good in irrigated crop production). The effects of this influence on the prices of other inputs and marketed goods and services translate into changes in individuals' welfare.

But the aggregate TEV of a given ecosystem's services, or combinations of such systems at the landscape level, may not be equivalent to the total system value. There are other sets of values that are supplementary to total economic value. These represent the role of wetlands in natural systems. They include the value of services that stabilize natural systems and perform protective and supportive roles for economic systems. These values are more usually presented in relation to biodiversity. They include the following (somewhat overlapping) categories of value that have appeared in the scientific literature:

- Inherent value: the value of those services without which there would not be the benefits provided by the system (Farnworth et al, 1981).
- Contributory value: this represents the economic-ecological importance of species diversity. Species that are not of use to humans are important because they contribute to increased diversity, which itself contributes to the generation of more species (Norton, 1986).
- Indirect use value: this is related to the support and protection that is provided to economic activity by regulatory environmental services (Barbier, 1994).
- Primary value: this incorporates the fact that the ecosystem structure exists prior to the range of service values (Turner and Pearce, 1993).
- Infrastructure value: this relates to a minimum level of ecosystem 'infrastructure' as a contributor to its total value (Costanza et al, 1997).

These values build on three important aspects of the ecology of natural systems:

1 **Complementary relationships**. Species co-exist within natural systems, defined by complex relationships of interaction and interdependence. Survival of one species depends on the existence of other species, which in turn depend on others. This 'contributory value' focuses on the survival of species within the web of interactive relationships with each species contributing to the survival of others. Contributory value is based on the limited substitutability of species. This occurs because every species performs very specific duties within the ecological system. The role of contributory values is not usually taken into account explicitly, because the required knowledge (on ecological interrelationships) is unavailable, but it can be incorporated through adoption of a precautionary approach to resource management.

2   **Keystone species.** The persistence of natural systems in their current existing states may be dependent on a limited number of biotic and physical processes. These processes are directed by groups of species with complementary functions, known as 'keystone species'. Other species are redundant, though can become keystone species under a change in environmental conditions. As long as species can substitute for each other under changing conditions, the balance of processes within the system can remain intact. Reductions in the diversity of species in the system do, however, diminish the possibilities for substitutions under a change in conditions. This limits the capacity of the system to persist in its current state in the face of stresses and shocks. More recently ecologists have highlighted the importance of keystone processes rather than individual species.

3   The services provided by a natural system are dependent on the **structure and functioning of the systems**. The services provided are inherently connected to the integrity of the natural system and the totality of the structure and functioning of the system (Farnworth et al, 1981). This can be understood in terms of the concepts of primary and secondary value (Gren et al, 1994). The primary value describes the system characteristics: the self-organizing capacity of the system including its dynamic evolutionary processes and capacity to absorb external disturbances. It relates to the aspects of the system that 'hold everything together' and is consequently also referred to as 'glue value'. Secondary value refers to the renewable flow of benefits generated by the natural system. It is dependent on the continued operation, maintenance and 'health' of the system as a whole.

Total economic value does not give credit to this set of values and, therefore, is not exhaustive. Such values are particularly relevant to single service natural systems, the contributory value of which can only be properly addressed when the site is viewed within the context of the larger catchment system. The recognition of complementary relationships implies that the total value of ecosystems is infinite. This is similar to the consideration of wetlands and water resources as a form of 'critical' natural capital (Dubourg, 1997). Here again, the value of these resources is infinite and the usual measures of value (market price; willingness to pay) do not reflect the true economic value of the resource. As a basis of human life, complementary relationships with wetlands are indispensable under realistic technological and economic conditions. However, apparently marginal decisions (as perceived by different stakeholders) are the stuff of the real world and therefore need to be considered. The problem is that knowledge about the consequences of resultant infringements on natural systems is incomplete. There is an unbridgeable gap in knowledge about natural system interrelationships and regularities. The benefits of protection may often only be discovered once the natural system has been disturbed or lost.

Socio-cultural and historical dimensions of natural values

The task of sustainable management can be defined as sustainable utilization of the multiple goods and services generated by natural systems, together with 'socially equitable' distribution of welfare gains and losses inherent in such usage. However, social welfare is affected not only by changes in economic welfare but also changes in properties of natural resources that are associated with people's sense of identity, their culture and those of historical significance. Such properties are particularly important in the case of wetlands, given the essential role of water for human life. The compilation of data for such properties is a qualitative exercise, involving more deliberative and inclusionary interest group approaches such as consensus conferences, citizen juries and focus group interviewing. Different cultural views of social relations are assumed to give rise to different degrees of support for alternative decision making procedures and for the underlying valuations elicited via the social discourse process (O'Riordan and Ward, 1997; Brouwer et al, 1999). This has similarities to the so-called 'approved process' approach (Morgan and Henrion, 1990) in which all relevant parties observe a specified set of procedures or concept of due process to make a decision that balances conflicting values at the political level.

Some environmental analysts claim that natural systems also have non-anthropocentric intrinsic value and that non-human species possess moral interests or rights, or that, though all values are anthropocentric and usually (but not always) instrumental, the economic approach to valuation is only partial. These environmentalist positions lead to the advocacy of environmental sustainability standards or constraints, which to some extent obviate the need for valuation of specific components of the environment. It is still necessary, however, to quantify the opportunity costs of such standards, or to quantify the costs of current and prospective environmental protection and maintenance measures. Nevertheless, some commentators view it as feasible and desirable to manage the environment without prices. For example, O'Neil (1997) found that in other arenas such as forestry and biodiversity management, issues concerning conflicts in value are resolved through pragmatic methods of argument between botanists, ornithologists, zoologists, landscape managers, members of the local community, and farmers.

There is a growing body of evidence that suggests that some of the conventional economic axioms are systematically violated by humans in controlled experiments and in everyday life. To take just one issue, it seems likely that individuals recognize 'social interest' and hold social preferences separate from self-interested private preferences. The origin of this social interest may be explained by theories of reciprocal altruism, mutual coercion, or by socio-biological factors. The distinction between the individual as a citizen and as a consumer is not, therefore, an either/or issue, but is more properly interpreted as the adoption of multidimensional roles by individuals.

As citizens, individuals are influenced by held values, attitudes and beliefs about public goods and their provision. In this context, property rights (actual and/or perceived), social choices and moral concerns can all be involved in the conflict between conservation and development of natural resources. The polar view to the conventional economic approach holds that the very treatment of ecological assets such as biodiversity in terms of commercial norms is itself part of the environmental crisis. The argument becomes one of the 'proper' extent of market influences and commodification (O'Neil, 1997). Advocates of this perspective argue that market boundaries should not be extended to cover as many environmental assets as possible. Instead society should give greater consideration to the nature of deliberative institutions for resolving environmental problems and the social and economic framework that sustains them (O'Neil, 1997). A counterbalancing argument is that some environmental goods and services that have mixed public and private good characteristics (e.g. forests, catchments, areas with ecotourism potential and some aspects of biodiversity services) could be privatized or securitized (shares issued). In this way self-interest and the profit motive can be made to work in favour of environmental conservation (Chichilnisky and Heal, 1998).

The ability to value wetland ecosystem services is also constrained by the complexity of the wetland ecosystem itself. In particular it is necessary to take into account the following issues:

- The spatial and temporal scale. Ecosystem processes operate over a range of spatial and temporal scales; the scales that are appropriate to study the management of one process may not be suitable for other processes
- The persistence of the services of a wetland are dependent on the complexity and diversity of its structures and processes. The diversity provides resistance and recovery from disturbances and capacity for long-term adaptation, as well as being a sensitive indicator of environmental change
- Ecosystems are dynamic in space and time. Change is the normal course of events. Natural or human-induced disturbance create an interrelated mosaic of change. This influences ecosystem processes at large spatial scales
- Uncertainty and surprise are inevitable. There is much that is not understood about wetland ecosystems. Progress will yield some new knowledge, but the complexity and interactions of non-linear processes mean that certain elements of wetlands will always be difficult to predict and that surprise outcomes are inevitable, hence the importance of the precautionary approach.

The 'production function' of wetland ecosystems is so complex, and little understood in many instances, that reliable estimates of all services cannot be made. Human intervention in these complex and large-scale systems can have results that we do not understand fully at present (Turner, 2000). An aspect of this complexity is that joint products are inherent in most wetland ecosystem processes. From an economic valuation standpoint it is thus important to recognize that some wetland services are complementary, others are competitive or even mutually exclusive, for example increased access and recreation versus conservation of breeding sites or ranges for rare/endangered species. Accounting for value must recognize all these joint product values and avoid double counting.

Finally it seems clear that all wetlands to a greater or lesser extent provide some valued services but that different wetland classes may yield different mixes of services. We have shown earlier that, nevertheless, a representative set of services and benefits can be distinguished and fitted to a very simple wetlands classification. But it is still the case that similar wetland classes may provide different mixes of 'valued' services depending on their location in different catchment contexts. These locational factors are particularly important and also serve to emphasize the importance of assessing wetlands within their relevant catchments or river basins, as discussed in the overview of approach and analytical stages at the beginning of this chapter. Relevant catchment level contextual factors that require consideration in appraisal will include:

- proximity of the wetland, and of the result of the services it performs, to human settlement;
- accessibility of the wetland to humans;
- land use in the vicinity of and downstream from the wetland;
- predominant local industries such as farming, manufacturing, mining, tourism, forestry – not limited to the catchment, but the local region;
- size and distinctiveness of the wetland in comparison with other nearby wetlands;
- likely changes in human factors in the catchment in the foreseeable future, such as urban expansion, change in farming practices, increasing nature conservation, road building, river management and so on;
- the existence of nature conservation schemes within or near the wetland;
- effluent discharge or nutrient seepage into a river upstream or downstream of the wetland;
- known or historical problems with the water environment, such as pollution of the river, flooding episodes.

In conclusion, a typology of values based on the total economic value concept is an appropriate way to represent the multifaceted nature of the benefits associated with wetland; and despite some grey areas around the precise demarcation of use and non-use value categories, such a distinction is meaningful and practical. We now look at the methods and techniques used to assess the TEV of wetland ecosystems.

Economic valuation techniques

There are numerous difficulties and problems in any attempt to estimate the various values associated with wetland services. Based on Renzetti's (2002) wider analysis of water resources, the following four problems are also particularly associated with valuing wetland ecosystem services:

- The paucity of market transactions in wetland ecosystem service outcomes (benefits); even where markets do exist prices may not reflect the social marginal costs of supply.
- The variety of regulations and legal institutions related to wetland ecosystems will influence the allocation of associated benefits and, thus, distort their value, for example trade barriers and subsidies.
- In general, the value assigned to the use of wetland ecosystem services is a function of their quality. For example, while the impact of changes in water quality on its value is relatively well understood, there are many wetland services where such knowledge is incomplete, for example between water quality and its many other ecological services.
- Difficulties related to the application of neo-classical valuation techniques due to the cultural and religious roles of wetland ecosystems that are emphasized by some societies.

Despite these difficulties a range of valuation methods and techniques exist and have been applied to estimate the value of wetland benefits. The various techniques presented here include the estimation of demand curves and the area beneath them, analysis of market-like transactions, use of production approaches that consider the contribution of wetlands to the production process, estimation of the costs of providing alternative sources of wetland services, as well other techniques used to estimate environmental resources more generally. The methods and techniques reflect the extent to which the services provided by wetlands touch on the welfare of society either as direct determinants of individuals' well-being (e.g. as consumer goods) or via production processes (e.g. as intermediate goods).

In applying these techniques to estimate wetland values, a number of general difficulties can be noted as follows:

- Data related to wetland use are often not available and are expensive to collect.
- Values for wetland service outcomes are usually site -specific, especially since such service outcomes (e.g. raw water) are 'bulky' and thereby exhibit high conveyance costs.
- Methods and assumptions across wetland resources are not standardized.
- The time frame of wetland resource use is important since it relates to the fixity of certain inputs and hence differences in long-run and short-run values.

- The measure of wetland values has to be commensurable in terms of a common denominator of place, form and time.
- Uncertainty (scientific and economic) related to wetlands may be quite high. Benefit estimation requires forecasting the behaviour of a number of economic, technological and social variables over a long time period. Highly unpredictable factors can be influential.

The aim here is to provide an overview of all the techniques before focusing on the practical application of some of those techniques to wetland benefit valuation. Further details of the underlying theory and application of all the techniques are provided in general texts including Braden and Kolstad (1991), Freeman (2003), Bateman et al (2002), Mitchell and Carson (1989), Champ, Boyle and Brown (2003), Kanninen (2007) and Bockstael and McConnell (2007). In addition, Turner et al (2003), Young (2005) and Renzetti (2002) provide a more detailed survey of the application of valuation techniques to wetlands and aquatic resources more generally. A useful summary of valuation methods and techniques is provided in Appendix A.

An important distinction to make is between market-based valuation techniques and non-market-based valuation techniques. Market valuation means that existing market behaviour and market transactions are used as the basis of the valuation exercise. Economic values are derived from existing market prices for inputs (production values) or outputs (consumption values), through more or less complex econometric modelling of dose-response and/or damage functions. Examples include the economic value of reeds from wetlands, which are sold in a market (market analysis), the costs of replacing impaired environmental riparian services such as nutrient retention and export through the installation of a wastewater treatment plant (replacement costs) or the costs of a water filter on tap water (avertive behaviour/defensive expenditures). The economic value of water abstraction from wetlands for agriculture, the food or paper industry, the energy sector or for drinking water purposes can also be measured directly through existing market prices for intermediate or final water products (e.g. drinking water price). The market price may have to be adjusted to provide social or shadow prices, but otherwise they are likely to provide a relatively simple means of assessing economic value. Wetlands may also provide marketed recreational activities. Examples include fishing. In some cases market-based recreational values can thus be derived from existing fishing permits or entrance fees.

Many wetland ecosystem benefits are not traded in markets and therefore remain unpriced. It is then necessary to assess their economic value with the help of direct and indirect non-market valuation methods. Non-market valuation means deriving economic values in cases where such markets are non-existent or distorted. Direct methods (also called stated preference methods) refer to contingent valuation (CV) and choice modelling (CM) techniques, where individuals are asked directly, in a social survey format, for their water treatment preference (WTP) for a prespecified environmental change. WTP can also be measured indirectly by assuming that this value is reflected in the costs incurred to travel to specific sites, such as with recreational visits (travel cost studies), or prices paid to live in specific neighbourhoods (hedonic pricing studies) (also called revealed preference methods). The latter two approaches are based on preferences being 'revealed' through observable behaviour, and are restricted in their application to where a functioning market exists. CV and CM, being based on surveys that elicit 'stated preferences', have the potential to value benefits in all situations, including non-use or passive-use benefits that are not associated with any observable behaviour. The legitimacy of these methods and results is still contested, especially in the context of non-use values, and conducting surveys can sometimes be a lengthy and resource-intensive exercise. Of these methods, CV is probably the most widely applied method in contemporary valuation research (Bateman et al, 2002).

Wetland resources can likewise be estimated when no market exists by, for example, measuring the value wetland resources add as an essential input factor in production processes. In this case, the economic value of wetland resources is derived, indirectly, through more or less complex production function approaches, where output is a function of labour, human-made capital, intermediate input and natural capital including the wetland resource. Regressing output on these input factors yields a marginal value for the wetland resource.

Sometimes, investments by public (especially government) bodies in wetland resources may represent a surrogate for aggregated individual willingness to pay and hence social value. These 'public prices' paid for resources have been used to approximate the value society places upon them, as for instance the costs of designating a wetland ecosystem as a nature reserve. For a variety of reasons, these are unlikely to accurately reflect aggregated individual values, although techniques exist for attributing economic value based on such 'collective choice' decisions.

It should be remembered that when using those valuation techniques that estimate costs as a proxy for benefits, for example Damage Costs Avoided, Defensive Expenditures, Replacement/Substitute Costs or Restoration Costs, it is understood that the costs are a reasonable approximation of the benefits that society attributes to the resources in question. The underlying assumption is that the benefits are at least as great as the costs involved in repairing, avoiding or compensating for damage. These techniques are widely applied due to the relative ease of estimation and availability of data, but it is important to be aware of the limitations in terms of the information they convey with respect to economic benefits. Where it can be shown that (a) replacement or repair will provide a perfect substitute for the original service and (b) the costs of doing so are less than the benefits derived from this service, then the costs do indeed represent the economic value associated with that service.

It is not always necessary to initiate a new study in a project area to determine how the well-being of individuals might be affected by some environmental change. If a similar project has previously been undertaken elsewhere, estimates of its economic consequences might be usable as an indicator of the impacts of the new project.

Such an approach has been termed 'benefits transfer' because the estimates of economic benefits are 'transferred' from a site where a study has already been completed to a site of policy interest. The benefits transferred from the study site could have been measured using any of the direct or indirect valuation techniques outlined above. There are three broad approaches to benefits transfer to consider here.

Transferring average benefit estimates

Here we assume that the change in well-being experienced on average by individuals at existing sites is equal to that which will be experienced at the new site. Previous studies are used to estimate the consumer surplus or average WTP of individuals engaged in, say, recreational activities of various kinds. The value of a 'person-day' for each recreational activity at existing sites is multiplied by the forecast change in the number of days at the new site, to obtain estimates of the aggregate economic benefits of recreation at the new site.

Transferring adjusted average benefit values

Here the mean unit values of the existing studies are adjusted before transferral to the new site, in order to account for any biases that are thought to exist, or to reflect better the conditions at the new site. These differences might be in socio-economic characteristics of households, in the environmental change being looked at, or in the availability of substitute goods and services.

Transferring benefit functions

Instead of transferring adjusted or unadjusted average values, the entire demand function estimated at existing sites could be transferred to the new site. More information is passed over in this way.

Benefits transfer is still in its infancy, in part because for many environmental policy issues only a limited number of high quality valuation studies have been completed. However, it is potentially a very important and useful estimation approach, as it could feasibly provide accurate and robust benefit estimates at a fraction of the cost of a full-blown valuation study. Further details regarding Benefits Transfer and the problems of transferring values are given in Appendix A.

Table 4.8 *Valuation methodologies relating to wetland services*

Valuation method	Description	Direct use values	Indirect use values[a]	Non-use values
Market analysis and transactions	Econometric procedures used to derive value from household's or firm's inverse demand function based on observations of wetland use behaviour	√	√	
	Observed prices from transactions for leases or sales of wetland resource rights			
Production and cost functions	Wetland resource treated as one input into the production of other goods. Econometric analysis used to relate output or cost of production of marketed good to wetland resource	√	√	
Hedonic Price Method (HPM)	Derives an implicit price for a wetland service from analysis of goods for which markets exist and which incorporate particular wetland characteristics	√	√	
Travel Cost Method (TCM)	Costs incurred in reaching a wetland site as a proxy for the value of recreation. Expenses differ between sites (or for the same site over time) with different environmental attributes	√	√	
Contingent Valuation (CVM)	Construction of a hypothetical market by direct surveying of a sample of individuals to state WTP amount for proposed wetland policy	√	√	√
Choice modelling	Construction of a hypothetical market by direct surveying of sample of individuals to make choices among alternative proposed wetland policies	√	√	√

Table 4.8 *Valuation methodologies relating to wetland services*

Valuation method	Description	Direct use values	Indirect use values[a]	Non-use values
Avertive behaviour/ defensive expenditures/ avoidance costs	Costs and expenditures incurred in mitigating the effects/avoiding damages of reduced environmental functionality		√	
Replacement/restoration cost and cost savings	Potential expenditures incurred in replacing the wetland, service or good/service that is lost, for example by the use of substitutes or 'shadow projects'; costs of returning the degraded wetland to its original state	√	√	
Public pricing	Public investment, for instance via land purchase or monetary incentives, as a surrogate for market transactions	√	√	√[b]

[a] Indirect use values associated with services performed by an ecosystem will generally be associated with benefits derived off site. Thus, methodologies such as hedonic pricing and travel cost analysis, which necessarily involve direct contact with a feature of the environment, can be used to assess the value of indirect benefits downstream from the ecosystem.

[b] Investment by public bodies in conserving ecosystems (most often for maintaining biodiversity) can be interpreted as the total value attributed to the ecosystem by society. This could therefore encapsulate potential non-use values, although such a valuation technique is an extremely rough approximation of the theoretically correct economic measure of social value, which is the sum of individual willingness to pay.

REFERENCES

Barbier, E.B. (1994) 'Valuing environmental functions: Tropical wetlands'. *Land Economics* 70(2): 155–173

Bateman, I.J., Carson, R.T., Day, B., Hanemann, W.M., Hanley, N., Hett, T., Jones-Lee, M., Loomes, G., Mourato, S., Ozdemiroglu, E., Pearce, D.W., Sugden, R. and Swanson, J. (2002) *Economic Valuation with Stated Preferences Techniques: A Manual.* Edward Elgar: Cheltenham

Bockstael, N.E. and McConnell, K.E. (2007) *Environmental and Resource Valuation with Revealed Preferences – A Theoretical Guide to Empirical Models.* Springer: Dordrecht, The Netherlands

Braden, J.B. and Kolstad, C.D. (1991) *Measuring the Demand for Environmental Quality*. North Holland: Amsterdam

Brouwer, R., Powe, N.A., Turner, R.K., Bateman, I.J. and Langford, I.H. (1999) 'Public attitudes to contingent valuation and public consultation'. *Environmental Values* 8(3): 325–347

Burbridge, P.R. (1994) 'Integrated planning and management of freshwater habitats, including wetlands'. *Hydrobiologia* 285: 311–322

Champ, P., Boyle, K.J. and Brown, T.C. (eds) (2003) *A Primer on Nonmarket Valuation*. Kluwer Academic Publishers: Dordrecht, The Netherlands

Chichilnisky, G. and Heal, G. (1998) 'Economic returns from the biosphere'. *Nature* 391: 629–630

Claridge, G.F. (1991) An Overview of Wetland Values: A Necessary Preliminary to Wise Use. PHPA/AWB Sumatra Wetland Project Report No 7. AWB: Bogor, Indonesia

Costanza, R., d'Arge, R., de Groot, R., Farber, S., Grasso, M., Hannon, B., Limburg, K., Naeem, S., O'Neill, R.V., Paruelo, J., Raskin, R.G., Sutton, P. and van den Belt, M. (1997) 'The value of the world's ecosystem services and natural capital'. *Nature* 387: 253–260

Cowardin, L.M., Carter, V., Golet, F.C. and LaRoe, E.T. (1979) *Classification of Wetlands and Deepwater Habitats of the United States*. US Fish and Wildlife Service: Washington DC

Farnworth, E.G., Tidrick, T.H., Jordan, C.F. and Smathers, W.M. (1981) 'The value of ecosystems: An economic and ecological framework'. *Environmental Conservation* 8: 275–282

Freeman, A.M. III (2003) *The Measurement of Environmental and Resource Values: Theory and Methods*. Resources for the Future: Washington DC

Gren, I.-M., Folke, C., Turner, R.K. and Bateman, I.J. (1994) 'Primary and secondary values of wetland ecosystems'. *Environmental and Resource Economics* 4: 55–74

Groot, R.S. de (1992) *Functions of Nature*. Wolters-Noordhoff: Amsterdam

Dubourg, W.R. (1997) 'Reflections on the meaning of sustainable development in the water sector'. *Natural Resources Forum* 21(3): 191–200

Hueting, R. (1980) *New Scarcity and Economic Growth*. North Holland Publishing Company: Amsterdam

Kanninen, B.J. (2007) *Valuing Environmental Amenities Using Stated Choice Studies*. Springer: Dordrecht, The Netherlands

King, A.W. (1993) 'Considerations of scale and hierarchy'. In Woodley, S., Kay, J. and Francis, G. (eds) *Ecological Integrity and the Management of Ecosystems*. St Lucie Press: Ottawa

King, D.M., Wainger, L.A., Bartoldus, C.C. and Wakely, J.S. (2000) Expanding Wetland Assessment Procedures: Linking Indices of Wetland Function with Services and Values. ERDC/EL TR-00–17. US Army Engineer Research and Development Center: Vicksburg, MS

Maltby, E., Holdgate, M., Acreman, M. and Weir, A. (1999) *Ecosystem Management: Questions for Science and Society*. Royal Holloway Institute for Environmental Research: Virginia Water, UK

Mitchell, B. (1990) *Integrated Water Management: International Experiences and Perspectives*. Belhaven Press: London

Mitchell, R.C. and Carson, R.T. (1989) *Using Surveys To Value Public Goods: The Contingent Valuation Method*. Resources for the Future: Washington DC

Morgan, M.G. and Henrion, M. (1990) *Uncertainty: A Guide to Dealing with Uncertainty in Quantitative Risks and Policy Analysis*. Cambridge University Press: Cambridge

Norton, B.G. (1986) *Towards Unity Among Environmentalists*. Oxford University Press: Oxford

O'Neil, J. (1997) 'Managing without prices: The monetary valuation of biodiversity'. *Ambio* 26: 546–550

O'Riordan, T. and Ward, R. (1997) 'Building trust in shoreline management: Creating participatory consultation in shoreline management plans'. *Land Use Policy*, 14(4): 257–276

Renzetti, S. (2002) *The Economics of Water Demands*. Kluwer Academic Press: Norwell, MA

Steele, J.H (1991) 'Marine functional diversity'. *Bioscience* 41: 470–474

Turner, R.K. (2000) 'Integrating natural and socioeconomic science in coastal management'. *Journal of Marine Sciences* 25: 447–460

Turner, R.K., Paavola, J., Cooper, P., Farber, S., Jessamy, V. and Georgiou, S. (2003) 'Valuing nature: Lessons learned and future research directions'. *Ecological Economics* 46(1): 493–510

Turner, R.K. and Pearce, D.W. (1993) 'Sustainable economic development: Economic and ethical principles'. In Barbier, E.B. (ed) *Economics and Ecology: New Frontiers and Sustainable Development*. Chapman and Hall: London

Turner, R.K., van der Bergh, J.C.J.M., Berendregt, A. and Maltby, E. (1997) 'Ecological-economic analysis of wetlands: Science and social science integration'. In: Soderquist, T. (ed) *Wetlands: Landscape and Institutional Perspectives*. Proceedings of the Fourth Workshop of the Global Wetlands Economics Network (GWEN). Beijer International Institute of Ecological Economics, The Royal Swedish Academy of Sciences, Stockholm, Sweden, 16–17 November

Young, R. (2005) *Determining the Economic Value of Water: Concepts and Methods*. Resources for the Future Press: Washington DC

5

Economic Valuation of Wetland Ecosystem Services in Practice

PRACTICAL CONSTRAINTS

As discussed in the earlier chapters, wetlands provide a variety of ecosystem services (intermediate and final services) that are beneficial to society. A distinction was made between hydrological, biogeochemical and ecological services.

In evaluating the economic value of the services performed by a wetland, a common approach is undertaken. The approach involves the identification of all the service outcomes (benefits) produced by each of the wetland services, followed by the valuation of each of the benefits.

The socio-economic benefits derived from these services can be measured in a variety of ways, as discussed in the previous chapter. In doing so, the following steps can be distinguished:

1   choice of the appropriate assessment approach (impact/damage analysis, partial valuation, total valuation);
2   definition and specification of the spatial system boundary of the wetland;
3   identification of the services of the wetland ecosystem and potential benefits provided by them;
4   assessment of their actual provision level (including quality), and what effect there would be if the wetland were removed;
5   identification of the groups of people in society who benefit from them (or will be suffering a loss when they are removed, destroyed or degraded);
6   identification of the possible values attributed to them by these different groups in society;
7   selection of the appropriate economic valuation technique(s);
8   estimation of the total economic value.

Steps 5 to 8 are important because it is not the degree to which the service is being performed that apportions economic value, but the influence that the service will have on resources regarded by society as worth conserving. The choice of valuation technique that can be employed to estimate the economic value of the good or service (step 7) will often be up to the analyst to decide. While some methods are theoretically preferable to others, other 'second-best' measures may often be easier to determine in practice. The choice of method is likely to depend, in part, on time, resources and data available for the investigation.

In considering the economic valuation of wetland services in practice, the following important issues also need to be borne in mind by appraisers.

Spatial and temporal scale

The scale of evaluation is determined by the issue that is under investigation. For a specific isolated external impact, evaluation may be restricted to a limited number of affected variables. Where broader changes are involved (e.g. a change in land use in a catchment), partial analysis of a number of integrated parameters may be required. Because of the costs and effort that are involved, full valuations are usually avoided unless they are absolutely necessary, for example, a situation where an entire catchment is under threat.

The spatial scale (or accounting stance) of a study is determined by the extent of the population that is affected by the impact under investigation. The accounting stance should be as encompassing in this respect as possible (see Bateman et al, 2006 for a more detailed discussion). Where the impact incurs only changes in direct uses of a wetland, the affected population is existing and potential resource users. This population does not, however, necessarily live in close proximity to the resource as they may travel considerable distances to use it. Indirect use values may not be site-specific in terms of those who benefit; for example, interception of flood waters by irrigation may yield benefits far downstream. Non-use benefits are derived over a wide geographical area, but are likely to be subject to 'distance decay' away from the site. In practice, a pragmatic accounting stance has to be adopted in specifying the scale, where the gains in accuracy are balanced against the costs of spreading the scale wider.

The temporal scale, combined with the discount rate (discussed below), influences the present value of the streams of costs and benefits. The calculation of expected future costs and benefits involves estimating future demand. This is necessarily unknown but a range of possible values can be obtained through the assessment of likely scenarios and application of sensitivity analysis. The temporal scale also determines the trade-off between considering long-run versus short-run values. Decisions are more constrained and responses quite different in short-run contexts. Most public policy contexts relate to the longer term, though there are some circumstances, such as drought planning, for which short-run values are more appropriate.

Aggregation and double counting

The adoption of an ecosystem services approach to wetlands involves considering the functioning outcomes provided by wetlands in relation to environmental structures and processes. This raises issues that require attention in the aggregation of data on the benefits provided:

- While the adoption of an ecosystem services perspective is advocated as the correct way to identify wetland outcomes, if each of them is identified separately, and then attributed to underlying services (i.e. intermediate and final service outcomes), there is a likelihood that benefits will be double counted. Benefits might therefore have to be allocated explicitly to connected intermediate and final service chains. For instance, Barbier (1994) noted that if the nutrient retention service (intermediate service) is integral to the maintenance of biodiversity (final service and benefit), then if both services are valued separately and aggregated, this would double count the nutrient retention which is already 'captured' in the biodiversity value. Some services might also be incompatible, such as water extraction and water recharge, so that combining these values would overestimate the feasible benefits to be derived from the wetland. Studies that attempt to value the wetland as a whole based on an aggregation of separate values tend to include a certain number of services, although these studies do not usually claim to encompass all possible benefits associated with the wetland.
- Some services of wetlands may be mutually exclusive and, therefore, cannot be aggregated. For example, aggregation of the values for both extraction of water and recharge of water would overestimate the benefits that could feasibly be derived from a wetland. The different values can only be added where they are consistent with a single allocation strategy for the wetland services.
- Interactions can occur between services. For example, conservation goals may require alteration to the harvesting regime employed for reed beds, which reduces the gross margins of the beds. Some services may be complementary; for instance, nutrient retention can promote biomass production.
- There will often be an imperfect fit or overlap between valuation methods and benefit types, so that even if benefit values are additive, the estimates of these values often are not. For example, measurement of beach recreation values may overlap with estimates of the earnings from beach-related tourism. As such, attempts to measure total economic value through the summation of individual values obtained using several methodologies may encounter problems with both inconsistency and non-additivity.

In practice, the ability to use wetlands repeatedly or simultaneously for different uses means that competition and complementarity are important considerations in valuing wetland ecosystems. Wetland management would ideally be considered under a general equilibrium framework, though this is in practice extremely difficult. This also means that total valuation (estimation of the full value of a wetland ecosystem) is undertaken only when necessary. Management decisions are more commonly assessed using impact analysis (which assesses the damage arising only from a particular impact) or partial valuation, based on a sectoral approach, or on specific services of a wetland. Such a partial approach means that a number of considerations must be taken into account. First, the different ways of calculating values may result in fundamentally different definitions of value, for example, which are specific to certain time frames that differ between the uses considered. Second, values may be based on average or marginal concepts, which are quite different concepts. Use of marginal values is required for the purposes of efficient allocation.

Allocation over time

It is frequently necessary to choose between options that differ in temporal patterns of costs and benefits, and those that differ in their duration. Discounting provides a common matrix that enables comparison of costs and benefits that occur at different points in time. Use of discounting is integral to cost–benefit analysis and cost-effectiveness analysis.

Discounting converts the stream of costs and benefits over time into a stream of 'present' values. The difference between the value of the discounted benefits and costs is referred to as the net present value (NPV). A management or policy option is economically viable only if NPV is positive, as described in Equation 1:

$$NPV = \sum_t \frac{(B_t - C_t)}{(1+r)^t} > 0 \qquad (1)$$

where B_t and C_t are benefits and costs in year t respectively, and r is the discount rate.

The rationale for discounting is that costs and benefits that occur in the future are not valued as highly as those that occur in the present. There are two explanations for this:

1 Time preference (or the 'consumption rate of interest'). Individuals prefer consumption in the present over consumption in the future. Reasons for this include:
   • the risks involved in delayed consumption;
   • anticipation of increased wealth in the future, which reduces the relative worth of postponed consumption (i.e. decreasing marginal utility of consumption);
   • 'pure' time preference or myopia.
2 The opportunity cost of capital. Financial capital that is not consumed in the present can be invested and expected to increase in value by the rate of interest. There is, therefore, an opportunity cost associated with present consumption of financial capital, which is the return that could be derived from its investment (as indicated by the rate of interest).

The choice of discount rate can have a significant effect on economic viability of management options and their relative economic ranking. It effectively signals the rate at which future consumption is to be traded against consumption in the present. Use of a high discount rate discriminates against the future. It discriminates against options that involve high initial costs and a stream of benefits that extends far into the future (e.g. creation or restoration of a wetland). Instead, it favours options that have immediate benefits and a lag in incurring costs. This has been described as the 'tyranny' of discounting (Pearce et al, 1989).

High discount rates tend to be justified based on the opportunity cost of capital, though to be correct this is relevant only for financial analysis, which is not examined here. In general, they are likely to encourage depletion of non-renewable natural resources and exploitation of renewable natural resources, reducing the inheritance of natural capital for future generations. Low discount rates favour the future but could discriminate against and hamper immediate economic development. They encourage investments which would otherwise have not been viable and which could be associated with an even more rapid depletion of natural resources (Fisher and Krutilla, 1975). The impact that the discount rate has on the environment is therefore ambiguous, and it is not clear that the call for use of lower discount rates to incorporate environmental concerns is generally valid.

A social rate of discount is used to evaluate the impact of management options on intergenerational welfare. Such evaluations take intergenerational welfare into consideration. The maintenance of future welfare can be regarded as a public good, in which private individuals will tend to underinvest. As a result, the social discount rate is lower than the equivalent rate of discount for individuals. The social discount rate is measured either as the social rate of time preference (SRTP) or the social opportunity cost of capital (SOC). Care has to be taken in developing country contexts, where the use of consumption rates of interest (which are likely to exceed 4–6 per cent) may not adequately account for concerns about the inheritance of environmental problems by future generations.

The social discount rate can also be adjusted to reflect temporal trends in the net benefits of environmental preservation and development. The net benefits of such preservation are likely to increase over time as demand for environmental services rises under conditions of limited or declining supply. Conversely, the net benefits of development projects are expected to decline over time due to technological advancement. These trends can be incorporated into economic evaluation through appropriate adjustment of the social discount rate, by decreasing the discount rate applied to preservation benefits and increasing the rate applied to development benefits (Hanley and Craig, 1991).

Risk and uncertainty

In the case of risk, meaningful probabilities can be assigned to the likely outcomes. In the case of uncertainty, probabilities are entirely unknown. Risk can be incorporated into an evaluation by attributing probabilities to possible outcomes, thereby estimating directly the expected value of future costs and benefits (Boadway and Bruce, 1984) or their 'certainty equivalents' (Markandya and Pearce, 1988). A premium for risk can be incorporated into the discount rate used for the analysis, but such adjustment is arbitrary, often subjective and attributes a strict (and unlikely) time profile to the treatment of risk and is not recommended for these reasons.

In an economic evaluation, uncertainty is associated with physical outcomes and their economic consequences. For wetlands, the necessary assessment of possible outcomes and the likelihood of perturbations to what is a highly complex system is inevitably fraught with difficulty. However, this is a necessary component of an economic evaluation. For each management or policy option under consideration, the range of possible impacts needs to be identified and quantified as far as possible. A particularly important issue relating to uncertainty in physical effects is the possible existence of thresholds beyond which disproportional and irreversible effects can occur. Such thresholds result in disproportional impacts and an inability to reverse consequences in the future (discussed further below).

There is also uncertainty that relates to the physical and economic conditions that will prevail in the future. For example, a change in regulations concerning agricultural production could cause farmers to respond with a change in land use, which could impact on nutrient concentrations in run-off and thereby affect the value of the nutrient retention service provided by a wetland. Likewise, individuals can alter their behaviour in response to changes in wetland services. For example, an increase in flooding might be responded to by farmers through a change in cropping patterns. Such uncertainties can influence projected benefits and so also need to be incorporated into any evaluation of options.

Uncertainty is incorporated into economic evaluations through the use of sensitivity analysis or scenario analysis. In sensitivity analysis, various possible values are used for key variables in the evaluation, such as the discount rate, the extent of services, and economic values. This provides a range of estimates within which the true result can be expected to fall. It can create ambiguity but is a necessary component of any economic evaluation. Scenario analysis can also be used to incorporate uncertainty through comparison of results using parameter values that represent different possible future scenarios.

Costanza (1994, p97) points out that 'most important environmental problems suffer from true uncertainty, not merely risk'. In an economic sense, such pure uncertainty can be considered as 'social uncertainty' or 'natural uncertainty' (Bishop, 1978). Social uncertainty derives from factors such as future incomes and technology, which influence whether or not a resource is regarded as valuable in the future. Natural uncertainty is associated with our imperfect knowledge of the environment and whether it has unknown features that may yet prove to be of value. This may be particularly relevant to ecosystems for which the multitude of services that are performed have historically been unappreciated. A practical means of dealing with such complete uncertainty is to complement the use of a cost–benefit criterion based purely upon monetary valuation with a safe minimum standards (SMS) decision rule (Ciriacy-Wantrup, 1952; Bishop, 1978; Crowards, 1996), as discussed below.

Irreversible change

Irreversible impacts, for instance the extinction of species or exhaustion of minerals, are not accounted for in the standard procedures for economic evaluation. Under such circumstances, account needs to be taken of the uncertain future losses that might be associated with potential irreversible change. Some protection to the interests of future generations can be offered through the imposition of the SMS decision rule (Ciriacy-Wantrup, 1952; Bishop, 1978; Crowards, 1996).

The SMS decision rule recommends that when a development activity that impacts on the environment threatens to breach an irreversible threshold, conservation is adopted unless the costs of forgoing the development are regarded as 'unacceptably large'. It is based on a modified principle of minimizing the maximum possible loss and therefore differs from routine trade-offs which are based on maximizing expected gains, for example, cost–benefit and risk analysis. However, activities that result in potential irreversible change are not rejected if the associated costs are regarded as intolerably high.

A critical aspect in the application of the SMS decision rule is specification of the threshold for unacceptable costs of forgoing development. The degree of sacrifice is determined through full cost–benefit assessment of the development option, including estimable costs of damage to the environment. The decision as to whether conservation of natural resources (and rejection of the development activity) can be justified is political, constrained by society's various goals. In this sense, SMS provide a mechanism for incorporating the precautionary principle into decision making: society may choose to conserve even in the absence of proof that damage will occur in order to limit potential costs in the future (Crowards, 1997).

The concept of safe minimum standards has usually been applied to endangered species. However, it could equally be applied to irreversible impacts that threaten wetlands. Where thresholds of wetland processes are threatened with irreversible change, the use of SMS provides a decision framework that gives more weight to concerns of future generations. It promotes a more sustainable approach to current development and can provide an appropriate supplement to standard analysis of economic efficiency.

SMS are closely related to sustainability considerations (Pearce and Turner, 1990). Sustainability essentially requires that the stock of natural capital available in the future is equivalent to that available at present. The concept of sustainability has been roughly partitioned into two approaches: weak sustainability and strong sustainability (Turner, 1993). Weak sustainability requires that the total stock of capital, whether human-made or natural, is maintained, and rests upon the assumption of substitutability between these two types of capital. Economic theory suggests that decreases in supplies of natural resources cause their prices to increase, which encourages more efficient use of natural resources, substitution with other goods, and technological advancement. However, complete substitution is not always possible due to physical limits on the efficiency and availability of opportunities for substitution, the question of whether human-made capital can fully compensate for all the services provided by complex ecosystems, and the existence of 'critical' natural capital and thresholds beyond which reversal is not possible. The more stringent interpretation of 'strong' sustainability requires that the total stock of natural capital is non-declining. Under this criterion, projects should either conserve the natural environment or ensure that losses incurred are replaced or fully compensated for in physical terms by the implementation of 'shadow projects' (Barbier et al, 1990).

An alternative mechanism that can be employed to account for potential irreversibility in the analysis of discrete development–conservation choices (e.g. if a development entails exploitation of a wetland to permanent loss) is to include the preservation benefits forgone as opportunity costs in the cost–benefit analysis. Future development benefits that occur as a result of relative price effects and technology changes are discounted and also included in the analysis. This approach is known as the Krutilla–Fisher algorithm (Krutilla and Fisher, 1985). Irreversible change can also be incorporated into the evaluation through adjustment of the social discount rate to allow for temporal trends in the benefits of preservation (discussed earlier).

Data limitations

It is inevitable that some of the data required for an economic evaluation will not be readily available. Budgetary constraints often limit extensive collection of original data. Where data are limited, this should be acknowledged and the measures taken in response to this limitation clearly specified. The results and recommendations should be made explicitly conditional on these limitations. The various techniques used to value non-marketed goods and services are each associated with specific data limitations.

WETLAND BENEFITS

We now provide a brief overview of some of the more economically significant benefits provided by wetlands (existing and potentially newly created), followed by a more detailed discussion of how each of the service outcomes is assessed in practice using the various valuation techniques. The services are characterized according to whether they are hydrological, biogeochemical or ecological. For any given assessment the type and number of outcomes that need to be valued will vary with the policy context in which the appraisal is being undertaken and with the choice of valuation approach.

It should be noted that although a number of economic valuation techniques can be deployed to value individual or a small number of wetland benefits, if an overall aggregate value for any given wetland is required, then only a survey-based willingness to pay (WTP) contingent valuation method is capable of simply yielding an appropriate monetary value.

The indirect use benefits from, for example, flood water detention mainly refer to potential damage avoided downstream. Besides the calculation of avoided damage costs, defensive expenditures related to flood warning or avertive action, and the replacement or substitution costs of building dikes if the wetland is removed, hedonic pricing studies have looked at the influence of risks of flooding on property prices (see Appendix B for an overview of studies). Contingent valuation studies have been used to estimate public WTP for flood protection (again see Appendix B for these and other studies related to the services also discussed below).

Ground (and surface) water recharge and discharge may include non-use values when water supplies are maintained for the sake of future generations. Based on market analysis, production function approaches and the calculation of replacement costs, the direct and indirect use value of wetlands for drinking water purposes and irrigation in agriculture have been estimated. Hedonic pricing studies have investigated the effect of access to water on property prices. Travel cost and contingent valuation studies have examined the recreational benefits associated with instream flow levels.

The direct and indirect benefits of wetlands retaining sediments from flood water and run-off water have been mainly estimated in terms of damage avoided (e.g. recreation, navigation, agriculture).

The direct and indirect use benefits from nutrient and trace element retention and export mainly refer to maintaining or improving water quality for various reasons, including drinking water and recreation. Market analysis and production function approaches have been used to estimate the value of clean water on human health and commercial fishing (forgone earnings). Defensive or avertive expenditures incurred by households have been assessed to avoid exposure to contaminated (ground)water supply. Replacement cost studies have looked at the costs of equivalent wastewater treatment methods. Travel cost studies have been used to assess the value of improved water quality at recreational sites, while hedonic pricing studies investigated the impact of differing water qualities on residential housing prices. Contingent valuation studies have assessed WTP for protecting and improving (ground)water quality for a variety of reasons (drinking water, health, recreation, habitat preservation etc.), including non-use motivations such as bequest or existence values.

The socio-economic value of a wetland's capacity to store carbon (peat accumulation) has been estimated through exercises looking at the damage caused by climate change. Although such studies have only assessed the indirect use value involved, the storage of carbon may also have non-use value (e.g. reducing climate change for the sake of future generations).

The socio-economic benefits of wetlands producing biomass (fish, reed, etc.) have been evaluated through market analyses and replacement cost estimations of shadow projects. Restoration cost studies have looked at the costs related to rehabilitating the ecology of wetlands (reed beds, cleaning up pollution, etc.). Hedonic pricing studies have been carried out to assess property prices in and near wetlands. Travel cost studies have estimated the recreational expenditures for waterfowl hunting, birdwatching, fishing and so on. Finally, contingent valuation surveys have been used to estimate the use and non-use values, separately or at the same time, through public WTP for species and habitat preservation.

The application of the various valuation techniques to many of the wetland goods and services outlined in the section of Chapter 4 addressing wetland functioning service benefits has already been extensively considered elsewhere (Gibbons, 1986; Young, 1996; National Research Council, 1997; Renzetti, 2002). A summary of wetland benefits and the techniques that are applied to them is shown in Table 5.1. In addition, Table 5.2 summarizes this information according to the main wetland service outcomes.

VALUATION OF HYDROLOGICAL SERVICE BENEFITS

Flood water detention

Definition: the short- or long-term detention and storage of waters from overbank flooding and/or slope run-off.

By diverting flood waters from entering rivers directly, for future more gradual release, wetlands reduce peak river discharges and consequently reduce flood damage downstream. In evaluating the benefits of the flood water detention service, an assessment is required of impacts on the extent of flooding as a consequence of the reduction in peak flow. Both the potential benefits of flood water detention and flood control will be assessed in this section. In addition, flood water detention can be important in terms of wildlife habitat provision, and as a component of other services such as sediment retention and nutrient retention/export.

Table 5.1 *Valuation methods used to estimate the socio-economic benefits of wetland ecosystem services*

Wetland ecosystem benefits	Direct use values	Indirect use values	Non-use values	Economic valuation technique[a]						
				MA	HP	TC	CV	DE	RC	PF
Hydrological services										
Flood water detention	√	√			√		√	√	√	
Groundwater recharge/discharge	√	√	√	√	√	√	√		√	√
Sediment retention	√	√						√		
Biogeochemical services										
Nutrient retention/export	√	√	√	√	√	√	√	√	√	√
Trace element storage/export	√	√	√	√	√	√	√	√	√	√
In-situ carbon retention	√	√	√					√		
Ecological services										
Ecosystem maintenance	√	√	√	√	√	√	√		√	
Food web support	√	√	√	√					√	

Note: [a]
CV: Contingent Valuation/Choice Modelling
DE: Defensive Expenditures/Averting Behaviour/Avoided Costs
HP: Hedonic Pricing
MA: Market Analysis
PF: Production Function
RC: Replacement/Restoration Costs
TC: Travel Cost

Table 5.2 *Wetland service outcomes and valuation techniques used*

Service provided	Effect on economic value (benefit)	Valuation techniques used to value
Potable water for residential use	Change in welfare from change in availability of potable water Change in human health or health risks	MA; PF; RC; CV; DE; HP
Water for landscape and turf irrigation Water for agricultural crop irrigation	Change in cost of maintaining public or private property Change in value of crops or production costs	MA; PF; RC; DE; CV
	Change in human health or health risks	MA; PF; RC; DE; CV; DE; HP
Water for livestock watering	Change in value of livestock products or production costs Change in human health or health risks	MA; PF; RC; CV; DE; HP
Water for food product processing	Change in value of food products or production costs Change in human health or health risks	MA; PF; RC; CV; DE; HP
Water for other manufacturing processes	Change in value of manufactured goods or production costs	MA; PF; RC; DE; CV
Water for power plants	Change in cost of electricity generation	MA; PF; RC; DE; CV
Water transport	Change in economic output	MA; PF; RC; DE;
Prevention of saline intrusion	Change in cost of maintaining public or private property	MA; PF; RC; DE; CV
Water/soil support for prevention of land subsidence	Change in cost of maintaining public or private property	MA; PF; RC; DE; CV
Natural erosion, flood and storm protection	Change in cost of maintaining public or private property	MA; PF; RC; DE; CV
Shoreline stabilization	Change in cost of maintaining public or private property	MA; PF; RC; DE; CV
Sediment removal	Change in human health or health risks Change in animal health or health risks Change in economic output or production costs	MA; PF; RC; CV; DE; HP
Transport, treatment and medium for wastes and other by-products of human activities	Change in human health or health risks Change in animal health or health risks Change in economic output or production costs	MA; PF; RC; CV; DE; HP
Improved air quality through the support of living organisms	Change in human health or health risks Change in animal health or health risks	MA; PF; RC; CV; DE; HP

Table 5.2 *Wetland service outcomes and valuation techniques used* (Cont'd)

Service provided	Effect on economic value (benefit)	Valuation techniques used to value
Improved water quality through the support of living organisms	Change in human health or health risks Change in animal health or health risks Change in economic output or production costs	MA; PF; RC; CV; DE; HP
Biological diversity provision	Change in quantity or quality of recreational activities Change in human health or health risks	MA; PF; RC; CV; TC; DE; HP
Recreational swimming, boating, fishing hunting, trapping and plant gathering	Change in quantity or quality of recreational activities Change in human health or health risks.	MA; PF; RC; CV; TC; DE; HP
Commercial fishing, hunting, trapping and plant gathering	Change in value of commercial harvest or costs. Change in human health or health risks.	MA; PF; RC; DE; CV
Energy production	Change in economic output	MA; PF; RC; DE
On-and off-site observation and study for leisure, education and scientific purposes	Change in quantity or quality of on/off-site observation or study activities	MA; PF; RC; DE; CV; TC
Micro-climate regulation, macro-climate regulation	Change in human health or health risks Change in animal health or health risks Change in economic output or production costs	MA; PF; RC; CV; DE; HP
Toxicant removal, toxicant export	Change in human health or health risks Change in animal health or health risk	MA; PF; RC; CV; DE; HP
Cultural value provision	Change in personal utility or well-being	CV
Historical value provision	Change in personal utility or well-being	CV
Aesthetic value provision	Change in personal utility or well-being	CV
Wilderness value provision	Change in personal utility or well-being	CV

Note:

CV = Contingent Valuation/Choice Modelling

DE = Defensive Expenditures/Averting Behaviour/Avoided Costs

HP = Hedonic Pricing.

MA = Market Analysis

PF = Production Function

RC = Replacement Costs/Restoration Costs

TC = Travel Cost

The procedures involved in assessing the economic value of the flood control service of a wetland involve four distinct stages. These are:

1   Assessing the potential for downstream flooding that will be influenced by the wetland (i.e. the assets at risk downstream).
2   Determining the extent to which the wetland influences downstream flooding, and how flooding would be affected were the wetland to be removed (the *with* and *without* comparison).
3   Identifying the potential for floods to damage resources and structures downstream.
4   Estimating the economic value of the wetland's flood control service.

Stages 2 and 3 are important because it is not the percentage of flood water that the wetland diverts, nor even the reduction in the physical extent of downstream flooding, that apportions economic value to the flood control service. It is the influence that this potential flooding will have on resources regarded by society as worth preserving that determines the value associated with the ability of a wetland to reduce flooding impacts.

In the final stage (4), there is a choice of methods that can be employed to estimate economic value of flood control, and it will be up to the analyst to decide which method(s) to employ. While some are theoretically preferable to others, in that they produce values based on the benefits that society derives from flood control, other second-best measures are often easier to determine in practice.

Assessing the potential for downstream flooding that will be influenced by the wetland
A Is the wetland providing storm water storage?
B Is there a potential flooding problem downstream?

1   Is there a history of flooding in the catchment?
2   Is there evidence of flood management activities (past or present) in the catchment?
3   Is there significant human activity (e.g. buildings or farming and land drainage) adjacent to the river downstream?
4   Is the wetland's water storage capacity 'significant' (i.e. could it influence downstream flood potential) compared to the discharge of the river?

If the answer to 1 **or** 2 is yes, then proceed with evaluation.
If the answers to 3 and 4 are yes, then proceed with evaluation.
If otherwise, there may be insufficient economic value attributable to the wetland's water storage service to warrant a detailed evaluation.

Determining the extent to which the wetland influences downstream flooding, and how flooding would be affected were the wetland to be removed (the with *and* without *comparison):*

A What is the likely influence of the wetland's water storage on downstream flooding?

1   As with 4 above: how 'significant' is the wetland's storage capacity compared to discharge of the river?

2   How much water is the wetland likely to divert from the river's storm discharge? (Require information on storm discharge at the point of the wetland to estimate probable future discharges, as well as the likely capacity of the wetland to reduce this discharge.)

3   How does the reduction in discharge correspond to flood levels downstream: for example does $1m^3$ of water storage correspond to $1m^3$ reduced flooding downstream?

4   What is the maximum additional water storage capacity of the wetland? Does this vary significantly according to factors such as time of year? (There will be a limit to the additional water storage capacity; so that the significant reduction in downstream peak discharge may be restricted to smaller flood episodes: the reduction is unlikely to remain a fixed percentage of discharge.)

5   How does flood water from the river in question synchronize with flood waters from other tributaries to produce peak flood levels?

(It is feasible that simply by delaying the discharge of water, flooding downstream could be made worse, depending upon the synchronization of different tributaries.)

A number of these points, especially those relating to catchment level issues are raised in Larson (1986). Interactions at the scale of the watershed are important, since 'although it is possible for an isolated wetland to perform a significant flood control service, effective flood control is more often the result of the interrelationship of a series of wetlands within a particular watershed' (Sather and Smith, 1984, p5).

B What is the likely degree of downstream flooding if the wetland remains undisturbed? For example historical episodes; flooding predictions or records; efficacy of flood mitigation measures. Factors such as location, area, depth and duration (especially, more or less than 12 hours) will be important.

C How frequently might such floods be expected (return periods or probabilities)? For example historical episodes; flooding records and predictions; efficacy of flood mitigation measures.

D From A, B and C above, what degree of (increased) flooding might be expected if the wetland's flood water storage was negated?

E Hence, to what (quantitative) extent is the wetland expected to influence downstream flooding (location, area, depth, timing and duration)?

Identifying the potential for floods to damage resources and structures downstream
What are the land (or river) uses in potential flood areas?

If, for instance, flooding is most likely to affect forest areas, parkland or other wetlands downstream, the damage may be minimal and short term. However, if an urban area is under threat, damage costs could be considerable and longer term.

Velocity reduction and erosion control

The flood control service can also have benefits in terms of control of bank erosion caused by peak river discharges. This is achieved through the retention and delayed gradual release of water. Some wetlands continually reduce the velocity of surface water flows, not only during high discharge episodes, further limiting erosion downstream. The value of erosion control is determined by the extent of potential erosion and its impact on social welfare. If erosion of a river bank would result in loss of marginal grazing land, for example, the value of its control is low, but if it were to undermine the foundations of a building, the value would be higher. The preceding sections on identifying the potential damage downstream are relevant here. The most likely valuation approach will be to assess the 'damage costs avoided' by maintaining the wetland, which is outlined in detail below.

Valuation techniques

- *Hedonic pricing.* Hedonic pricing can be used to analyse the price differential for properties that are at risk from flooding. It entails analysis of all variables that could affect price, such as location, size, aspect and age of property. Use of hedonic pricing requires the existence of a property market and the existence of known and distinct risks of flooding. It is a complicated procedure. Impacts of flooding on property prices can be countered by defensive expenditures to reduce flood damage (Holway and Burby, 1990). A further complication is that perceived risk of flooding and the resultant impact on house prices can diminish as memories of previous flooding episodes fade (Tunstall et al, 1994). Also, house prices may reflect flood hazards only where flooding has occurred relatively recently, regardless of the expected frequency of flooding (Tobin and Newton, 1986).
- *Contingent valuation.* Flood water control can be valued by asking the affected population what they would be hypothetically willing to pay to either avoid flooding (of some area of interest) or to avoid an increase in the frequency of flood episodes. Given the analytical and resource demands of contingent valuation survey, this is best limited to valuation of the impacts of flooding that are non-marketed, such as impacts on unique ecosystems.

- Damage costs avoided. The costs that would be incurred if flood control provision (e.g. the flood protection provided by a wetland) was not present are given by the damage costs. These can be divided into direct costs, indirect costs and intangible costs.

  The direct costs of flooding are incurred by physical contact with the flood waters. Costs of damage to the built environment are determined by the type of building (e.g. residential, commercial, industrial) and factors such as the design, function, density and age of the buildings. Cost estimates can be obtained from relevant publications (e.g. the 'FLAIR blue book' used in the UK (N'Jai et al, 1990)), government agencies, or site-specific surveys conducted by government agencies or insurers. In determining the costs of damage to movable assets, account needs to be taken of avertive action. For example, Tunstall et al (1994) found in a study of flooding in Maidenhead in the UK that the reduction in damage due to avertive action was 'substantial'. Higgs (1992) allows for a 5 to 10 per cent reduction in damage costs due to items being moved away in advance from flood-prone areas.

  Flooding also imposes costs on productive activities in the non-built environment. Damage to natural ecosystems (wetlands, woodlands and meadows) may be minor and temporary. However, the costs can be substantial for intensive agriculture. Losses in returns to agricultural production are determined by the depth, extent and duration of flooding, the effluent and silt content of the flood waters, types of crop, expected yields and price. Silt exacerbates the volume of flooding and is itself a cause of damage; Clark (1985) estimated that silt accounted for 20 per cent and 7 per cent of urban and rural flood damage respectively for a study in the US. Returns from agriculture, as the opportunity cost of wetland preservation, are calculated by Turner et al (1983) based on detailed analysis of output, fixed and variable costs and transfer payments (agricultural subsidies). Estimates of standard losses in agricultural gross margins due to flooding may also be available from official publications (e.g. the *Farm Management Pocketbook* for the UK). Long-term impacts on agricultural production through continued exposure to inundation are reflected in the value of the land. Flooding affects the land use categorization of land and this is reflected in the market price (Boddington, 1993); average price data for land use categories is often available from official publications.

  Flooding also results in indirect and intangible costs. Indirect costs are caused by disruption to physical and economic linkages in the economy. They include costs of implementing immediate emergency measures; reduced production, and the knock-on effects of this on production elsewhere; impacts on transport; and increases in living expenses. Intangible costs by definition cannot be readily quantified. Examples include psychological effects (stress caused by flooding and worry about future events) and poor health caused by flooding. Some costs formerly described as intangibles are now being quantified such as the effects of disruption and evacuation (Green and Penning-Rowsell, 1986; 1989). Intangible costs could be more significant than the direct damage of a flood episode (Green and Penning-Rowsell, 1989). It is best to acknowledge that such costs are expected but cannot be valued and that the total cost of damage (and hence the value of the wetland flood protection service) is underestimated as a result.

- *Defensive expenditures.* Defensive expenditures provide only a minimum estimate of the benefits of flood water control as they may omit costs of flooding against which defensive actions are not taken. Furthermore, defensive expenditures tend to be low relative to potential damage as individuals underestimate the likelihood of flooding and overestimate their ability to cope with its effects (Tunstall et al, 1994). Defensive expenditures include relocation of assets (buildings, nature reserves and livestock (Boddington, 1993), rewiring of electrical points above expected flood levels and raising of houses on stilts or piles (Tunstall et al, 1994). Relocation may not be to a site that is a direct substitute. Costs of relocation therefore need to be attributed accordingly between the various benefits, and any disadvantages also need to be taken into account.

- *Replacement cost.* The replacement cost of flood control can be determined, for example, through the use of shadow projects. In the case of the flood water control service of a wetland, a shadow project could entail creation or restoration of another wetland that would perform the same service within a given catchment. This would also replace other services of the wetland and would, therefore, be particularly appropriate in a situation where total loss of a wetland is threatened. Locally relevant costings for wetland creation or restoration are likely to be sparse (though mitigation banking has led to considerable creation and restoration of wetlands in the US). There is uncertainty associated with 'engineered' ecosystems and the services that they can perform. This will be more pronounced the more geographically distant are the original and new locations, and economic values in terms of who can derive the benefits are also likely to alter with increasing distance. There is also the question of 'authenticity', where the natural or original version of a resource may be preferred to even an exact replica, thereby influencing the value (especially amenity and non-use values) attributed to the ecosystem. For instance, Kosz (1996) finds a strong preference among Austrians for wetlands in an unchanged state, even if artificial manipulation allows natural conditions to be simulated 'perfectly'. For shadow projects that entail a change in land use for a site (e.g. taking land out of agricultural production) the opportunity costs of this must also be included in the analysis.

- *Current flood protection measures.* Identifying flood protection measures already in place in the catchment can provide useful indicators as to the potential extent and possible costs associated with any increased flooding:

- If flood protection measures are in place, then presumably there *is* considerable flooding potential; costs of improving facilities already in place may be substantially less than building entirely new facilities.
- If there are no flood protection measures in place, then flooding might not be expected to be a major problem; even if it is, costs of implementing new flood protection schemes could exceed the benefits of reduced flooding.

Artificial flood control measures:

A Given the expected degree of increased flooding, what preventive measures would be required?
Possible measures could involve construction of drainage channels, levees, barrages and flood walls, pumping and drainage systems, channel alteration, or dam construction; or improving such facilities already in place.

B What are the estimated costs of such an enterprise?
This information may be available from local water authorities, agricultural authorities, environmental authorities, engineering consultancies or local councils.

C What ongoing maintenance costs would this entail in the future?
This could be based on similar cases elsewhere, from sources such as those outlined in B.

D Are the current and future costs of flood protection likely to exceed the damage that floods could cause if they are not checked? (See damage costs avoided, above.)
The type of land use that would be flooded as a result of the wetland service being lost may give a rough indication. The possible damage costs (see previous section) can approximate the benefits to be derived from maintaining the flood control service.

E Will the flood protection measures themselves incur indirect costs or benefits?
There is frequently a 'risk–environment trade-off' (Fordham and Tunstall, 1990) between reduced risks of flooding through construction of flood defence measures, and impacts on local environmental quality. Such impacts might involve a loss of landscape amenity in terms of open spaces, river views and accessibility, or local ecosystem damage. There is also the potential that flooding could simply be increased elsewhere downstream. There could be *benefits* associated with protective structures, such as increased recreation possibilities or energy production potential, suggesting that construction costs cannot be

attributed solely to achieving flood protection. This information is likely to derive from local experts and planners or previous cases elsewhere.

Groundwater recharge

Definition: the recharge of groundwater by infiltration and percolation of detained flood water into a significant aquifer.

A wetland's ability to recharge groundwater will only be of value if that groundwater is then of some benefit to society. It is important to identify a subsequent use of groundwater, or perhaps non-use motivations for maintaining supplies of groundwater, for economic value to be associated with the wetland's recharge service. Again, to assess the economic value of this recharge service, the following procedures must be used:

1   Assessing the potential for the wetland recharge to influence groundwater.
2   Determining the extent to which the wetland influences levels of groundwater, and how these would be affected were the wetland to be removed (the *with* and *without* comparison).
3   Identifying the potential uses of groundwater – for example abstraction, maintenance of groundwater discharge services, and for future use.
4   Estimating the economic value of the wetland's groundwater recharge with respect to each of these 'uses'.

The benefits may be direct, such as abstraction of water for irrigation or domestic use, or indirect, such as the maintenance of water table levels. In addition to these use values, there may be non-use values of maintaining groundwater supplies. Non-use values can be attributed to the maintenance of groundwater supplies for subsequent generations, but only if use of the reserves is anticipated.

Valuation techniques

As far as extractive uses are concerned, the techniques involved in assessing the economic value of groundwater recharge are much the same as those outlined for the 'groundwater discharge/surface water generation' below. Studies that have considered values for groundwater supply are outlined as they illustrate techniques that may also be useful for assessing the value of surface water. They include hedonic pricing based on variations in availability of groundwater irrigation supplies; costs of establishing substitute well sites; and contingent valuation of willingness to pay for alternative piped water supplies. A number of studies have assessed values associated with maintaining the quality of groundwater (which may be relevant to the in-situ uses of the recharge service) and these are considered under the 'nutrient retention' service. Two other in-situ use values arising from groundwater recharge include prevention of land subsidence and saltwater intrusion.

Prevention of land subsidence

- *Hedonic property pricing.* Hedonic pricing is used to analyse a price differential in property that is attributable solely to the risk of subsidence. If identical sets of housing exhibit variation in prices, and the only non-constant attribute is the risk of subsidence, then price differences can be related to the buyers' willingness to pay to avoid subsidence. However, it is necessary to assess all relevant variables that could affect price (e.g. location, size, aspect, age of property, etc.), and to isolate the effect of subsidence from these.

- *Damage costs avoided.* Predominant land uses are identified and the various costs of potential subsidence assessed. Estimation of the damage costs that are avoided due to groundwater recharge provides an upper bound estimate of the value of this service as it does not technically value society's willingness to pay to avoid the subsidence. Instead, it values the full extent of costs expected to result from subsidence, which could exceed the cost of alternative measures that might be used to negate the economic impacts. However, it may not be feasible to estimate all the costs involved, particularly the intangible costs.

Salt water intrusion

- *Residual imputation and variants.* Intrusion of salt water can occur due to falling groundwater levels areas near to the coast. Saltwater intrusion can render groundwater unusable for irrigation, thereby impinging directly on agricultural production. The change in net returns that this would cause can be used to assess the value of maintaining groundwater levels to prevent the intrusion of salt water.

Groundwater discharge

Definition: the upward seepage of groundwater to the wetland surface.

The discharge of groundwater contributes to the surface water within a wetland and to downstream flow. Whether water originates from direct precipitation, groundwater discharge or another source will not in itself influence the value attributable to a wetland's surface water generation. Groundwater discharge at a wetland is not considered as a separate service in terms of valuation. The discharge will contribute to surface water within the wetland and therefore can be valued with the same techniques as outlined in the section above. Characteristics of discharged groundwater, such as temperature and chemical constituents, might influence other wetland services such as primary productivity and the ability to retain nutrients, but any benefits that may be associated with these will be included in the valuation of specific services. Identifying the source of water could become important if the focus of valuation is extended to a level beyond the wetland – perhaps to the catchment level. In this case, benefits associated with surface water could be linked to its previous sources, thereby attributing value, perhaps, to ecosystems that have facilitated the previous recharge of groundwater elsewhere.

Surface water generation

Definition: the discharge of groundwater into the surface water system.

Groundwater discharge and surface water generation can be considered as one outcome for the purposes of valuation. Whether water originates from direct precipitation, groundwater discharge or another source does not influence the value attributable to surface water generation. The surface water that is generated contributes to the stocks and flows of surface water, which support a variety of in-situ and extractive uses as well as non-use values.

Extractive uses of surface water include use of water for irrigation and domestic purposes. In-situ uses of surface water are more varied and can include maintenance of habitats and provision of aesthetic and recreational value, for example chalk streams, which are Biodiversity Action Plan priority habitat. A number of the in-situ uses of surface water are also considered within other services. For instance, the reliance of characteristic wetland ecology on surface water and anaerobic conditions resulting from inundation (and the subsequent capacity to retain excess nutrients) are considered under the 'ecological' and 'nutrient retention' services, respectively. Downstream habitat and biodiversity maintenance are considered below only insofar as they might contribute to recreational and amenity value. Other benefits associated with maintaining biodiversity could be significant (e.g. non-use values) and valuation methods for these are outlined under the subsection on 'ecological' services.

Valuation techniques[1]

As mentioned earlier, the techniques outlined below for valuing extractive and in-situ uses of surface water are also applicable to the extractive uses listed under groundwater recharge. The main extractive and in-situ uses and possible techniques used to value them have already been comprehensively considered in, for example, Gibbons, 1986; Young, 1996; National Research Council, 1997; Renzetti, 2002; hence we only provide a few illustrative application examples here.

- *Market-based transactions.* Surface water abstraction for use in irrigation can be valued using market prices observed in rentals and sales of water rights. In order for traded water rights (either for use of water over a specified period or for a permanent right to water use) to reflect the economic value of water use, allocation and enforcement of property rights is required. If necessary, prices should be adjusted to reflect long-term considerations (i.e. social values). In practice rental rates may be affected by factors other than the marginal value of water. Although observations of prices on markets for perpetual water rights are more appropriate for long-run planning contexts, some degree of care is required in converting this capitalized asset value into the annual values conventionally used in planning and policy analysis (Young, 1996). Furthermore, the use of water right prices, in circumstances where crop prices are supported by agricultural subsidies, will lead to overestimation of the social value of irrigation water.

- *Residual imputation and variants.* This is one of the techniques that is most widely used to value irrigation water. It was employed by Ruttan (1965) in an early study that demonstrated the difference between the value of irrigated and non-irrigated agricultural production. Some degree of care has to be taken with its use to ensure that statistical problems, such as multicollinearity between variables, do not bias the analysis. Linear programming models have been applied to farm budget data to derive shadow values on irrigation water (e.g. Colby, 1989). Here, crop type is the most important determinant of the marginal value of irrigation water. The presence of uncertainty makes valuation of agricultural water use difficult, with uncertainty in the need for irrigation (arising from climatic variation, for example) and in water supplies. Farmers' attitudes towards risk must therefore be considered when undertaking studies. Market distortions and externalities also need to be taken into account.

- *Derived demand functions.* This technique has been used to estimate households' valuation of domestic water supplies employing relatively easily acquired price and quantity data, for example in Young and Gray (1972) and Gibbons (1986). Though these studies address households' valuations of a given quantity of water, they did not address complications created by variations in water quality or service reliability. These issues have been considered in studies using contingent valuation and avoided cost approaches.

- *Hedonic pricing.* Hedonic pricing can, in principle, be used to derive the value of maintenance of river flows by surface water generation (Loomis, 1987a). Individuals or businesses (including farms) might pay a premium for property located close to a river. It may be difficult to distinguish use of water in the river from other locational factors, such as benefits associated with aesthetics, recreation or transportation that result from proximity to the river. It is also difficult to determine the contribution made by the discharge of groundwater to maintenance of water levels in the river. Few studies have used hedonic pricing to value surface water generation, presumably due to these complications and demands of the technique. One of the few examples decomposes the value of agricultural land as a function of its attributes including the use of irrigation water (Faux and Perry, 1999).

- *Replacement cost/avoided cost.* Avoided cost has been used to value hydroelectric power generation (see Gibbons, 1986). The cost that would be incurred if the capacity to generate power were provided from an alternative source is used to impute the value of the hydroelectric power generated. However, the method is problematic as it ignores the price elasticity of demand for electric energy. The approach can also be applied to valuation of surface water generation where water is abstracted to provide drinking water. The expense of finding an alternative water supply, though considerable, is likely to be exceeded by benefits of continued use of the existing source. The technique may be particularly suited to this application if there is difficulty in valuing the health implications of restrictions in water supply.

Sediment retention

Definition: the net retention of sediments carried in suspension by waters inundating the wetland from river overbank flooding and run-off from the contributory area.

The benefits of a wetland's ability to retain sediments that settle out as the water velocity passing through the wetland decreases relate essentially to the reduced sediment load in waters downstream. However, the retention of sediments also contributes to other potential benefits *within* the wetland, such as the support of ecological services, as this deposition of sediments maintains inputs and improves water quality within the wetland. Sedimentation within a wetland maintains biodiversity and biomass harvesting and is thus closely linked to the ecological services; the evaluation of this benefit will be examined within the context of the 'ecological services' section.

Valuation of the damage resulting from sediment loading (or benefits of reduced loading due to a wetland's sediment retention service) is considered. Again, assessing the economic value of the sediment retention by a wetland involves:

1   assessing the potential for sediment to be retained by the wetland;
2   determining the extent to which the wetland reduces the sediment load of the downstream flow and how this will be affected if the wetland were to be removed (*with* and *without* comparison);
3   identifying any adverse effects of increased sediment loads that result in a loss in economic welfare; linking possible (quantified) increases in sediment load to these adverse effects;
4   estimating the economic value of each of the benefits of reduced sediment loading due to the wetland's sediment retention.

In order for the wetland to perform sediment retention, there must be sediment within the water entering the wetland and the conditions for the deposition of sediment must be met. The sediment load of water entering a wetland is dependent upon the upstream catchment, for example recent logging or intensive cultivation/soil compaction can lead to higher levels of sediment being released into the watercourse. For this sediment to be deposited, the conditions within the wetland must be such that the water is moving slowly.

Valuation techniques

Retention of sediment reduces the load in water downstream and thereby improves water quality. The value of this may be most readily estimated in terms of the additional costs that would be incurred by industrial and municipal users of water through the necessity for water treatment in the absence of sediment retention. Higher water quality may also lead to increased opportunities downstream (e.g. for recreation and commercial fisheries) and will have biological impacts on survival of habitats and species. Habitats and biodiversity are considered here only insofar as they might contribute to recreational and amenity value. Techniques for valuing the benefits of improved water quality (or, conversely, the costs of poor water quality) are covered under the nutrient retention service.

Additional benefits of reduced sediment loads include mitigation of damage to water conveyance facilities, for example through deposition of sediment in rivers, drainage ditches and irrigation canals, which can lead to adverse effects on navigation and water storage capacity and can increase flooding and costs of maintenance. Some of the techniques that may be used to value those benefits, which have not already been considered, are discussed below.

- *Avoided cost/damage costs.* The benefits of maintaining navigation can be estimated in terms of the avoided costs of alternative transport. This approach does not usually account for the differences in speed between alternative modes of transport. Alternatively, the benefits of maintaining navigation can be valued as the damage costs avoided in terms of reduced accidents and groundings. However, values are likely to be low, especially if the costs of infrastructure have already been accounted for. The benefits of mitigating damage to water conveyance, such as deposition in drainage ditches and irrigation canals, is peculiar to the sediment retention service. Estimating the damage costs avoided in terms of the costs of reversing possible adverse impacts is the most appropriate valuation technique to use.
- *Residual imputation and variants.* The presence of fine silt particles in water used for irrigation can lead to a loss in productivity, as these can seal the surface of the soil, making it impermeable. However, the addition of sediment can also increase soil fertility and thereby improve productivity. As sediment impinges directly on agricultural production, for which market prices exist, then changes in marketed outputs can be used to assess the value of sediment retention.

VALUATION OF BIOGEOCHEMICAL SERVICE BENEFITS

Nutrient retention

Definition: the storage of excess nutrients (nitrogen and/or phosphorus) via biological, biochemical and geochemical processes in biomass (living and dead) and soil mineral compounds of a wetland.

In storing nitrogen and phosphorus, the nutrient retention service has the effect of improving water quality downstream of the wetland. However, the retention of nutrients contributes to other potential benefits *within* a wetland such as the support of ecological services, as these nutrients contribute to high levels of productivity. As this productivity contributes to biodiversity maintenance and biomass harvesting, it is closely linked to the ecological services and will be evaluated in that section.

The assessment of the economic consequences of damage to wetlands relating to nutrient retention involves the following steps:

1   assessment of the potential for nutrients, species, nitrogen and phosphorus to be retained by the wetland;
2   determination of the degree to which nutrient release into water sources is reduced by the wetland (*with* and *without* comparison);
3   identification of potential adverse effects of increased nutrient levels and where they might occur;
4   assessment of the degree to which an increase in nutrient levels that results in adverse effects represents a loss in economic welfare.

As nutrient retention refers to the *storage* of nutrients within a wetland site, a further stage of assessment is required. Since retention implies a comparatively short time horizon, if no subsequent *removal* of these nutrients from the wetland occurs, then potential thresholds of nutrient levels, and the limited time frame before higher nutrient levels once again enter the water stream, must be considered. The permanent removal of nutrients from the wetland is discussed in the next section on 'nutrient export'. Presumably, if no export occurs, then continual nutrient retention cannot be sustained indefinitely. This could be due to impacts on the wetland itself or an overloading of the capacity of the wetland to perform the service, thereby crossing some threshold beyond which the service is either degraded or is not able to process any further nutrients. Where the service is sufficiently degraded, it may be possible that increased levels of nutrients are released as a result of additional recourse to this service. Where nutrient retention dominates, without any subsequent export, it might be appropriate to consider concepts such as critical loads, sustainability and maintaining safe minimum standards in addition to economic valuation.

Thus, a further stage of analysis involves questions as to the physical capacity of a wetland to continue to absorb nutrients:

5   determination of whether a possible threshold level of nutrients above which the wetland service is overburdened exists, and whether current or predicted future nutrient levels threaten to cross such a threshold.

Assessing the potential for retention

Nutrient retention is only performed when excess nutrients enter the wetland ecosystem, where excess nutrients refer to a level of nutrients that would not be expected under natural conditions. To determine whether nutrients are being retained within a wetland depends on certain conditions being met. Input of nitrogen, ammonia or phosphorus is an essential prerequisite, whether through a direct or indirect source, with other factors including vegetation type, soil–water regime and the pH of soil, depending on which process is influencing the retention of nutrients.

Determining the reduction in nutrient release

It is essential that the quantities of each of the nitrogen, ammonia and phosphorus nutrient inputs to the wetlands are identified. Once in a wetland, nutrients can be retained through storage in living (plants) and dead (soil organic matter) biomass, through biogeochemical interactions with the mineral component of soil, and through the deposition of particulate matter within the wetland (Figure 5.1). It is possible for a wetland to store nutrients in all these ways or in any combination. Thus it is essential to determine the nutrient retention capacity and how much it is being utilized for each possible means of storage within the wetland.

Identifying adverse effects of increased nutrient levels

The impact on aquatic ecosystems of nutrient enrichment is no different to the impact on the wetland ecosystem, in that biological productivity will increase. However, although wetlands are typically able to withstand substantial increases in the concentration of available nutrients, many other aquatic habitats are not nearly so tolerant. While the increased biological productivity within aquatic ecosystems can be beneficial, if the capacity of an ecosystem to assimilate the nutrient-enhanced productivity is exceeded, water quality degradation will occur with detrimental impacts on the components of an ecosystem and ecosystem functioning, and consequently human welfare. Caddy (1993) demonstrated the effect of this assimilation threshold for fisheries, where a positive relationship exists between yield and nutrient loading up to a maximal point, after which the fisheries' yield declines as nutrient load increases.

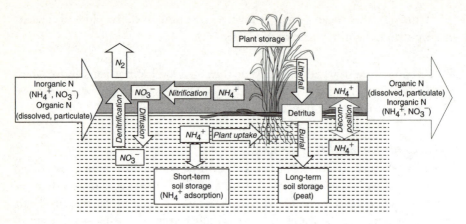

Figure 5.1 *Summary diagram of the fate of nitrogen entering a wetland*

Source: DeBusk, 1999.

Effect on human welfare

Improvements to water quality will only be of value if human welfare is affected. The effects of eutrophication and acidification of surface waters have the following impacts on human welfare:

- water flow and movement of boats impeded by increased vegetation;
- loss of habitats and biodiversity;
- unsuitability of water for drinking, even after treatment;
- decrease in the amenity value of water, for example for water sports;
- disappearance of commercially important species.

Thus, the nutrient retention service performed by a wetland produces economic benefit in terms of navigation, biodiversity and water quality downstream of the wetland. The navigation of waterways downstream of the wetlands is covered in the section on 'sediment retention', and downstream habitat and biodiversity maintenance are considered here only insofar as they might contribute to recreational and amenity value.

The benefits of wetlands in reducing water pollution can be classified and therefore valued as (Freeman, 1982):

- Recreation, such as fishing, boating, hiking and aesthetic appreciation of the water-body or waterside site.
- Non-use benefits, from knowing that water quality and ecosystem health are maintained for the sake of others.
- Diversionary uses, including health aspects associated with abstracting drinking water, costs associated with treatment of municipal water supplies,

costs to households of possible corrosion of pipes and appliances, and treatment costs of water used in industrial processes and cooling.
- Commercial fisheries, whose productivity may be heavily affected by levels of pollutants.

Valuation techniques

The main impact of storage of nitrogen and phosphorus is improved water quality; thus this service is discussed here with respect to water quality. A few illustrative examples of valuing benefits of improved water quality are outlined below. Impacts on recreation can be valued using the travel cost method. The benefits for drinking water supplies can be considered via defensive expenditures. Nutrient retention benefits can be considered generally in terms of the costs of providing substitute treatment facilities. Potential increases in the costs of industrial production processes are not considered here. The residual imputation methodology, discussed with reference to the 'surface water generation' service, could also be employed to value the benefits of improved water quality as an input to production processes.

- *Contingent valuation.* CV-based research has been widely used to consider water quality. Jordan and Elnagheeb (1993) used the approach to assess households' valuations of improvements in drinking water supplies (due to reductions in nitrate levels). One of the most challenging aspects of using this approach is the manner in which water quality information is conveyed to survey respondents, and specifically whether objective or subjective measures of water quality are used. Poe (1998) argues that objective measures are preferable because people do not have reliable and well-informed reference points. Conjoint analysis and contingent ranking have also been used to value water quality improvements. For example, Georgiou et al (2000) used contingent ranking to value urban river water quality improvements. Appendix C contains a case study that examines water quality in the Philippines.
- *Travel cost.* The travel cost method has been used to assess the value of improved water quality at recreational sites. A complex form of travel cost analysis, which includes measures of water quality as independent variables, is applied to sites which vary in water quality (but are similar in other attributes) or to one site for which water quality changes over time. This is an extremely involved procedure, which measures only the recreational benefits associated with improved water quality downstream. There are a number of difficulties with such analysis. In particular, for a multi-site study, the influence of water quality between sites needs to be isolated from other varying attributes that might affect recreation demand. In the case of a single site temporal study, changes in water quality need to be isolated from other attributes that might change over time. Smith and Kaoru (1990) undertook

a meta-analysis of travel cost studies that relate to water-based recreational values. They found that the following five features consistently had an influence on results: type of recreational site, the definition of a site's usage and quality, measurement of the opportunity cost of time, the description of substitutes, and specification of the demand model.

- *Hedonic price method.* The price of properties in close proximity to water bodies can be affected by the quality of the water and therefore by nutrient retention. The value of the nutrient retention service is derived from (a) property values that are attributable to water quality and (b) the role of the service in maintaining the water quality. This entails analysis of prices for otherwise similar properties that are located close to polluted and unpolluted water bodies. The data demands are, however, considerable. A rough approximation of value can be derived directly from a summation of adjustments in property prices, which could be based on assessments of experts, such as estate agents, rather than actual observed price differentials in the property market.

- *Defensive expenditures/avoided cost.* The value of improved water quality can be estimated based on the expenditures undertaken by people to avoid consumption of poor quality water. The sum of defensive expenditures on marketed goods such as water purification equipment represents the lower boundary of society's willingness to pay for improved water quality. This accounts only for changes in behaviour made by consumers in response to poor water quality. It does not take into account consumers who do not undertake defensive actions but would nonetheless prefer improved water quality. Such individuals may be inhibited from acting by inconvenience associated with the defensive activities, or lack of information about pollutant levels and possible adverse effects. Abdalla et al (1992) use this valuation approach to determine the time and money that households expend to avoid risk arising from groundwater contamination. Their approach assumes that households undertake a two-step decision making process in which they first decide whether to undertake any avertive action, and then decide on the intensity of those actions. Abdalla (1994) also provides a survey of the literature on averting cost methods.

- *Replacement cost.* The retention of nutrients can be valued using the replacement cost in terms of the cost of substitutes. Substitute activities include reduction of nitrate and phosphate pollution at source by limiting applications of agricultural fertilizers or the installation of water treatment facilities. The replacement cost is particularly useful for situations where the benefits of reduced nutrient loading are difficult to estimate. Examples include estimation of the benefits of avoiding deleterious health effects or the benefits of maintaining water quality and ecosystems for future generations.

Nutrient export

Definition: the removal of excess nutrients (nitrogen and/or phosphorus) from a wetland via biological, biochemical, physical and land management processes.

The sources of value attributable to nutrient export are the same as for nutrient retention (previous section). The important difference, however, is that *export* implies a permanent removal of the nutrients, while *retention* suggests that nutrients might once more enter the water stream. The level of nutrients that can be diverted from the water stream by a wetland may alter according to which of these two services is being performed.

The initial valuation techniques for improvements to the water quality will be the same for both nutrient retention and export (hence, the section 'Nutrient retention' should be referred to for valuing the nutrient export service). The same initial stages of analysis should be undertaken to assess the economic consequences of damage to the wetlands relating to this nutrient export:

1   assessing the potential for the nutrients, nitrogen and phosphorus, to be retained by the wetland;
2   determination of the degree to which nutrient release into water sources is reduced by the wetland (*with* and *without* comparison);
3   identification of potential adverse effects of increased nutrient levels and where they might occur;
4   assessment of the degree to which an increase in nutrient level that results in these adverse effects represents a loss in economic welfare.

Assessing the potential for nutrient release to be reduced
Within the nutrient export service, there are three major processes by which the nutrients are removed or 'exported' from wetlands: via gaseous export of nitrogen, export through land management and physical processes (Figure 5.1).

Nitrogen can be released into the atmosphere through bacterial reduction to either nitrous oxide or atmospheric nitrogen (Mitsch and Gosselink, 2000). If nitrogen is present in the form of ammonium or ammonia, this can be released to the atmosphere through volatilization. The uptake of nutrients by plants increases ecosystem productivity, and the nutrients can be removed through land use management practices. Land use practices may export the nutrient directly, through the burning of wetland vegetation (loss to the atmosphere), harvesting of vegetation (e.g. crops for consumption), and harvesting of the produce of animals (which have assimilated the nutrients through the consumption of vegetation). Further uses of the land that could lead to the export of nutrients are forestry and hunting, fishing and shooting. The final method of export is when nutrients are removed from the wetland by water or wind transport processes. While the nutrients are permanently removed from the wetland in question, they can then act to support other ecosystems or be a source of nutrient contaminants for other ecosystems.

Determining how actual nutrient release is affected by wetlands

The quantities of nitrate, ammonia and phosphorus entering the wetland must be identified. In addition to determining how much of each nutrient is retained, further analysis is required to determine whether nutrients previously stored within a wetland are now being exported, and if so, in what quantities, as this could adversely affect water quality and this service could represent a *cost* rather than a benefit. This is a direct consequence of the export service releasing nutrients back into the aquatic ecosystem. Otherwise the means of analysis are the same as for nutrient retention.

Identifying adverse effects of increased nutrient levels

In reducing the levels of nutrients entering waters downstream of the wetland, this service has the same effects as the previous service. However, a further consideration exists over where the nutrients ultimately end up, having been exported from the wetland. Will the means of export simply transfer the problem elsewhere? The value attributable to the wetland for such export should take account of any such external effects that might result off site. For example, a consequence of denitrification could be increased environmental pollution, with nitrous oxide released into the atmosphere being oxidized to nitric oxide, which is a contributor to acid rain. Also, as the export through land use management involves biomass harvesting, these values are closely linked to the ecological services and will be evaluated in that section.

Valuation techniques

Again, the same methods as used in the previous service are used for the effects on water quality, except that a release of nutrients will decrease water quality downstream of the wetland.

Trace element storage

Definition: the storage of trace elements via biochemical and physical processes in the mineral compounds of the wetland soils.

Trace elements (including heavy metals) are natural constituents of the Earth's crust and are present in varying concentrations in all ecosystems. At trace levels, many of these elements are necessary to support life. The essential metals include cobalt (Co), copper (Cu), iron (Fe), manganese (Mn), molybdenum (Mo), strontium (Sr), vanadium (V) and zinc (Zn). However, at elevated levels they become toxic and significantly detrimental to living organisms. They are stable and persistent environmental contaminants since they cannot be degraded or destroyed. They tend to accumulate in soils, seawater, freshwater and sediments. Excessive levels of metals in the marine environment can affect marine biota and pose risks to human consumers of seafood. Non-essential heavy metals of particular concern to surface water systems are cadmium (Cd), chromium (Cr), mercury (Hg), lead (Pb), arsenic (As) and antimony (Sb).

Sources of trace elements found in watercourses include fertilizer input (organic and inorganic), aerial input through atmospheric or gaseous industrial discharge and organic industrial waste or sewage sludge. Trace elements can enter the wetland through groundwater discharge, run-off from slopes, atmospheric deposition and from river water entering the wetland through overbank flooding.

This storage service has the effect of improving water quality downstream of the wetland, and is thus treated in a similar fashion to the nutrient retention service. The assessment of the valuation of trace element retention follows the same five processes as for nutrient retention, since there is the potential for trace elements to be released if thresholds are exceeded. For further detail refer to the nutrient retention service:

1   assessment of the potential for trace elements to be retained by wetlands;
2   determination of the degree to which trace element concentrations in water sources are reduced by wetlands (*with* and *without* comparison);
3   identification of potential adverse effects of increased trace element concentrations and where they might occur;
4   assessment of the degree to which an increase in trace element concentrations represents a loss in economic welfare;
5   determination of whether there exists a possible threshold level of nutrients above which the wetland service is overburdened, and whether current or predicted future nutrient levels threaten to cross such a threshold.

Assessing the potential for trace element concentrations to be reduced
Within a wetland, trace elements can be retained through either physical or biogeochemical means. If the conditions are right for deposition of sediments, for example, when the wetland is inundated with polluted water, trace elements can be deposited in the solid form of particulate matter. Trace elements are bound biogeochemically within the soil, and are thus immobilized. Whether this process occurs depends on the speciation of the elements themselves and the soil conditions.

Determining the reduction in trace element concentrations
It is essential that the trace elements entering the wetlands are identified and quantified. Once in a wetland, the trace elements can be stored through the two major processes of physical and biogeochemical retention. It is possible for a wetland to store trace elements by either or both of these methods. Thus it is

essential to determine the capacity of the wetland to store trace elements by each possible means of storage.

Identifying adverse effects of increased trace element concentrations

In reducing the concentrations of trace elements entering the waters downstream of the wetland, this service has the effect of improving water quality. The impact of increased levels of trace elements within the aquatic ecosystem is in bioaccumulation, where the trace elements enter the food chain through uptake in living plants. Concentrations of the elements increase the further up the food chain one goes, with an increase in the toxicity resulting in a decrease in the survival, size and density of some fish, and the loss of other fish and aquatic biota from lakes and streams.

As the ability of the trace elements to be deposited with other sediments suspended in the water flow is not constrained to wetland areas, in other areas of the watercourse where sedimentation occurs trace elements will be deposited and their effect may be limited. However, in areas where flow rates are high or the water is constantly disturbed, for example in streams and rivers in the upper reaches of a catchment and in tidal estuaries, the concentration in the water column will be high, as the elements do not settle. Additionally, sediments previously deposited may be disturbed, releasing further trace elements and causing high levels of toxicity.

Valuation techniques

The ecological changes resulting from contamination of water by trace elements impact human populations by changing the availability of seafood and creating a risk of consuming contaminated fish or shellfish; reducing our ability to use and enjoy our coastal ecosystems; and causing economic impact on people who rely on healthy coastal ecosystems, such as fishermen and those who cater to tourists. Thus, the same methods of evaluation used for valuing water quality within the nutrient service can be applied here.

Trace element export

Definition: the removal of trace elements from a wetland via biological, biochemical and physical processes.

The sources of value attributable to trace element export are the same as for trace element storage. The important difference however is that *export* implies a permanent removal of the trace elements, while *retention* suggests that trace elements might once more enter the water stream. The level of trace elements that can be diverted from the water stream by a wetland may alter according to which of these two services is being performed.

The initial valuation techniques for improvements to the water quality will therefore be the same for both trace element storage and export. The 'Trace element storage' section should be referred to for evaluating the trace element export service.

The same initial stages of analysis should be undertaken to assess the economic consequences of damage to the wetlands relating to this trace element export service:

1   assessment of the potential for trace elements to be retained by a wetland;
2   determination of the degree to which trace element concentrations in water sources are reduced by the wetland (*with* and *without* comparison);
3   identification of potential adverse effects of increased trace element concentrations and where they might occur;
4   assessment of the degree to which an increase in trace element concentrations that results in these adverse effects represents a loss in economic welfare.

Assessing the potential reduction in trace element release

Trace element export represents a closely linked service affecting water quality in interaction with trace element storage. There are three major processes by which trace elements are removed or exported from a wetland: the uptake of trace elements by plants, and the physical or biogeochemical remobilization of the elements. The remobilization of trace elements can either happen in a physical manner, where the trace elements retained in the particulate matter re-enter the drainage system when the soil in which they are deposited is eroded; or alternatively, biogeochemical remobilization occurs when the chemical bonds between the trace element and the soil break and the trace elements then re-enter the watercourse.

Determining the actual effect on trace element concentrations

It is essential that the trace elements entering wetlands are identified and quantified. A direct consequence of the export service is that trace elements can be released back into the aquatic ecosystem or can enter the food chain. Analysis is required to determine whether trace elements previously stored within the wetland could, with a change in the wetland, shift to being exported, and if so in what quantities, as this could adversely affect water quality. In this way, this service could represent a *cost* rather than a benefit.

An assessment is required into the trace elements exported from the wetland through plant uptake as this not only has implications for the food web, it is the only means by which the elements are actually removed from the wetland.

Identifying adverse effects of increased trace element concentrations

In reducing the levels of trace elements entering the waters downstream of the wetland, this service has the effect of improving water quality. The impact of increased levels of trace elements within the aquatic ecosystem is in bioaccumulation, where the trace elements enter the food chain through biological uptake into living plant matter. These bioaccumulation effects are not constrained to the aquatic ecosystem due to the export of the trace elements through plant uptake, thus the ecological services of biomass maintenance and harvesting can be affected by increased concentrations of heavy metals.

As the ability of the trace elements to be deposited with other sediments suspended in the water flow is not constrained to wetland areas, in other areas of the watercourse where sedimentation occurs trace elements will be deposited and their effect will be limited. However, in areas where flow rates are high or the water is constantly disturbed, for example streams and rivers in the upper reaches of a catchment and tidal estuaries, the concentration will be high as the elements do not settle. Additionally, sediments previously deposited may be disturbed, releasing further trace elements, and causing high levels of toxicity.

Valuation techniques

The ecological changes resulting from contamination of water by trace elements impact human populations by changing the availability of seafood and creating a risk of consuming contaminated fish or shellfish, reducing our ability to use and enjoy our coastal ecosystems, and causing economic impact on people who rely on healthy coastal ecosystems, such as fishermen and those who cater to tourists. Thus, the same methods of evaluation used for valuing water quality within the nutrient service can be applied here.

In-situ carbon retention

Definition: the retention of carbon in the form of partially decomposed organic matter or peat in the soil profile due to environmental conditions that reduce rates of decomposition.

Where hydrological and geomorphological conditions combined with appropriate climatic conditions create wet soils and a low rate of decomposition, partially decomposed organic matter may accumulate within the soil in the form of peat deposits. This leads to the storage of the carbon bound in the organic matter, which is a major benefit of a wetland's ability to accumulate peat. Ecosystems that can act as carbon sinks are becoming increasingly important, as the link between carbon compounds in the atmosphere and global warming becomes apparent (Maltby and Immirzi, 1993). The accumulation of peat can create a substrate for rare and unique plants and animals, which is closely linked to the ecological service of biodiversity maintenance and will be evaluated in this context in that section.

The assessment of the economic value of in-situ retention of carbon through the accumulation of peat requires the degree of accumulation and storage to be estimated, along with their significance in terms of global carbon emissions. The following assessment procedures are required:

Assessing the potential of the wetland for peat accumulation and carbon sequestration

1 determination of the extent to which a wetland acts as a carbon store (the *with* and *without* comparison);
2 identification of the potential uses of accumulated peat;
3 estimation of the economic value of the in-situ carbon retention service.

Assessing potential for peat accumulation

For wetlands the accumulation of carbon may be offset by the simultaneous production of the greenhouse gas methane. In order to ascertain whether a wetland is a carbon sink/source/neutral with respect to greenhouse gas emissions, there is a need to know whether the wetland emits more methane than it stores as organic carbon. Although data on the amount of organic carbon stored by a wetland is easily generated, it is difficult to calculate the production of methane, and as such, little data on wetland methane production currently exists for the UK. While it is known that emissions of methane are lower from high salinity and high altitude wetlands, Parkes (2003) demonstrates how the use of different estimations of methane emissions can lead to substantially different assertions as to whether a wetland is a greenhouse gas sink or source. Parkes found that for the Wash saltmarshes, eastern England, the use of estimates of methane fluxes at the lower end of those reported led to the conclusion that saltmarshes act as a carbon store, while the use of high methane fluxes found the saltmarshes were acting as a source of carbon. Due to these difficulties, and the range of conditions that can influence methane production, it is impossible to generalize which wetlands in the UK will act as carbon stores and which will act as sources. However, when peat wetlands do act as stores of previously accumulated peat this may be associated with a considerable value in terms of containing a potential source of atmospheric carbon. Conversely, if a wetland acts as a source of methane then this will be associated with a considerable cost, given its effects as a greenhouse gas.

Extent of peat accumulation

The conversion of a peatland to another use would result in a considerable release of carbon. Peat is an excellent growing medium; however, it requires drainage and cultivation to be used as pasture or for crops to be grown. The drainage of this peatland leads to increased run-off cutting into the peat layers, with the resulting drying-out as the peat is exposed, enabling the carbon to be oxidized to carbon dioxide, which is ultimately released to the atmosphere. This is in addition to the destruction of habitat. If excessive drainage occurs at the edges of a peat bog, this will affect the continued accumulation of peat and lead to a change in the species formulation.

Uses of accumulated peat

While the slow rates of current accumulation might not generate significant value, the continued storage of carbon could be associated with considerable economic benefits.

Alternative uses of the accumulated peat exist, providing a source of fuel or horticultural materials. However, these are extractive uses of peat bog and due to the considerable length of time that it takes peat to accumulate, any benefit being attributed to the accumulation service based on extraction is ruled out within the temporal framework of an economic study. While these uses are in conflict with the use of peat bogs as a store of carbon and represent a wholly unsustainable degradation of the ecosystem, they do provide a source of value that must be taken into account in any valuation of the wetland ecosystem – if only to ensure that negative economic and social values are considered.

Valuation techniques

The value of peat accumulation as a store of carbon is not easily assessed. Estimating the benefits associated with accumulating and maintaining a carbon store will inevitably represent an extremely rough approximation, the main reason being that the benefits of global warming mitigation are truly global, making their accurate estimation a complex exercise. Damage cost estimates vary between £7 and £70 per tonne of carbon (depending on assumptions about adaptive behaviour); the carbon permit market also provides a possible source of economic data in that a market price for carbon reduction permits is becoming established. Chapter 6, case study B, on managed coastal realignment policy deals with the carbon storage issue in more detail.

VALUATION OF ECOLOGICAL SERVICE BENEFITS

Ecological services relate primarily to maintenance of habitats within which organisms survive. In terms of economic benefits, habitats and their overall structure are not themselves of value. It is the diversity of species (and their genes), landscapes and services that are assigned economic value. It is therefore the biodiversity that is supported by a wetland that forms the basis for valuation of ecological services. An example of the relationship between individual wetland ecological services and economic valuation is illustrated in Figure 5.2, and is outlined below. Essentially, there is considerable overlap in the list of 'Ecological Services'; so, for instance, biomass exports (whether via abiotic or biotic media) are necessarily dependent upon biomass production (allowing for any biomass import). To avoid double counting, economic valuation will concentrate therefore on only a limited number of ecological services. It is biodiversity within, or supported by, a wetland that is most clearly linked to economic value, whether in maintaining it or in harvesting it. In terms of deriving the total economic value

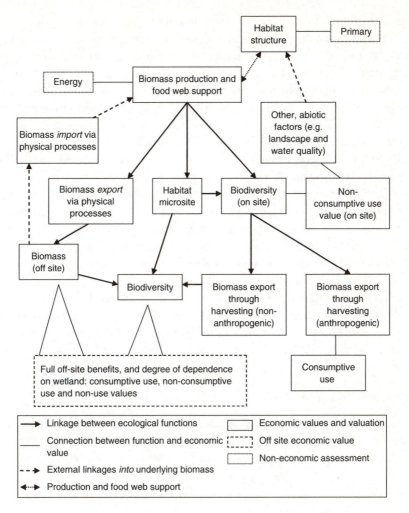

Figure 5.2 *Ecological services and economic value*

of the ecological services of a wetland, estimation focuses specifically upon biodiversity maintenance and anthropogenic harvesting of biomass.

The schematic of Figure 5.2 shows the links between the various ecological services that may be performed by a wetland. These are seen to derive ultimately from biomass production and food web support, although economic value is related to the end product of biodiversity within (and beyond) the wetland. Biomass production, deriving ultimately from utilization of solar energy, is a fundamental process within any ecosystem. However, a simple measure of the quantity of biomass (or perhaps the amount of embedded energy) does not give an indication of whether or not given *qualities* of biomass – the way in which it is structured and organized or its physical location, may be of use or concern to humans. Habitat structure, which serves to encapsulate biomass production and all of the goods and services that may derive from it, is also not of direct use or concern to humans. The system framework within which an ecosystem services may be attributed some form of primary or prior value, although it is not clear that this can be meaningfully quantified. Biodiversity, on the other hand, can be directly linked to satisfying human wants and needs. On-site biodiversity may be associated with non-consumptive use values (such as recreation) or non-use values (such as a bequest for future generations). Direct (anthropogenic) harvesting of the biota can provide consumptive use benefits (such as in providing building materials or foodstuffs). Wetlands that act as habitat microsites might also be valued for their biodiversity, although the degree to which the value of each species can be attributed to the wetland will depend on their reliance upon the wetland. Abiotic export and non-anthropogenic harvesting are not in themselves services that are of value. However, depending on the extent to which this contributes to benefits to be derived from ecosystems elsewhere, some economic value might be attributable to the wetland as a result of such export.

Economic valuation of ecological services performed by wetlands will therefore concentrate on the specific services of biodiversity maintenance and anthropogenic biomass harvesting, although each of the other services under the ecological heading will be considered briefly in turn.

Ecosystem maintenance

Definition: the provision of habitat for animals and plants through the interaction of physical, chemical and biological wetland processes.

The service of ecosystem maintenance is composed of three processes:

- provision of overall habitat structural diversity;
- provision of microsites;
- provision of plant and habitat diversity.

However, it is only through contact with, or concern for, the biological organisms that make up an ecosystem that economic value is generally derived from the ecological services that a wetland performs. It is thus biodiversity within the wetland, the (anthropogenic) export of this biodiversity (*biomass export*) and the wetland's contribution to biodiversity elsewhere that form the basis of the valuation of a wetland's ecological services. While a wetland's biodiversity may derive ultimately from the process of *biomass production* and food web support and is dependent upon overall ecosystem health and habitat structure (*provision of overall habitat structural diversity*), these processes are not in themselves of economic value to society. It is therefore on aspects of a wetland's biodiversity (both quantity and variety of organisms) that economic valuation is focused. A brief overview of the first two processes is given below.

Provision of overall habitat structural diversity

The overall structure of the ecosystem and its habitats is clearly fundamental to continuing ecological processes and interactions. However, as with biomass production, habitat structure is not in itself a source of economic value. A possible caveat to this is in its contribution to the overall landscape, from which amenity benefits may be derived, although this will be included with the benefits to be derived from a wetland's biological features (*biodiversity maintenance*). It is possible that value might be associated with habitat or ecosystem structure: the so-called primary value (see the section in Chapter 4 on wetlands valuation/evaluation). Such a consideration might suggest employing some form of safe minimum standard (Bishop, 1978), which recommends favouring preservation when confronted with irreversible damage, unless the benefits to be derived from the damaging action are considered to be too great to forgo. The concept of incorporating other such criteria into an economic evaluation framework is considered in previous sections.

Provision of microsites

A wetland's provision of habitat microsites for feeding and breeding can generally be valued in the same manner as biodiversity maintenance. However, in the case of habitat microsites, it is explicitly acknowledged that there is only a partial dependence of species on the wetland, so, for instance, any recreational and amenity value they might provide may be restricted to a particular (perhaps seasonal) time frame.

A number of studies have sought to value the benefits of maintaining habitats specifically as breeding microsites. For instance, Boddington (1993) claims to estimate the existence value associated with providing nesting habitat for wading birds, based on the difference in gross margins that are derived from farming (that is conducive to this nesting) compared with what the maximum returns might be under alternative management regimes. Cummings et al, (1994) employ contingent valuation to estimate willingness to pay to preserve habitat that acts as a breeding site for the endangered Colorado Squawfish. Hanley and Craig (1991) refer to the importance of the Scottish Flow wetlands as a breeding site for birds in their contingent valuation study of use and non-use benefits for the area. Loomis (1987b) estimates willingness to pay to preserve a wetland habitat using a contingent valuation survey, where one of the main advantages highlighted was maintaining a site for gull nesting.

While these studies focus specifically on the value of habitat as a breeding site, the valuation techniques and means of apportioning total value between alternative possible microsites – a number of which may be important for the survival of species – are identical to those for biodiversity maintenance in general. In assessing the economic value of biodiversity maintenance the following steps are required:

1   assessment of potential sources of value from maintaining biodiversity;
2   determination of a wetland's contribution to biodiversity maintenance;
3   identification of impact on human welfare;
4   estimation of the economic value of the wetland's flood control service.

Assessment of sources of value

Activities that result in the deliberate export or removal of material are dealt with in the next section on 'Biomass export through harvesting', and relate to 'consumptive use values'. Values associated with maintaining rather than harvesting biodiversity will be associated with non-consumptive use (based on aesthetic benefits such as enjoying scenery or bird watching, and distant use benefits such as reading magazine articles or watching television programmes that involve wetland biodiversity) or non-use values (for instance in preserving natural heritage for future generations). Any indirect use values that derive from the services provided by a wetland are included in Chapters 1 and 2, relating to hydrological and biogeochemical services.

Determining a wetland's contribution

It may be that some types of biodiversity within the wetland that are of value do not depend entirely upon the wetland. So, for instance, in the case of endangered species, there may be substitute sites available with suitable habitat, or species may be only partly reliant on the type of habitat that the wetland provides. This dependence will influence the extent to which the value of biodiversity maintenance can be attributed to the wetland. One possible management (and valuation) approach might involve relocating organisms to alternative sites. Another might be providing replacement or substitute sites where there is suitable habitat. The degree to which the wetland is integral to the preservation of biological attributes will clearly be a matter of scientific enquiry.

Dixon (1989) demonstrates how a wetland can provide a habitat for species that are then utilized off site; although this survey of 'indirect products' was undertaken for mangroves, a wetland habitat type not found in the UK, it nevertheless highlights the range of indirect products that a wetland can provide. Dixon found that mangroves can provide important habitats for a range of fauna, including fish, crustaceans, molluscs, bees, birds, mammals and reptiles, while the benefits derived from these species, either for consumptive use or for recreation, are often derived outside the ecosystem. Part of the value derived from these species is therefore attributable to the wetlands that provide an occasional, but often essential, habitat.

Identification of impact on human welfare
Possible indicators that a wetland's biodiversity may be of value to society follow.

Non-consumptive use values:
• recreation activities such as bird watching, hiking, boating;
• official designation as a site for recreational purposes, perhaps as a national park.

Non-use values:
• Recreational and amenity interest in scenic beauty or specific wildlife could indicate value attributed both by users and non-users to the continued existence of these features based on non-use motivations such as for the sake of future generations.
• Official designation as a protected area based on unique natural features may well indicate social value not dependent on any use being made of the area.
• If the area is known to be home to unique or endangered species, society may well attach value to ensuring the continued existence of these species for their own sake.

Ongoing or historic public (or possibly private) projects designed to enhance or protect biological features might also be an indication of either amenity or non-use benefits deriving from such features.

Valuation techniques
The economic values deriving from biodiversity maintenance are potentially considerable and could be an important component of a wetland's total economic value. However, more so than other (hydrological and biogeochemical) wetland services, maintaining biodiversity and healthy ecological functioning have the potential to be associated with highly uncertain, irreversible and ethically charged outcomes. The loss of species, genetic information or even whole habitat structures may be truly irreversible and the consequences in terms of ecosystem stability and future economic benefits may be wholly uncertain, with the potential for large impacts on the well-being of future generations. In addition to any ethical concerns for other species, moral and ethical issues relating to intergenerational equity are therefore raised when impacts upon biodiversity are threatened. This would suggest that other criteria than simply economic efficiency should be considered, such as applying sustainability constraints or safe minimum standards.

Given the extreme uncertainty that surrounds both the complex interactions within and between ecosystems, as well as the benefits that humans could derive from them both now and in the future, there is a strong argument for supplementing purely economic analysis to allow for such considerable uncertainties. Therefore, particularly with regard to maintaining biodiversity and the linkages within ecosystems, issues such as ensuring sustainability of a given service, preserving critical components of 'natural capital', and maintaining safe minimum standards of species populations and habitat requirement are extremely important.

Where the benefits of maintaining biodiversity are difficult to quantify and/or we can assume that the benefit of maintaining biodiversity is greater than the cost, or goals or targets have been set by alternative methods, then cost-effectiveness analysis is a useful way of appraising management options.

With respect to biodiversity maintenance the valuation techniques of relevance include:

- *Contingent valuation.* Contingent valuation can be particularly useful for assessing the value of biodiversity maintenance, indicating willingness to pay for conservation of biodiversity. Contingent valuation is the only technique currently regarded as suitable for estimating non-use values associated with the maintenance of species diversity and population sizes. By definition, these values are not reliant on individuals visiting the site (so are not associated with measurable changes in behaviour). Brouwer et al (1997) provide a meta-analysis which attributes values to various ecological services estimated from a large number of contingent valuation studies.
- *Hedonic pricing.* Differences in property prices that can be attributed to aesthetic and amenity benefits of proximity to a wetland can provide a value for maintenance of biodiversity on the wetland site. This requires analysis of prices for otherwise similar properties that are located close to and distant from wetlands with a diversity of species.
- *Replacement cost.* The replacement cost of the biodiversity maintenance service is based on the costs of creation or renovation of an alternative. To provide a replacement, the alternative is required to provide similar habitats to the original site. Indeed, a possible management option would entail relocation of species to an alternative site. To have corresponding value, the alternative site is required to provide the same benefits. These are influenced by the location of the alternative site, the proximity to population centres, ease of access and availability of substitute sites. There is also the question of 'authenticity': the original naturally occurring site may be preferred to an exact replica, thereby affecting amenity and non-use values. Valuation using the replacement cost is most straightforward for sites that predominantly provide the single service of biodiversity maintenance. For sites that provide multiple services, the costs of replacement are attributed between the respective services. Opportunity costs of the conversion of the alternative site and any externalities are also taken into account.

Food web support

Definition: the support of food webs within and outside a wetland through the production of biomass and its subsequent accumulation and export.

The service of food web support comprises three processes:

- biomass production;
- biomass import;
- biomass export,

where:
On-site Food Web Support = Production + Import – Export.

Of this food web support service, it is only the export of biodiversity from the wetland that is of economic value. While the export of biomass can result from physical (the water course, overland flow, wind transport) or biological means (associated with the movement of macro-invertebrates, birds, fish and mammals), it is only export by anthropogenic means that is of economic value.

Biomass production

Biomass production occurs in any ecosystem, but it does not of itself provide economic value. Not all biomass will be equally beneficial in terms of the goods and services it provides, nor will all biomass necessarily be associated with any positive benefits in terms of satisfying human wants and needs.

Some work has been done to assess the productivity of wetlands in terms of energy flows (Gosselink et al, 1974; Farber and Costanza, 1987; Folke, 1991) which is then converted into monetary terms according to the equivalent costs of deriving this energy from alternative sources (e.g. fossil fuels). The underlying assumption of such analysis is that all the energy-potential stored in wetlands is economically useful (and equivalent to the alternative energy source). Since this will not be the case, and since there is no link between embodied energy and benefits derived from a wetland (apart from, perhaps, as an upper bound on consumptive use values: Costanza et al, 1989) such 'energy analysis' cannot provide a realistic estimate of the value of a wetland. So long as all possible benefits to be derived from a wetland are identified, any value attributable to biomass production (and embodied energy) will be accounted for in the value estimates for other services.

Biomass import

The transfer of biomass *into* the system, or biomass import, is also not a valuable service in itself. Biomass import may contribute to services within a wetland that are regarded as valuable. However, whether the biomass within a wetland derives from primary production or from import does not directly influence economic value. Even if these two different sources lead to distinct wetland functioning, it is the end result of qualitative variations in ecosystem structure and biodiversity that determine the value of ecological services. The value attributed to the maintenance of a given form of biodiversity will not alter according to the source of the biomass.

Identifying the source of a wetland's biomass might become important if the valuation exercise is extended to systems beyond the wetland – perhaps to the catchment level – when services performed within the wetland could be identified as relying upon the import of biomass from other ecosystems under scrutiny. Just as services off site can be linked to *export* of biomass from the wetland, services within the wetland could be linked to the export of biomass by other ecosystems within the catchment.

Biomass export through harvesting (non-anthropogenic)

The biomass harvesting service is split into two distinct units for the purposes of valuation. The first, referring to *non-anthropogenic* or natural harvesting of biota, is considered here. The second, referring to *anthropogenic* export or harvesting, is considered in detail in the next section. The reason for splitting the service in this fashion for the purposes of assessing economic values is that deliberate harvesting suggests that benefits are being derived from the wetland's ecology, while a natural process of export need not necessarily be associated with any benefit to society.

The natural, or non-anthropogenic, harvesting of biomass is not of direct economic value: there is no demand for the physical process of biomass export. However, the biomass that is transferred to an alternative ecosystem by this process could be potentially valuable. Estimating the value involves assessing the benefits derived from the services to which this biomass contributes in the alternative ecosystem, and attributing a portion of these benefits to the original wetland. As with other ecological services that are associated with benefits derived from off-site locations (i.e. provision of habitat microsites), quantifying possible economic values is likely to be a highly resource-intensive exercise. It involves assessing the value of relevant goods and services provided by an off-site ecosystem and then attributing a portion of this value to the wetland's export service. Only where the wetland makes a significant contribution to off-site services will such analysis be justified. This will involve repeating an assessment of the relevant services being performed by an off-site ecosystem, determining the degree to which these are influenced by the transfer of biomass from the wetland, and applying appropriate valuation techniques to these services.

Biomass export through harvesting (anthropogenic)

The anthropogenic – as opposed to natural – export or harvest of biota from a wetland represents consumptive use value of the wetland. The assessment of the economic value of this service is simpler than for the other services as the value of harvesting biomass is directly attributable to the wetland. All that is required is the identification of the impact on human welfare and the valuation techniques required.

Such export is associated with commercial exploitation of wetland resources, subsistence provision or recreational use.

1   Commercial exploitation: commercial value of wetland resources, for instance for fish, reed, grass/hay or timber harvesting, can generally be assessed by analysis of market prices.
2   Subsistence use: subsistence value of wetlands is harder to estimate due to the fact that the products are not marketed. However, market prices may exist for the products, or market prices for alternative products or for the inputs to production (in particular labour), may act as surrogates for the price of wetland products.
3   Consumptive recreation: recreational value, such as fishing or hunting, is generally not associated with a functioning market. However, non-market valuation techniques such as the Travel Cost Method or the Contingent Valuation Method can be employed to assess these values.

An important aspect of valuation with regard to such consumptive uses is the degree to which extraction or exploitation is sustainable. While harvesting of a wetland's resources might provide a valid justification for its conservation, when compared with the opportunity costs of alternative uses of the land, the temporal scale over which these resources will continue to be available, and whether they may be overexploited, will need to be considered. Where extraction is not sustainable, the impact that this could have on other services and on future human generations should be assessed, as well as its effect on the economic value associated with the extracted resource. A pioneering study by Hammack and Brown (1974) considered the ability of wetlands to withstand pressure from recreational hunting, introducing this concept into their analysis via a biometric model. Concepts such as sustainability constraints and safe minimum standards might usefully be applied.

Commercial exploitation and subsistence use

Market analysis based on commercial exploitation of wetland products is based on observing prices that currently exist in markets for these products. However, market prices are often *not* a clear indication of the benefits derived by society from particular resources. For instance, taxes and subsidies, monopoly competition and quantitative restrictions in markets for final goods or for inputs of labour and materials can distort prices. It may therefore be necessary to calculate 'shadow' or social prices for the relevant outputs and inputs, in order to derive *economic* value (as opposed to observed *financial* value) of the wetland service. Furthermore, if significant changes in supply or demand for resources are expected to result from wetland alteration, then any influence this might have on prices should also be taken into account. This is most likely to be a problem where large changes in resource availability are anticipated.

Consumptive recreation

Consumptive recreational activities most often involve fishing and hunting. Since these activities are generally not associated with a functioning market, non-market valuation techniques can be employed. For instance, the Travel Cost Method, which uses expenditures on marketed goods involved in reaching a site, can be used to estimate the value attributable to recreation at that site. The Contingent Valuation Method can also be applied to elicit willingness to pay directly for recreational experience.

NOTE

1   It should be noted that the use of irrigation in the UK is supplemental to rainfall and that many crops are not irrigated (Weatherhead and Knox, 2000). However, where irrigation does take place, the valuation techniques in this section are applicable.

REFERENCES

Abdalla, C. (1994) 'Groundwater values from avoidance cost studies implications for policy and future research'. *American Journal of Agricultural Economics* 76: 1062–1067

Abdalla, C.W., Roach, B.A. and Epp, D.J. (1992) 'Valuing environmental-quality changes using averting expenditures: An application to groundwater contamination'. *Land Economics* 68(2) 163–169

Barbier, E.B. (1994) 'Valuing environmental functions: Tropical wetlands'. *Land Economics* 70(2): 155–173

Barbier, E.B., Markandya, A.A. and Pearce, D.W. (1990) 'Environmental sustainability and cost–benefit-analysis'. *Environmental Planning* 22(9): 1259–1266

Bateman, I.J., Day, B.H., Georgiou, S. and Lake, I. (2006) 'The aggregation of environmental benefit values: Welfare measures, distance decay and total WTP'. *Ecological Economics* 60(2), 450–460

Bishop, R.C. (1978) 'Endangered species and uncertainty: The economics of a safe minimum standard'. *American Journal of Agricultural Economics* 60: 10–18

Boadway, R.W. and Bruce, N. (1984) *Welfare Economics*. Basil Blackwell: Oxford

Boddington, M.A.B. (1993) 'Financial and economic measurement of environmental factors'. *Journal of the Institute of Water and Environmental Management* 7: 125–133

Brouwer, R., Langford, I.H., Bateman, I.J., Crowards, T.C. and Turner, R.K. (1997) 'A meta-analysis of wetland contingent valuation studies'. Global Environmental Change Working Paper GEC 97–20. Centre for Social and Economic Research on the Global Environment (CSERGE), University of East Anglia and University College London

Caddy, J.F. (1993) 'Towards a comparative evaluation of human impacts on fishery ecosystems of enclosed and semi-enclosed seas'. *Reviews in Fisheries Science* 1: 57–95

Ciriacy-Wantrup, S.V. (1952) *Resource Conservation: Economics and Policies*. University of California Press: Berkeley

Clark, E.H. (1985) 'The off-site costs of soil erosion'. *Journal of Soil and Water Conservation* Jan–Feb: 19–21

Colby, B. (1989) 'Estimating the value of water in alternate uses'. *Natural Resources Journal* 29(2): 511–527

Costanza, R. (1994) 'Three general policies to achieve sustainability'. In Jansson, A-M., Hammer, M., Folke, C. and Costanza, R. (eds) *Investing in Natural Capital: The Ecological Economics Approach to Sustainability*. Island Press: Washington DC

Costanza, R., Farber, C.S. and Maxwell, J. (1989) 'Valuation and management of wetland ecosystems'. *Ecological Economics* 1: 335–361

Crowards, T.M. (1996) 'Addressing uncertainty in project evaluation: The costs and benefits of safe minimum standards'. Global Environmental Change Working Paper GEC 96–04. Centre for Social and Economic Research on the Global Environment (CSERGE), University of East Anglia and University College London

Crowards, T.M. (1997) 'Combining economics, ecology and philosophy: Safe minimum standards of environmental protection'. In O'Connor, M. and Spash, C. (eds) *Valuation and Environment: Principles and Practices*. Edward Elgar: Aldershot, UK

Cummings, R.G., Ganderton, P.T. and McGuckin, T. (1994) 'Substitution effects in CVM values'. *American Journal of Agricultural Economics* 76: 205–214

DeBusk, W.F. (1999) *Nitrogen Cycling in Wetlands*. A fact sheet of the Soil and Water Science Department, Florida Co-operative Extension Service, Institute of Food and Agricultural Sciences, University of Florida: Gainesville, FL

Dixon, J.A. (1989) 'Valuation of mangroves'. *Tropical Coastal Area Management Manila* 4(3): 2–6

Farber, S. and Costanza, R. (1987) 'The economic value of wetland systems'. *Journal of Environmental Management* 24(1): 41–51

Faux, J. and Perry, G.M. (1999) 'Estimating irrigation water value using hedonic price analysis: A case study in Malheur County, Oregon'. *Land Economics* 75(3): 440–452

Fisher, A.C. and Krutilla, J.V. (1975) 'Resource conservation, environmental preservation, and the rate of discount'. *Quarterly Journal of Economics* 89: 358–370

Folke, C. (1991) 'The societal value of wetland life-support'. In Folke, C. and Kaberger, T. (eds) *Linking the Natural Environment and the Economy: Essays from the Eco-Eco Group*. Kluwer: Dordrecht, The Netherlands

Fordham, M. and Tunstall, S. (1990) *The Trade-Off between Flood Alleviation and Environmental Values*. Publication given at the joint XII/Middlesex Polytechnic Workshop 'Risk and Environmental Management', Flood Hazard Research Centre, Middlesex Polytechnic

Freeman, A.M. (1982) *Air and Water Pollution Control*. John Wiley: New York

Georgiou, S., Bateman, I.J., Cole, M. and Hadley, D. (2000) 'Contingent ranking and valuation of river water quality improvements: Testing for scope sensitivity, ordering and distance decay effects'. Global Environmental Change Working Paper GEC 2000–18. Centre for Social and Economic Research on the Global Environment, University of East Anglia: Norwich

Gibbons, D.C. (1986) *The Economic Value of Water*. Resources for the Future: Washington DC

Gosselink, J.G., Odum, E.P. and Pope, R.M. (1974) *The Value of the Tidal Marsh*. Center for Wetland Resources Publ.LSU-SG-74–03. Louisiana State University: Baton Rouge

Green, C.H. and Penning-Rowsell, E.C. (1986) 'Evaluating the intangible benefits and costs of a flood alleviation proposal'. *Journal of Institution of Water Engineers and Scientists* 40(3): 229–248

Green, C.H. and Penning-Rowsell, E.C. (1989) 'Flooding and the quantification of "Intangibles"'. *Journal of the Institute of Water and Environmental Management* 38: 27–30

Hammack, J. and Brown, G.M. (1974) *Water and Wetlands: Towards Bioeconomic Analysis.* Resources for the Future: Washington DC

Hanley, N.D. and Craig, S. (1991) 'Wilderness development decisions and the Krutilla–Fisher model: The case of Scotland's Flow country'. *Ecological Economics* 4(2): 145–164

Higgs, A.W. (1992) 'Purley on Thames Flood Alleviation Scheme'. Paper to the Economic Appraisal Group, National Rivers Authority

Holway, J.M. and Burby, R.J. (1990) 'The effects of floodplain development controls on residential land values'. *Land Economics* 66(3): 259–271

Jordan, J.L. and Elnagheeb, A.B. (1993) 'Willingness to pay for improvements in drinking water quality'. *Water Resources Research* 29(2):237–245

Kosz, M. (1996) 'Valuing riverside wetlands: The case of the "Donau-Auen" National Park'. *Ecological Economics* 16: 109–127

Krutilla, J.V. and Fisher, A.C. (1985) *The Economics of Natural Environments.* Johns Hopkins University Press: Baltimore

Larson, L.A. (1986) 'Wetland and flooding: Assessing hydrologic functions'. In Kusler, J.A. and Riexinger, P. (eds) *Proceedings of the National Wetland Assessment Symposium,* Association of State Wetland Managers, Portland, Maine, 17–20 June 1985

Loomis, J.B. (1987a) 'The economic value of instream flow: Methodology and benefit estimates for optimum flows'. *Journal of Environmental Management* 24: 169–179

Loomis, J.B. (1987b) 'Balancing public trust resources of Mono Lake and Los Angeles' water right: an economic approach'. *Water Resources Research* 23(8): 1449–1456

Maltby, E. and Immirzi, C.P. (1993) 'Carbon dynamics in peatlands and other wetland soils: Regional and global perspectives'. *Chemosphere* 27(6): 999–1023

Markandya, A. and Pearce, D.W. (1988) 'Environmental considerations and the choice of discount rates in developing countries'. Environment Department Working Paper No 3. World Bank: Washington DC

Mitsch, W.J. and Gosselink, J.G. (2000) *Wetlands.* 3rd edition. Wiley: New York

National Research Council (1997) *Valuing Groundwater: Economic Concepts and Approaches.* Committee on Valuing Groundwater; Water Science and Technology Board; Commission on Geosciences, Environment and Resources; National Research Council. National Academy Press: Washington DC

N'Jai, A., Tapsell, S.M., Taylor, D., Thompson, P.M., Witts, R.C., Parker, D.J. and Penning-Rowsell, E.C. (1990) Flood Loss Assessment Information Report. Flood Hazard Research Centre, Middlesex University, UK

Parkes, D. (2003) 'Storage and cycling of organic carbon and nutrients in Holocene coastal sediments'. PhD thesis, University of East Anglia, Norwich

Pearce, D.W., Markandya, A. and Barbier, E.B. (1989) *Blueprint for a Green Economy.* Earthscan: London

Pearce, D.W. and Turner, R.K. (1990) *Economics of Natural Resources and the Environment*. Harvester Wheatsheaf: London

Poe, G. (1998) 'Valuation of groundwater quality using a contingent valuation-damage functions approach'. *Water Resources Research* 34(12): 3627–3633

Renzetti, S. (2002) *The Economics of Water Demands*. Kluwer Academic Press: Norwell, MA

Ruttan, V. (1965) *The Economic Demand for Irrigated Acreage: New Methodology and Some Preliminary Projections, 1954–1980*. Resources for the Future: Baltimore

Sather, J.H. and Smith, R.D. (1984) An Overview of Major Wetland Functions and Values. FWS/OBS-84/18, Fish and Wildlife Service: US Dept of the Interior

Smith, V.K. and Kaoru, Y. (1990) 'Signals or noise? Explaining the variation in recreation benefit estimates'. *American Journal of Agricultural Economics* 72(2): 419–433

Tobin, G.A. and Newton, T.G. (1986) 'A theoretical framework of flood induced changes in urban land values'. *Water Resources Bulletin* 22(1): 67–71

Tunstall, S.M., Tapsell, S.M. and Fordham, M. (1994) Public Perception of Rivers and Flood Defence: Final Report. R&D Note 444, National Rivers Authority: Bristol

Turner, R.K. (1993) *Sustainable Environmental Economics and Management: Principles and Practice*. Belhaven Press: London and New York

Turner, R.K., Dent, D. and Hey, R.D. (1983) 'Valuation of the environmental impact of wetland flood protection and drainage schemes'. *Environment and Planning A*, 15: 871–888

Weatherhead, E.K. and Knox, J.W. (2000) 'Predicting and mapping the future demand for irrigation water in England and Wales'. *Agricultural Water Management* 43(2) 203–218

Young, R.A. (1996) 'Measuring economic benefits for water investments and policies'. World Bank Technical Paper No 338

Young, R.A. and Gray, S.L. (1972) Economic Value of Water: Concepts and Empirical Estimates. Technical Report to the National Water Commission

6

Valuation of Multi-functional Wetland:
Case Studies

Following on from the previous chapter, a number of actual case studies are outlined in detail in order to illustrate some of the procedures and challenges involved in assessing the value of wetland ecosystems and their services. The case studies address a number of different problems across different temporal and spatial scales – from individual wetland service valuation, through whole area management in the context of a single/few environmental pressures, to catchment/landscape scale problems.

The first case study (A) consists of two examples concerned with the valuation of nature conservation, recreation and other economic interests at risk from flooding. The first example has been chosen to illustrate the use of a fully fledged contingent valuation survey to obtain monetary willingness to pay values, which assess the benefits of preserving the existing landscape, ecology and recreational characteristics of the Norfolk Broads area relative to their expected values in the absence of a Broadland-wide flood alleviation scheme. The study was conducted in answer to a real-world question regarding the funding of flood defences in Broadland. The second example extends the analysis to a wider consideration of the economic costs and benefits of flood deserves. These include protection of agriculture and property as well as any damage avoidance to infrastructure. Although the benefit–cost ratio of the latter items was calculated at 0.98, when conservative measures of WTP for the recreational and environmental benefits of flood prevention are considered, the benefit–cost ratio increases substantially to 1.94, indicating that the benefits of a flood alleviation strategy are almost twice the associated costs. The case study illustrates the importance that non-market values can have in providing justification for central government funding support for a proposed flood alleviation strategy.

The second case study (B) illustrates an example concerned with the use of economic valuation and appraisal in the context of wetland creation. Managed realignment is now becoming an important element in coastal zone policy, and is being increasingly utilized for flood defence purposes. The case study, which centres on the Humber Estuary, has been included in order to show how the economic approach can be combined with future scenario analysis in order to provide policymakers with an array of possible options.

The **final case study** (C) relates to the valuation of benefits from wetland restoration. It illustrates an example of the contingent valuation method being used to assess the economic benefits of increasing the landscape, ecology and recreational characteristics of the Culm Grasslands in south-west England – a scientifically important habitat supporting many endangered species including the Marsh Fritillary butterfly and Curlew. This study is important because it encompasses a conservation policy context in which experts value the sites and their amalgamation into a more coherent whole very highly. However, the public were by and large ignorant of the sites and their ecological significance. The analysis illustrates how a survey-based economic analysis can be deployed and can yield an aggregate/composite value estimate for the wetland as a whole; and how information can be provided to help survey respondents articulate their preferences.

CASE STUDY A: FLOOD WATER DETENTION

Example 1 The introduction of a flood alleviation scheme in the Broads and its effect on recreational visitors: A contingent valuation study

As a consequence of the ongoing and increasing risk of flooding within Broadland, in 1990 the National Rivers Authority (NRA)[1] initiated a wide-ranging study to develop an 'effective and cost-effective strategy to alleviate flooding in Broadland for the next 50 years' (Bateman et al, 1992, p31). The study consisted of five main components: hydraulic modelling; engineering; cost–benefit analysis (CBA); environmental assessment, and consultations. Given prior work on the market costs and benefits of flood alleviation schemes (Turner and Brooke, 1988), the principal task of the CBA was to estimate values for the non-market goods concerned. In particular, the estimation of the environmental and informal recreational values was seen as a central objective of this study. To address these values, in 1991 a contingent valuation (CV) study was commissioned to assess the benefits of preserving the existing landscape, ecology and recreational characteristics of the area relative to their expected values in the absence of a Broadland-wide flood alleviation scheme (Bateman et al, 1992). The study consisted of two surveys: (1) a postal survey of households across the UK designed to capture the values which non-users might hold for preservation of the present state of Broadland, and (2) an investigation of the values held by users for the same scenario as elicited through an on-site survey. Details of these studies are presented below.

The 1991 study of non-users
Non-user values were estimated by means of a mail survey questionnaire sent to addresses throughout the UK selected so as to capture both socio-economic and

distance decay effects upon stated WTP and thereby provide the basis for calculation of aggregate values. Full details of this study are provided in Bateman and Langford (1997).

The survey questionnaire was designed in accordance with the 'Total Design Method' of Dillman (1978) and pre-tested through focus group and pilot exercises. The questionnaire contained visual, map and textual information detailing the nature of Broadland, the flooding problems and flood defence options together with necessary details supporting a WTP question such as payment vehicle, payment time frame and so on. The survey achieved a typically modest response rate of some 31 per cent. However, initial analysis showed that this was heavily supported by past users of Broadland who represented well over one-third of responses in each distance category. Although experience of visiting the Broads declines significantly with distance from the area (p < 0.0001) it cannot therefore be claimed that the sample is nationally representative; rather it is biased towards past users and can perhaps be best characterized as being a sample of present non-users for comparison against results from the on-site survey of present users described subsequently.

When asked whether or not they agreed with the principle of incurring extra personal taxes to pay for flood defences in Broadland (the 'payment principle' question),[2] of the respondents 166 (53.5 per cent) answered positively to the payment principle question.

Those respondents who accepted the payment principle were presented with an open-ended format valuation question asking them to state the maximum amount of extra taxes they would be willing to pay per annum to ensure the preservation of Broadland from the effects of increased flooding. Including, as zeros, those respondents who refused the payment principle (i.e. those who stated they were not willing to pay to prevent flooding), this question elicited a whole-sample mean WTP of £23.29 per annum (95 per cent CI: £17.53–£32.45). Table 6A.1 decomposes these bids across a zonal distance variable, showing a marked decrease in mean WTP as distance from Broadland increases, and according to previous visitation

Table 6A.1 *Mean WTP per annum by distance zone and visitation experience (payment principle refusals included as zeros)*

Distance zone	No of respondents	Mean WTP (£ pa)	Visit experience	No of respondents	Mean WTP (£ pa)
1(closest)	58	39.34	Holiday	118	27.86
2	66	27.67	Day trip	82	25.65
3	139	13.97	Never visited	110	12.29
4 (furthest)	47	14.72			
All	310	23.29	All	310	23.29

experience, which shows that those who have previously visited Broadland express a substantially higher WTP than those who have not.

Analysis of WTP responses showed that bids were negatively related to distance from the Broads and positively related to income (or more precisely to that portion of disposable income which was spent annually upon recreational and environmental goods).[3]

Aggregation was conducted using three approaches:

1   *Aggregation using sample mean WTP.* This approach was adopted in a high-profile benefits assessment conducted by the Environment Agency (EA) in respect of an application by Thames Water to abstract water at Axford on the River Kennet, a low-flow chalk stream in southern England. Following existing guidelines, the EA multiplied a sample mean WTP by the entire population of the Thames Water catchment, yielding a very high estimate of preservation benefits which was rejected at a subsequent planning inquiry (which allowed the proposed abstraction to proceed). Following this procedure, the approach (1) (in Table 6A.2) multiplies the sample mean by the population of Great Britain.

2   *Aggregation adjusting for distance zones.* Here a simple procedure was used, which could readily be adopted by policy analysts, wherein the mean WTP in each distance zone (detailed in Table 6A.1) is used as the basis of aggregation. Multiplying the mean WTP by the population of each zone captures a simple distance decay effect.

3   *Aggregation by bid functions.* Here the consistent drivers of responses are recognized to have been the distance at which the respondent lives from Broadland and their socio-economic circumstances (specifically some measure of income), both in terms of the probability of replying to the questionnaire, of responding positively to the payment vehicle question and to the determination of the WTP amount.

Results from these various approaches to aggregation are detailed in Table 6A.2.

Table 6A.2 *The present non-user's benefits of preserving the present condition of Broadland aggregated across Great Britain using various procedures (£million/annum)*

Aggregation approach	Untruncated	Truncated
(1) Aggregation using sample mean WTP	159.7	98.4
(2) Aggregation adjusting for distance zones	111.1	98.0
(3) Aggregation by bid functions:		
i. using distance zone and national income	27.3	25.3
ii. using county distance and regional income	25.4	24.0

Examination of Table 6A.2 shows that aggregate benefits estimates vary very considerably across the procedure used. Considering the untruncated sample we can see that the simplest approach (type (1) used by the EA in the Axford inquiry) results in an aggregate benefits estimate which is very much higher than that provided by even the crude incorporation of distance decay effects given under approach (2). However, benefits estimates reduce by an even wider margin when we move to the bid function approach (3) with the latter being around one-sixth of the initial estimates. Interestingly the bid function is relatively stable with respect to the scale of data used to calculate results although we would recommend the use of more detailed data wherever possible. Truncation effects are highly marked for the cruder aggregation approaches while the more detailed bid function approach yields estimates which are reassuringly stable (see Bateman et al, 2006 for a more detailed examination of aggregation issues).

In summary, the study of present non-users yields a consistent picture and provides the basis for some defensible estimates of aggregate benefits, which in turn yield an interesting commentary upon current practice. We now turn to consider the various on-site CV surveys of visitors to Broadland.

The 1991 study of users

From a decision making perspective, the 1991 on-site survey of those who directly use Broadland was primarily intended to estimate the benefits to this group of preventing saline flooding in the study area. However, the study also had an academic objective, namely to investigate the impact upon stated values of varying the way in which responses are elicited. Five WTP elicitation methods were investigated:[4]

1   *Open-ended* (OE). Here the respondent is asked, 'How much are you willing to pay?', and is therefore free to state any amount.
2   *Single bound dichotomous choice* (1DC). Here respondents face a single question of the form, 'Are you willing to pay £X?', with the bid level X being varied across the sample.
3   *Double bound dichotomous choice* (2DC). Here those respondents previously asked the 1DC question are asked a supplementary dichotomous question on the basis of their prior response. Those who agreed to pay the 1DC bid face a higher 2DC amount while those refusing to pay the 1DC bid face a lower 2DC amount.
4   *Triple bound dichotomous choice* (3DC). This extends the previous procedure by adding a further question.
5   *Iterative bidding* (IB). Here the bidding game formed by the various dichotomous choice questions is extended by a supplementary open-ended question asking respondents to state their maximum WTP. Such a procedure is appropriate to all respondents in the DC bidding game irrespective of whether they answer positively or negatively to individual DC questions.

The study itself generally conformed to the CV testing protocol laid down subsequently by the NOAA blue ribbon panel (Arrow et al, 1994). Survey design was extensively pretested with any changes to the questionnaire being retested over a total pilot sample of some 433 respondents. One of the many findings of this process was that a tax-based annual payment vehicle appeared optimal when assessed over a range of criteria (details in Bateman et al, 1993).

The finalized questionnaire was applied through on-site interviews with visitors at representative sites around Broadland with 2897 questionnaires being completed. This sample was composed of 846 interviewees being administered with the OE WTP questionnaire and the remaining 2051 facing in turn the 1DC, 2DC, 3DC and IB questions. Prior to any WTP question, respondents were presented with a 'payment principle' question. Negative responses to this question reduced sample sizes to 715 and 1811 respectively. Except where indicated, all those refusing the payment principle were treated as having zero WTP in calculating subsequent WTP measures. Table 6A.3 details various measures of WTP estimated from these various elicitation methods.

Table 6A.3 indicates that there were strong elicitation effects at work in this case, although the direction of differences was as expected with OE estimates below those from DC approaches, and with IB values, the product of both methods, yielding intermediate results. There is considerable disagreement regarding the interpretation of such results. However, most commentators agree that OE responses are liable to represent more conservative estimates of

Table 6A.3 *Measures of users' WTP to preserve the Norfolk Broads from saline flooding obtained using various elicitation techniques*

Elicitation method	Mean WTP (£ pa)	Median WTP (£ pa)
OE	67.19	30
	(59.53–74.86)	(18–46)
1DC	144	144
	(75–261)	(75–261)
2DC	a	88
		a
3DC	a	94
		a
IB	74.91	25
	(69.27–80.55)	(19–35)

Notes: [a] = not estimated.

Figures in parentheses are 95 per cent confidence intervals.

underlying WTP. Given this, these results can be used as the basis for estimating lower values for the aggregate benefits to users of preserving the Norfolk Broads from saline flooding.

The Norfolk Broads CV study was conducted in answer to a real-world question regarding the funding of flood defences in Broadland. The study fed into a wider cost–benefit analysis which also examined the agricultural, property and infrastructure damage-avoided benefits of such defences. The benefit–cost ratio of the latter items was calculated at 0.98 (National Rivers Authority, 1992). However, even when the conservative OE measure of WTP for the recreational and environmental benefits of flood prevention is considered, the benefit–cost ratio increases substantially to 1.94 (NRA, 1992) indicating that the benefits of a flood alleviation strategy are almost twice the associated costs. These results, including the findings from the CV study, were submitted to the relevant Ministry of Agriculture, Food and Fisheries as part of an application for central government funding support for the proposed flood alleviation strategy. Following lengthy consideration of this application, in 1997 the Environment Agency announced that it had received conditional approval for a programme of 'bank strengthening and erosion protection' (Environment Agency, 1997).

Example 2 Sea level rise and the threat to Broadland: A cost–benefit analysis

The physical vulnerability of the East Anglian coastline derives from large areas of low-lying land, both immediately adjacent to the shoreline and inland, and stretches of soft erosive cliffs. Coastal defences, mainly hard engineering structures built largely after the very destructive 1953 North Sea storm surge flood, and river flood embankment defences play a crucial role in the maintenance of the current shoreline, levels of economic activity and environmental resources in the immediate hinterland. The coastal erosion and flooding threat, enhanced as it may be by sea level rise associated with global climatic changes (Wigley and Raper, 1993), is directly related to the maintenance and ecological integrity of the Broads.

The policy options open in the face of this threat to the East Anglian coast include:

- *Retreat*: the abandonment of the land and structures in vulnerable areas and resettlement of population; this option can also include managed retreat linked to specific measures aimed at restoring or creating desirable habitat, landscape or amenity features.
- *Accommodation*: continued occupancy and use of vulnerable areas.
- *Protection*: continued full defence of vulnerable areas, especially population centres, economic activities and natural resources.

All these options have direct consequences for the freshwater Broads themselves. The impact of accelerated sea level rise on the hazard zone depends greatly on how the coastline is managed. An economic approach to assessing which of the strategies is desirable for the overall coast and for each section of the coast involves the quantification of costs and benefits. In this section, we restrict consideration to the two 'active' management response options: accommodation and protection, comparing these to the retreat option (full details of this and further analyses being presented in Turner et al, 1995). As in the case of the flood alleviation schemes considered previously, the cost–benefit analysis is restricted to the economic benefit of protection to properties, agriculture and the indirect value of recreation and amenity in Broadland.

Cost–benefit analysis seeks to identify that strategy which maximizes net present values. The benefits of protection and accommodation are the impacts avoided, taking the accommodation option as the baseline scenario. These benefits therefore include the marginal value of the agricultural output, the other economic activity, and the amenity value of Broadland saved through active management. The costs of the active strategies include hard and soft engineering defence maintenance; replacement cost of defences; cost of repairing breaches in defence, and necessary beach nourishment. Similar studies for developed and natural coastlines faced with the threat of climate change induced sea level rise include West and Dowlatabadi (1999), Yohe et al (1995) and Yohe and Neumann (1997).

The total benefits of adopting either an accommodation or protection strategy are given by the size of the avoided damage costs, i.e. the change in costs compared to those incurred under the abandon defences (retreat) option. The net benefits of each response strategy can be computed by subtracting the capital and maintenance defence system costs from the value of total benefits (damage costs avoided).

The results of the cost–benefit analysis are summarized in Table 6A.4. The present value of flood and erosion defence costs for each response strategy is the accumulated cost of defence over the period 1990–2050, discounted at 6 per cent.[5] There were no defence costs associated with the retreat response strategy as this involves allowing natural erosion and flood processes to dominate the coastal zone. Benefits of the accommodation and protection strategies substantially exceeded those of the retreat option and are shown as differences from the latter in Table 6A.4.

Although in the accommodation response strategy, the physical scale of the defences was assumed to remain the same, there was still a gradual increase in defence costs with increasing values of sea level rise, due to an increased frequency of flooding events and consequent defence repair costs. In the case of the protection response strategy, defence costs rise gradually, reflecting the need for progressively higher defences and increased volumes of beach nourishment required to counter sea level rise and enhanced erosion. The highest sea level rise projection (0.80m) produces a significant increase in costs due to the necessity to employ relatively expensive engineering methods.

Table 6A.4 *Costs and benefits of policy responses to sea level rise in East Anglia*

	Net present value over period 1990–2050 (£million)[c]			
Sea level rise	0.20m	0.40m	0.60m	0.80m
Protection costs (PC)				
Retreat	–	–	–	–
Accommodate	132	137	151	157
Protect	187	232	292	485
Flood and erosion[d] damage costs (EC)				
Retreat	1333	1355	1405	1436
Accommodate	194	257	320	397
Protect	77	74	81	85
Benefits (B)[a]				
Accommodate	1141	1108	1098	1058
Protect	1259	1284	1326	1352
Net benefits: (B-EC-PC)				
Accommodate	1009	971	947	901[b]
Protect	1072[b]	1052[b]	1034[b]	867

Turner et al, 1995.
Notes:
[a] Benefits of defence relative to the do-nothing option (retreat).
[b] Optimal strategy between accommodate and protect, given the sea level rise projection.
[c] NPV estimated at 6 per cent discount rate.
[d] Erosion accounts for around 20–30 per cent of the total defence cost.

As far as the two active response strategies are concerned, the protection response had the highest NPV, indicating that this would be the preferred approach to coastal management for all sea level rise scenarios, with the exception of 0.80m sea level rise. In this extreme case, the high cost of maintaining a protection-style defence line meant that an accommodation response strategy becomes more desirable from an economic perspective. Due to the nature of the study area, the analysis was dominated by the flood hazard. In contrast to the overall results, when the erosion hazard alone was considered, the NPV was negative in almost all cases in the accommodation and protection response strategy simulations.

While physical parameters such as the assumed rate of sea level rise did have an effect on the results, socio-economic parameters were equally significant in this case study. Thus the extent and value of property at risk in the hazard zone dominated the damage cost calculations, although the environmental asset valuation is only a proxy variable and undoubtedly underestimates the full costs involved. Similarly the assumed discount rate had a major influence on the results. Sensitivity analysis of discount rates, from 3 to 9 per cent, have the effect of doubling and halving the net present value of benefits and costs, from the base level rate of 6 per cent. More importantly, they changed the rank order of the desirable policy options under some assumptions (Turner et al, 1995).

CASE STUDY B: ECOSYSTEM MAINTENANCE

With climate change leading to rising sea levels and increased storminess and many of the existing defences reaching the end of their design life and in need of repair or replacing, the sea defences and coastal protection strategies of the UK are currently under review. The traditional method of flood management has been to construct structural or 'hard' defences, such as sea walls to protect land; however, a reorientation in thinking about response strategies is leading to an abandonment of 'coastal armouring' (i.e. the building and maintenance of hard engineering structures and works) in favour of a mixed approach which will include substantial elements of more flexible 'soft engineering' measures, such as setback or managed realignment. The term 'managed realignment', also referred to as 'managed retreat' or 'coastal setback', involves deliberately breaching engineered defences to allow the coastline to recede to a new line of defence further inland. See Figure 6B.1.

Although the contemporary belief was that hard defences were best practice, it is now recognized that these are unsustainable both from an environmental and economic perspective given recent understanding of coastal dynamics. Not only do these hard defences provide a false sense of security and encourage development immediately behind the defences, they show little regard for natural processes. The

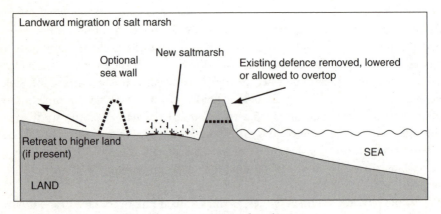

Figure 6B.1 *Managed realignment*

construction of coastal defences effectively immobilizes a naturally dynamic and adaptive ecosystem at the land–sea interface. In response to rising sea levels, a modified coast is unable to adapt by migrating landwards with the result that valuable intertidal habitats are eventually lost through erosion ('coastal squeeze'). This is illustrated in Figure 6B.2. There are two main consequences of this 'squeeze' effect. It can be argued that the ability of the intertidal zone to absorb energy and water and thereby contribute to sea defence will be diminished. The loss of a 'first line' of defence against waves and tides, especially during storm conditions, can result in increased capital and maintenance costs for engineered defences. Second, 'squeeze' results in degraded or destroyed mudflats, sandflat and saltmarsh habitats. These habitats are significant reservoirs of biodiversity and have attracted a range of conservation designations. Under the EU Water Framework Directive loss of conservation area must be compensated for on a like for like basis. Managed retreat seems to offer a way of mitigating this problem by deliberately breaking defences, allowing the coastline to recede and the intertidal zone to expand. However, the situation is further complicated because many freshwater coastal sites protected by coastal defences are also designated as protected areas on nature conservation grounds. Pethick (2002) has claimed that a stalemate might develop between the requirements of freshwater and intertidal habitats conservation. If sea defences are removed the freshwater habitat is compromised; if the defences are maintained then the intertidal habitat is reduced.

Managed realignment schemes generally aim to realign defences in a manner that will not only reduce the length of defence required, but will also increase the overall area of intertidal habitat. This is partly to create intertidal habitat as a means to comply with the Habitats Directive and also because it has recently been recognized that the intertidal zone may act as a natural sea defence by absorbing energy and water, reducing the potential for a flood to be hazardous.

Managed realignment in the Humber

This case study is based on 'A cost–benefit appraisal of coastal managed realignment policy' in *Global Environmental Change* (Turner et al, 2007).

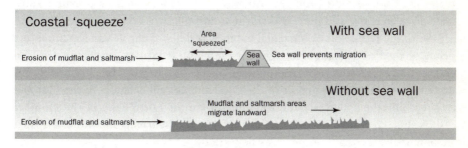

Figure 6B.2 *Coastal squeeze*

The macrotidal Humber estuary is one of the largest in the UK, fed by two principal river systems, the Ouse and the Trent. With a maximum tidal length of 147km from Cromwell Weir on the Trent to the Humber's mouth, and a maximum width of 15km, it is comparable with the Thames and Severn estuaries. Draining over one-fifth of the land area of England (24,000km²), the Humber estuary is the largest source of fresh water (approximately $250m^3s^{-1}$) flowing into the North Sea from all the British rivers. Much of the land surrounding the estuary is the result of historical land reclamation, created from the enclosure of salt marshes and mudflats. Consequently, approximately 90,000ha of land surrounding the Humber estuary is below high spring tide level and is currently protected by 235km of flood and coastal defences (405km including those defences along the tidal reaches of the Rivers Trent and Ouse). This area comprises mainly agricultural land (85 per cent), limited housing (8 per cent) and commercial or industrial activities (3 per cent).

The Humber estuary is of international importance for wildlife, particularly birds, with a large area of intertidal habitat of between 10–11,000ha. This intertidal habitat plays an important role within the estuary by recycling nutrients, and acting as soft sea defences, dissipating wave energy. It is highly productive biologically in terms of bird species. The entire estuary has been proposed as a marine Special Area of Conservation (SAC) while the Humber Flats are designated a Special Protection Area (SPA), Site of Special Scientific Interest and Ramsar site.

However, through land-claim, the Humber estuary has an uncharacteristically low extent of saltmarsh for an English estuary and more than 90 per cent of the intertidal area and sediment accumulation capacity of the Humber estuary has been lost over the last 300 years. The natural succession of marine to terrestrial environments has been truncated by the construction of sea walls.

In addition to the loss of intertidal habitats through reclamation and coastal squeeze, there is also concern regarding the state of traditional sea defences within the Humber estuary. As many of the defences in the estuary were built following the 1953 flooding disaster on the East Coast, they are now reaching the end of their design life and are currently unsatisfactory and in need of repair or replacing. Both of these problems are likely to be exacerbated by climate change related sea level rise and increased storm conditions.

With the reduction of intertidal habitats and increasing costs of maintaining defences, the flood defence strategies for the Humber estuary are being reassessed and a limited amount of realignment work has begun. In 2003, the EA undertook the first realignment of the flood and coastal defences in the Humber by breaching the defences at Thorngumbald, on the north bank of the Humber east of Hull, creating 80ha of intertidal habitat, and by having identified a further 11 potential sites (Environment Agency, 2000).

Investigations using GIS have identified suitable areas for realignment within the Humber based on the following five key issues:

1   area below the high spring tide level (maximum area of potential intertidal habitat);
2   present land use – undeveloped land more suitable for conversion (physical ease and its economic value); however, SSSIs, SACs and other similarly protected areas may not be considered suitable;
3   infrastructure (transport network, including roads, railway lines and canals);
4   historical context;
5   spatial context of the areas:

   - size: realignment is not cost-effective for areas under 5ha;
   - shape: trade-off between a wide intertidal area to maximize benefits and length of realigned defences to protect the surrounding land;
   - elevation: higher ground can be used as a natural defence to absorb wave energy to minimize defences required and reduce maintenance costs of the realigned defences;
   - proximity to existing intertidal habitats facilitates the movement of species between habitats.

To help reduce uncertainty and aid decision making, Ledoux et al (2005) applied future scenario analysis to help scope possible management strategies for the Humber estuary. The case study presented here adopts the five scenarios (a *hold-the-line* approach versus four other possible states of the world with increasing reliance on managed realignment measures) of possible futures set out by Ledoux et al (2005).

The five scenarios are based on the following assumptions:

1   *Hold-the-line (HTL)*: the existing defences are maintained to a satisfactory standard, but intertidal habitat will be lost due to continued development and coastal squeeze.
2   *Business as usual (BAU)*: this option takes into account existing realignments; however compliance to the Habitats Directive is also lax, with continued economic development leading to an overall net loss of habitat due to coastal squeeze.
3   *Policy Targets (PT)*: economic growth is combined with environmental protection, with realignment being undertaken to reduce flood defence expenditure and compensate for past and future intertidal habitat loss in compliance with the Habitats Directive.
4   *Deep Green (DG)*: environmental protection takes priority over economic growth, while development continues; the maximum feasible area of intertidal habitat is created.

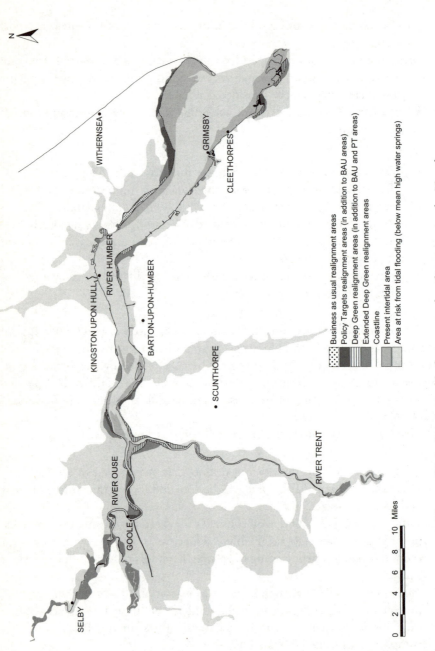

Figure 6B.3 *Areas suitable for managed realignment in the Humber*

Legend:

- Business as usual realignment areas
- Policy Targets realignment areas (in addition to BAU areas)
- Deep Green realignment areas (in addition to BAU and PT areas)
- Extended Deep Green realignment areas
- Coastline
- Present intertidal area
- Area at risk from tidal flooding (below mean high water springs)

SELBY

RIVER OUSE

GOOLE

RIVER TRENT

SCUNTHORPE

BARTON-UPON-HUMBER

KINGSTON UPON HULL

RIVER HUMBER

WITHERNSEA

GRIMSBY

CLEETHORPES

N

0   2   4   6   8   10 Miles

5   *Extended Deep Green (EDG)*: A greater emphasis is placed on habitat creation, with less restrictive criteria being used to identify suitable areas for realignment.

Details of the extent of the areas of habitat that would be created under each of the scenarios is shown in Figure 6B.3, and Table 6B.1 gives detailed information on each scenario with the implications of realignment on defence length, the amount of habitat that could be created, and the subsequent impacts on carbon sequestration.

Cost–benefit assessment of the managed realignment schemes

Cost–benefit analysis (CBA) was used to determine the economic efficiency (whether benefits exceed costs) of each of the managed realignment scenarios.

Table 6B.1 *Details of areas suitable for realignment*

	Scenarios				
	HTL	BAU	PT	DG	EDG
Length of defences before realignment (km)	405.3	405.3	405.3	405.3	405.3
Length of defences after realignment (km)	405.3	396.8	361.6	318.2	284.5
Length of realigned defences (km)	0.0	7.0	30.8	69.0	102.7
Length of unsatisfactory defences after realignment (km)	64.6	61.9	42.2	38.2	34.0
Amount of intertidal habitat created by realignment (ha)[a]	0.0	80.0	1320.9	2332.4	7493.6
Estimated tonnes of carbon stored each year[b,c]	0	38.4	634.1	1119.4	3597.1

Notes:
[a] Due to uncertainty over the loss of intertidal habitat due to coastal squeeze over the next 50 years, it is assumed that no further coastal squeeze takes place. Therefore, the HTL scenario as the baseline scenario assumes no loss of intertidal habitat and no carbon sequestration, and that habitat creation and sequestration in the other scenarios are relative to this base.
[b] Estimates of the carbon storage capacity of newly created intertidal habitat are derived from Andrews et al, 2000.
[c] Intensively managed arable land is a net source of carbon and we assume that the agricultural land that is sacrificed to realignment is managed in this way. Note, however, that minimal or no-till management practices can reduce carbon emissions from agricultural soils or even convert them to carbon sinks on a scale that is equivalent to, or greater than, the carbon storage potential of intertidal habitat.

Table 6B.2 *Values used to estimate the costs and benefits of realignment*

Costs/benefits	Value
Capital costs of realignment[a]	£878,159/km
Opportunity costs:	
Grades 1 and 2 agricultural land[b]	£4790/ha
Grade 3 agricultural land[b]	£5458/ha
Maintenance costs of defences[c]	£3560/km/yr
Replacement costs[d]	£668,441/km
General habitat creation benefits[e]	£621/ha/yr
Carbon sequestration benefits	£7.77/tonne CO_2 equivalent

Notes:
All values are converted to 2005 prices using the GDP deflators published by HM Treasury
(www.hm-treasury.gov.uk/).
[a] Costs based on contemporary realignment schemes (Halcrow, 2000).
[b] Based on sale prices (DEFRA, 2004) and adjusted downwards for the effects of the single farm payment
following Penning-Rowsell et al, 2005.
[c] Maintenance costs are taken from Black and Veatch/Halcrow (2005). These are assumed to increase in
the future due to the effects of climate change. Following current government guidance (Penning-Rowsell
et al, 2005) maintenance costs are increased by a factor of 1.5 for the period between 20 and 50 years
into the future and by a factor of 2 for years further into the future.
[d] Only the costs of replacing unsatisfactory defences (DEFRA, 2001) not affected by realignment are
included.
[e] Assumed to be gained immediately, although in practice habitat establishment may take some time
before maturity is achieved.

The main elements of the analysis are summarized in the three equations and
Table 6B.2 and follow the standard *with* and *without* procedure which in this case
sets the net discounted benefits of realignment against the net discounted benefits
of the hold-the-line traditional sea defence strategy.

Hold-the-line 'status quo' defences

where:

$$C_t^{sq} = \sum_{t=0}^{T} \frac{1}{(1+r)^t} [l^{sq}(C_{r,t}^{sq} + C_{m,t}^{sq}) + C_{br,t}^{sq}]$$

C_t^{sq} = Present value of total cost of status quo defences at time t (£million).

r = Discount rate.

l^{sq} = Length of the status quo defences (km).

$C_{r,t}^{sq}$ = Replacement cost of the status quo defences at time t (£/m).

$C_{m,t}^{sq}$ = Maintenance cost of the status quo defences at time t (£/km/yr).

$C_{br,t}^{sq}$ = Cost of repairing breaches in the status quo defences at time t (£/km).

Managed realignment

where: $$C_t^{mr} = \sum_{t=0}^{T} \frac{1}{(1+r)^t} [l^{mr}(C_{k,t}^{mr} + C_{m,t}^{mr}) + a^{mr}(L_{agr,t}^{agr} - B_{e,t})]$$

C_t^{mr} = Present value of total cost of managed realignment at time t (£million).

r = Discount rate.

l^{mr} = Length of the managed realigned defences (km).

$C_{k,t}^{mr}$ = Capital cost of realignment at time t (£/km).

$C_{m,t}^{mr}$ = Maintenance cost of realignment at time t (£/km/yr).

a^{mr} = Area of intertidal habitat created by realignment (ha).

$L_{agr,t}^{agr}$ = Forgone agricultural land value if realignment takes place (£/ha).

$B_{e,t}$ = Environmental value gain associated with realignment, for example, habitat services, functions and products (£/ha).

Net present value

where: $$NPV_t^{mr} = \sum_{t=0}^{t} (C_t^{mr} - C_t^{sq})$$

NPV_t^{mr} = Net present value of managed realignment in comparison to hold-the-line for a given stretch of coastline (£million).

Cost–benefit analysis results and sensitivity analysis

To estimate the net present value (NPV) of providing defences for each of the scenarios, the present value of all the costs were subtracted from the present value of all the benefits. The present value for the HTL scenario was then subtracted from the present values for the BAU, PT, DG and the EDG scenarios respectively, to calculate the NPV of realignment for each scenario. The results of this process are presented in Table 6B.3 (using a declining discount rate, following UK government guidance given in HMT, 2003). This shows that while no scenario NPVs are positive after 25 years, the PT and EDG managed realignment scenarios become more economically efficient the longer the time horizon over which the appraisal is undertaken. Neither the BAU nor the DG scenarios have positive NPVs over any period of appraisal.

Table 6B.3 *Net Present Values at 25, 50 and 100 years of providing flood defence for the BAU, PT, DG and EDG scenarios as compared to the hold-the-line scenario using a declining discount rate*

Scenario	25 years	50 years	100 years
Business as usual			
BAU	−72,748,196	−88,545,279	−106,964,304
HTL	−70,404,389	−87,805,060	−107,611,098
NPV	−2,343,807	−740,219	646,794
Policy Targets			
PT	−73,335,164	−83,405,325	−96,795,875
HTL	−70,404,389	−87,805,060	−107,611,098
NPV	−2,930,775	4,399,735	10,815,223
Deep Green			
DG	−97,509,518	−102,165,512	−110,870,115
HTL	−70,404,389	−87,805,060	−107,611,098
NPV	−27,105,129	−14,360,452	−3,259,017
Extended Deep Green			
EDG	−94,906,735	−73,084,078	−59,184,503
HTL	−70,404,389	−87,805,060	−107,611,098
NPV	−24,502,346	14,720,981	48,426,595

Note: A declining discount rate is used following current HM Treasury guidance for project appraisal (HMT, 2003): 3.5 per cent for years 1 to 30, 3 per cent for years 31 to 75 and 2.5 per cent for years 76 to 100.

The sensitivity of the results of the cost–benefit analysis to changes in key parameters (type of discount rate, level of maintenance costs, the value of habitat and the value of carbon) is indicated by the figures presented in Table 6B.4 which show the 'switching points', that is, the year at which NPV becomes positive, for each scenario.

Discount rate
Results are calculated in Table 6B.4 using differing types of discount rate; a constant rate (3.5 per cent), a declining rate (3.5 per cent for years 1 to 30, 3 per cent for years 31 to 75, 2.5 per cent for years 76 to 125, 2 per cent for years 126 to 200), and the hyperbolic gamma discounting method following Weitzman (2001). The first set of results in Table 6B.4 corresponds to the results presented in Table 6B.3,

Table 6B.4 *Year in which NPV (scenario costs – HTL costs) becomes positive under alternative discount rates and alternative cost and benefit value scenarios*

Scenario	Discount rate type		
	Constant[a]	Declining[b]	Gamma[c]
1: Assuming equal maintenance costs non-realigned and realigned defences			
Business as usual	Never	Never	228
Policy Targets	34	34	30
Deep Green	Never	Never	63
Extended Deep Green	40	40	33
2: Assuming maintenance costs of realigned defences are 50% lower			
Business as usual	Never	Never	147
Policy Targets	30	27	27
Deep Green	Never	80	54
Extended Deep Green	37	34	31
3: As 1 + habitat creation benefits values reduced to £145/ha			
Business as usual	Never	Never	Never
Policy Targets	Never	Never	Never
Deep Green	Never	Never	Never
Extended Deep Green	Never	Never	Never
4: As 1 + carbon sequestration benefits increased to £222/tonne carbon			
Business as usual	Never	Never	194
Policy Targets	28	28	25
Deep Green	Never	114	53
Extended Deep Green	32	32	28
5: As 1 + carbon sequestration benefits reduced to £4/tonne carbon			
Business as usual	Never	Never	237
Policy Targets	36	36	31
Deep Green	Never	Never	66
Extended Deep Green	43	43	35

Notes:

[a] Discount rate constant at 3.5 per cent.

[b] See note for Table 6B.3.

[c] The hyperbolic gamma discounting method described by Weitzman (2001) is used here.

directly for the DDR figures and in terms of the values for the various aspects of the analysis for the constant and gamma discount rates. For all these sets of results the effect of the type of discount rate (as would be expected) is to shift the time at which NPV becomes positive closer to the present as one moves from the constant rate, to the DDR and then to the gamma discount rate. It is also notable that under all the changes (excepting the habitat value change) set out in Table 6B.4, the gamma discount rate is the most stable, that is, there is a relatively smaller variation in switching values in response to these changes.

Maintenance costs

Edwards and Winn (2006) state that the intertidal habitat created by managed realignment can produce benefits by dissipating wave energy and hence reducing the estuary's erosive impact on flood defences. Maintenance cost savings will vary from site to site according to wave climate, coastal topography and consequent defence works. It therefore seems reasonable to assume that across an estuary or extensive stretches of coast, realignment strategies will yield significant maintenance cost savings. We take this possible effect into account within the analysis by comparing the situation where the costs of maintaining defences are equal across non-realigned and realigned defences (results set 1 in Table 6B.4) with one where the costs of maintaining realigned defences are 50 per cent lower (results set 2). Switching points for the PT and EDG scenarios are slightly lower with lower maintenance costs, but the DG switching point is substantially lower under the DDR schedule, as is the BAU switching point for the gamma discount rate.

Habitat values

In order to avoid double counting problems, the environmental benefits derived from realignment schemes, as intertidal habitats are created, were treated as one composite value. An estimate of £621/ha/yr was used, based on the results of a meta-analysis of wetland values (Woodward and Wui, 2001). It is also the case that ecosystems such as saltmarshes act as sinks for organic carbon (C) and nitrogen (N) and particle reactive phosphorus (P) (Andrews et al, 2000; Jickells et al, 2000). The nutrients (N and P) storage function has not been separately valued because its human welfare impact is felt via better water quality and consequent amenity/recreational quality enhancement. This impact, we have assumed, is already encompassed by our composite wetland value. The same is not the case for carbon burial which we have included as an independent and separately valued benefit of realignment.[6]

Results set 3 in Table 6B.4 shows the effect on the analysis of the use of a lower value for wetland habitat. The value of £145/ha/yr is drawn from the Brander et al (2006) wetland value meta-analysis and is the median value for salt/brackish marsh (converted from 1995 US$). Table 6B.4 demonstrates that results for all scenarios are very sensitive to the value used for habitat creation since a positive

NPV is not achieved under any discount rate type over any time period. Note that this value is low compared to the mean value for salt/brackish marsh of about £2276/ha/yr taken from the same study. As such we would expect the value of £145/ha/yr to represent a lower bound to the range of possible values.

Carbon values

Various approaches exist for estimating the monetary value of carbon storage. In this study we based the monetary estimate on the environmental damage done per tonne of carbon dioxide (or equivalent) emitted into the atmosphere – the 'damage cost avoided' by storing rather than releasing a given quantity of carbon dioxide equivalent units. A recent meta-analysis undertaken by Tol (2005), using only peer-reviewed studies, estimated that the mean marginal damage cost of carbon dioxide emissions was $50/tC (in 1995 US$, equivalent to about £45 in 2005) and this value is used in the CBA. We also use a value of £222/tC (again derived from Tol, 2005) to represent an upper estimate of the value of carbon storage, and a lower value estimate of £4/tC (derived from Pearce, 2003). Switching values, results for these values are shown in results sets 4 and 5 in Table 6B.4. These results indicate that the analysis is relatively insensitive to the value of carbon used, with significant effects on the timing of NPV becoming positive only occurring for the BAU and DG scenarios, under the DDR and gamma schedules.

Concluding comments

The Humber CBA shows that limited managed realignment assessed over an extensive spatial and temporal scale and with non-constant discounting provides an economic efficiency gain. However, the critical importance of the estimated magnitude of the composite ecosystem/habitat value in the CBA outcomes serves to highlight the need for careful scrutiny of the original research and benefits transfer from which the estimates have been derived and the importance of original site-specific valuation studies. Only the latter can provide the full degree of confidence necessary for actual policy implementation.

CASE STUDY C: WETLANDS RESTORATION

The restoration of the Culm Grasslands: A scientifically important wetland ecosystem

This case study looks at the current state and potentially future-threatened status of the highly prized (in biodiversity, landscape and amenity terms) Culm Grasslands. The Culm Grasslands are semi-natural grasslands in south-west England which have resulted from traditional low-intensity farming practices. These grasslands are a scientifically important habitat, home to many endangered species including the Marsh Fritillary butterfly and the Curlew. Approximately 75 per cent of the grasslands are under some form of management agreement (Saunders, 2003). However, the grasslands are highly fragmented and are only a small remnant of their former occupation within Devon and Cornwall, an estimated 92 per cent of the grassland having been lost since 1905 (English Nature, 1991). Agricultural improvement has frequently been cited as the principle driving force behind these massive losses (Devon Biodiversity Partnership, 1998). Despite their importance in biodiversity terms the grasslands are, however, not well recognized by the general public.

The remaining grassland is therefore vulnerable to the effects of adjacent land use and neglect (Saunders, 2003). The main threat to the conservation of the Culm Grasslands not under management agreements is land use change, either through further agricultural intensification, or more probably, through neglect due to changes in CAP regime and the diversification of farming, often towards tourism. However, the longer term ecological viability of the majority of the Culm Grassland sites (whether under management agreements or not) is seriously in doubt given their small size and patchwork pattern (Saunders et al, 1991).

To maintain the Culm Grasslands, both wildlife enhancement and countryside stewardship schemes are used. The case study reports the results of a contingent valuation study used to estimate the benefits of a proposed expansion in the area of Culm Grasslands in Devon and Cornwall. These benefit estimates are then incorporated into a cost–benefit analysis to assess whether net societal benefits are gained through providing these management agreements.

Benefits of the Culm Grasslands

The characteristics of these grasslands offer the potential for a range of benefits which are of value to humans. In order evaluate these benefits a link has to be made between the functioning of the grasslands system and the consequent provision of goods and services from which humans can derive welfare gains (or losses if the grasslands disappear). A functional assessment of the Culm Grasslands was undertaken with the following functions being found to be performed: groundwater recharge and discharge; nutrient retention and export; organic carbon concentration control; in-situ carbon retention and ecosystem maintenance. A combination of the above functions produces a number of socio-economic benefits including recreation, landscape and amenity, agricultural output, water quality, water generation, flood control, in-situ carbon retention, and biodiversity.

In this study, we focus on the ecosystem maintenance function and its related socio-economic function of biodiversity and landscape amenity. This is to avoid the issue of double counting, but is not to deny that further benefits from the Culm Grasslands exist.

The contingent valuation of the Culm Grasslands

The contingent valuation survey was designed to fit into the Culm Grasslands conservation conflict context, by determining the benefits accruing from a 10 per cent expansion of the grasslands, which could be achieved through a combination of agri-environmental schemes (chiefly that of countryside stewardship) and land purchases. Thus, the focus was on the benefits deriving from the expansion rather than the valuation of the means by which it is achieved.

In addition to enhancement of biodiversity and landscape attributes, other benefits will result from the expansion which are not covered in this study. Consequently, the values estimated in this study are an underestimate of the total economic value of the grasslands. The use here of environmental change scenarios to define the valuation scenarios assists in visualization of a world in which everything is exactly the same except the aspect which is to be evaluated. The scenarios are given below:

Business-as-Usual (BAU). Continued losses to the remaining areas of Culm Grasslands. This is a result of further land use change due to reform of the CAP as well as decreased ecological viability of the remaining sites. The long-term viability of the Culm Grasslands is seriously in doubt under the BAU scenario.

Policy Targets (PT). As a consequence of the ongoing risk to the future integrity of the Culm Grasslands, in 2003 the Devon Wildlife Trust set a target to increase the grasslands by 10 per cent over the next ten years (Saunders, 2003). This target is implemented under the PT scenario. There will not only be improvements in the quality and longevity of the grasslands, but these can be added to the sustainable rural development that will draw on and enhance the environmental and cultural assets of the Culm.

Deep Green (DG). Protection of the Culm Grasslands is given maximum priority. There would be a push to extend the grasslands back to their pre-1905 extent. The long-term viability of the grasslands will be increased under this scenario.

An economic approach to assess which of these three scenarios would be most desirable for the Culm Grasslands requires a quantification of the costs and benefits. In this section we present a simplified analysis, with full details being presented in the CSERGE (Centre for Social and Economic Research on the Global Environment) working paper 'Assessing the value of a scientifically important wetland ecosystem: The case of the Culm Grasslands' (Burgess et al, 2008). The cost–benefit analysis is restricted to the economic benefits of increasing the landscape, ecology and recreational characteristics of the Culm Grasslands, relative to their continued decrease due to land use change and reducing ecological viability.

In order to assess the benefits of implementing an expansion scheme a contingent valuation (CV) study was undertaken. The study consisted of a survey which attempted to capture the values which members of the public might put on the preservation of the Culm Grasslands, obtained through face-to-face interviews throughout Devon and Cornwall. Respondents were asked their willingness to pay, in the form of extra household taxation, for a 10 per cent expansion of the Culm Grasslands through the restoration of converted and neglected land adjacent to the existing grasslands, in the expectation that this would provide protection and enhancement of the ecological, landscape and recreational characteristics of the area.

To elicit the WTP of respondents, use was made of both a coercive payment vehicle (an increase in council tax for residents and the imposition of a tourist tax on visitors to the area) and a voluntary donations payment vehicle to elicit WTP for the expansion of the Culm Grasslands. Within the survey, a one-and-a-half-bound elicitation format approach (Cooper et al, 2002) was used, whereby the survey respondent was initially given a range of costs (BID_L for the lower cost and BID_U for the higher cost) for implementing the scheme and asked whether they would be willing to pay either the lower cost or the higher one, and depending on the response a second question would be asked.

The survey was conducted through Devon and Cornwall during the month of August and the beginning of September, a time selected to coincide with the summer holidays to gain the values of tourists as well as local residents. A range of locations were covered and these included towns, cities, holiday resorts, National Trust properties, an agricultural show and even a balloon festival. Approximately 700 people were interviewed, 73 per cent of whom had no prior knowledge of the Culm Grasslands. The sampling frame for the survey was a random sample of people approached in a variety of locations and times with the aim of interviewing a wide spectrum of people. The sample could be split broadly into two categories, those respondents who are resident in either Devon or Cornwall and those respondents who were visiting Devon or Cornwall.

Results

To obtain population estimates of the benefits deriving from the 10 per cent expansion of the Culm Grasslands, individual WTP must be aggregated across the population. However, care must be taken in defining the relevant population which derives benefit from the good in question in the aggregation process. As this valuation study focuses on the biodiversity and landscape attributes of the Culm Grasslands, the relevant population is potentially large as a result of the non-consumptive use values of recreation/amenity and non-use values deriving from the ecosystem maintenance function. Thus, benefits from the Culm Grasslands scheme will be derived from a number of sources, those in the immediate area, visitors from outside the area and the general public. Hence, the relevant population for the Culm Grasslands relates to 'users' (visitors to the areas) and potential 'non-users' (both nearby and distant).

To aggregate the individual estimates of WTP for the Culm Grasslands, the relevant population was taken to be the local population of Devon and Cornwall and visitors to the region. This entailed splitting the sample into 'locals' and 'tourists' and deriving the WTP for each of these sub-samples and then aggregating up to the affected population.

For brevity, the values obtained from the sample of respondents under the voluntary payment scheme will be used. Of the 248 respondents within this payment vehicle, 167 were local to Devon and Cornwall. The measures of WTP are shown in Table 6C.1. As can be seen, the median WTP falls into the range £0–5 as fewer than 50 per cent of respondents who were offered a bid level of £5 rejected it. The mean value of WTP for the local population of Devon and Cornwall for the 10 per cent expansion of the Culm Grasslands was £12.50 per household per year, with a 95 per cent confidence interval of £7.01–17.99.

Within Devon and Cornwall there are 514,271 households (UK Census, 2001), thus the annual benefit for the local population of increasing the Culm Grasslands by 10 per cent is £6.4 million. The benefits of the biodiversity and landscape attributes of the Culm Grasslands will occur over a ten-year time horizon of the scheme. To gain the net present value of the benefits accruing from the Culm Grasslands expansion scheme over that period, the population estimates of WTP are discounted over ten years at a rate of 3.5 per cent (HM Treasury, 1997). This gives a total value for the local population of £53.5 million.

In addition to the local population, a third of the sample was composed of tourists visiting Devon and Cornwall. The measures of WTP for the tourist sub-sample are shown in Table 6C.2. Again, the median WTP falls into the range £0–5 as only 30 per cent of respondents offered a bid level of £5 accepted it. The mean value of WTP for tourists to Devon and Cornwall to expand the Culm Grasslands by 10 per cent was £9.21 per household per year, with a 95 per cent confidence interval of £2.11–16.86.

In aggregating the estimated WTP of the individual tourist to obtain the total benefit to the population, care must be taken in determining the relevant population. Based on a number of assumptions (for details see Burgess et al, 2008), the number of visitors is estimated at 1.08 million per year. With a mean estimated WTP of £9.21 this gives an annual benefit of expanding the Culm Grasslands of £9.97 million. Discounting this annual benefit over the ten-year lifespan of the scheme using the 3.5 per cent discount rate gives the total benefit from tourists to Devon and Cornwall as £82.75 million.

Table 6C.1 *Results from the non-parametric modelling of the voluntary payment scheme data (local sub-sample)*

	WTP (£ per household per year)	Confidence interval (95%)
Median (WTP)	0–5.00	–
Mean (WTP)	12.50	7.01–17.99

Table 6C.2 *Results from the non-parametric modelling of the voluntary data (tourist sub-sample)*

	WTP (£ per household per year)	Confidence interval (95%)
Median (WTP)	0–5.00	–
Mean (WTP)	9.21	2.11–16.86

Together with the benefits accruing to the local population, expanding the Culm Grasslands will result in a total benefit of £136.25 million. This figure can now be compared with the costs of implementing the scheme to determine whether it should be implemented.

Cost–benefit analysis

The implementation of any scheme designed to increase the area of Culm Grassland will incur costs. The costs of three different options for the expansion of the Culm Grasslands by 400ha and maintenance of the existing area of 4000ha are estimated as follows (for details see Burgess et al, 2008):

Option 1
Purchase of all 4400ha, plus costs of restoration on the 400ha expansion, as well as costs of maintaining Culm Grassland (annual costs which are assumed to be at a conservative level of £50/ha and represent costs associated with low-intensity grazing and rush and purple moorgrass management). Costs are calculated for a lower and upper bound determined by the range of land prices elicited from estate agents operating in the area as well as other local experts (£2100–6175). Restoration costs amount to one-off payments of £500/ha for scrub clearance and £375/ha for hedge restoration.

Option 2
Costs of forgone agricultural production brought about by reversion to Culm Grassland are represented by annual payments made under agri-environmental management schemes. These costs are bounded at lower and upper levels with payment under the various schemes available. All management agreement payments are also assumed to attract annual extensification payments of £29.74/ha (we assume, not unrealistically, that pasture reverting to Culm Grassland will be predominately used for extensive beef production). We also assume that 20 per cent of the 4400ha will attract additional Countryside Stewardship Scheme small field supplements of £30/ha and that restoration costs will be incurred over the 400ha expansion in Culm Grassland (as in option 1).

Table 6C.3 *Costs of alternative 10 per cent Culm Grassland expansion schemes (current £million)*

	Option 1		Option 2		Option 3	
	Lower bound	Upper bound	Lower bound	Upper bound	Lower bound	Upper bound
Land purchase	11.11	32.67	0	0	5.56	16.34
Management agreement payments	0	0	2.26	4.57	1.13	2.29
Restoration costs	0.42	0.42	0.42	0.42	0.42	0.42
Maintenance costs	1.89	1.89	0	0	0.95	0.95
Totals	13.42	34.98	2.68	4.99	8.06	20.00

Option 3

A combination of 50 per cent option 1 and 50 per cent option 2. Note that all costs are discounted over a ten-year time horizon, following usual practice, at a rate of 3.5 per cent. Costs for these three options are summarized in Table 6C.3 above.

The highest cost option is the upper bound of option 1, land purchase, at £35 million and the lowest cost option is the lower bound of option 2 at £2.68 million.

Do costs exceed benefits?

With the determination of both the benefits and the costs of implementing this expansion scheme, a cost–benefit analysis can be undertaken, whereby the benefits are compared with costs to establish whether any net benefit (benefits minus costs) exists . The net benefit of each possible option in creating this policy target environmental change scenario is shown in Table 6C.4.

As can be seen from Table 6C.4, substantial net benefit exists for introducing this 10 per cent expansion scheme, irrespective of the method used to achieve it, although option 2, using the management agreements, is the cheapest way of

Table 6C.4 *The net benefits of implementing the 10 per cent expansion scheme (current £million)*

	Cost	Benefit	Net benefit
Option 1	35	136	101
Option 2	5	136	131
Option 3	20	136	116

achieving the 10 per cent expansion, and therefore produces the largest net benefit. Thus, as a result of this CBA, the 10 per cent expansion scheme can be said to be economically efficient and should be introduced.

NOTES

1   National Rivers Authority (NRA), precursor to the UK Environment Agency with responsibility for the rivers.
2   The main aim of this question was to validate refusals as it was felt that respondents presented directly with a request to state how much they would pay might feel either intimidated about stating a zero amount (and consequently state false positives) or offended at the presumption of some positive WTP (which might lead to 'protest' behaviour; see Sagoff, 1988).
3   Further analyses shown included an assessment of WTP as a lump sum amount and the period of commitment for payments. Details are given in Bateman and Langford, 1997.
4   Results from the open-ended format are presented in Bateman et al, 1994 and contrasted with dichotomous choice and iterative bidding formats in Bateman et al, 1995. Analysis of the triple bounded format is given in Langford et al, 1996; Langford and Bateman 1999; and Bateman et al, 1999.
5   This was the UK Treasury specified discount rate at the time of the study.
6   Note however, that in a recent review of the long-term impacts of managed realignment, French (2006) states that the establishment of saltmarsh is not inevitable following realignment. Even if satmarsh is not created post-realignment, some kind of wetland (e.g. mudflats) will be created, and these will have associated amenity, and nutrient and carbon storage functions – albeit possibly at a lower level. For the purposes of this study we assume that saltmarsh is created after realignment.

REFERENCES

Andrews, J.E., Samways, G., Dennis, P.F. and Maher, B.A. (2000) 'Origin, abundance and storage of organic carbon and sulphur in the Holocene Humber Estuary: Emphasising human impact on storage changes'. In Shennan, I. and Andrews, J. (eds) *Holocene Land–Ocean Interaction and Environmental Change around the North Sea*. Geological Society: London, Special Publications, 166: pp145–170

Arrow, K., Solow, R., Schuman, H., Ragner, R. and Portney, P. (1994) 'Report to the NOAA Panel on Contingent Valuation'. *US Federal Register* 58(10): 4602–4614

Bateman, I.J., Day, B.H., Georgiou, S. and Lake, I. (2006) 'The aggregation of environmental benefit values: Welfare measures, distance decay and total WTP'. *Ecological Economics* 60 (2): 450–460

Bateman, I.J. and Langford, I.H. (1997) 'Non-users' willingness to pay for a national park: An application and critique of the contingent valuation method'. *Regional Studies* 31(6): 571–582

Bateman, I.J., Langford, I.H. and Rasbash, J. (1999) 'Elicitation effects in contingent valuation studies'. In Bateman, I.J. and Willis, K.G. (eds) *Valuing Environmental*

Preferences: Theory and Practice of the Contingent Valuation Method in the US, EU, and Developing Countries. Oxford University Press: Oxford, pp511–539

Bateman, I.J., Langford, I.H., Turner, R.K., Willis, K.G. and Garrod, G.D. (1995) 'Elicitation and truncation effects in Contingent Valuation Studies'. *Ecological Economics* 2: 161–179

Bateman, I.J., Langford, I.H., Willis, K.G., Turner, R.K. and Garrod, G.D. (1993) 'The impacts of changing willingness to pay question format in contingent valuation studies: An analysis of open-ended, iterative bidding and dichotomous choice formats'. GEC Working Paper 93–05, Centre for Social and Economic Research on the Global Environment (CSERGE), University of East Anglia and University College London

Bateman, I.J., Willis, K.G. and Garrod, G.D. (1994) 'Consistency between Contingent Valuation estimates – a comparison of 2 studies of UK National Parks'. *Regional Studies* 28(5) 457–474

Bateman, I.J., Willis, K.G., Garrod, G.D., Doktor, P., Langford, I.H. and Turner, R.K. (1992) Recreation and environmental preservation value of the Norfolk Broads: A contingent valuation study. Report to the National Rivers Authority, Environmental Appraisal Group, University of East Anglia, p403

Black and Veatch/Halcrow (2005) Humber Estuary Flood Defence Strategy: Strategy Development Study Technical Report. Report to the Environment Agency, Leeds

Brander, L.M., Raymond, J.G., Florax, M. and Vermaat, J. (2006) 'The empirics of wetland valuation: A comprehensive summary and a meta-analysis of the literature'. *Environmental and Resource Economics* 33: 223–250

Burgess, D., Jackson, N., Hadley, D., Turner, K., Georgiou, S. and Day, B. (2008) 'Assessing the value of a scientifically important wetland ecosystem: The case of the Culm Grasslands'. CSERGE Working Paper, Centre for Social and Economic Research on the Global Environment, University of East Anglia, Norwich (forthcoming)

Cooper, J.C., Hanemann, M. and Signorello, G. (2002) 'One-and-one-half-bound dichotomous choice contingent valuation'. *Review of Economics and Statistics* 84(4): 742–750

DEFRA (Department for Environment, Food and Rural Affairs) (2001) FCDPAG3 Flood and Coastal Defence Project Appraisal Guidance: Economic Appraisal. www.defra.gov.uk/environ/fcd/pubs/pagn/fcdpag3/default.htm

DEFRA (2004) Agricultural land sales and prices in England Quarterly. Online edition (16 June 2004). http://statistics.defra.gov.uk/esg/statnot/alpxls

Devon Biodiversity Partnership (1998) The Nature of Devon: A Biodiversity Action Plan – Rhôs Pasture. www.devon.gov.uk/biodiversity/pasture.shtml

Dillman, D.A. (1978) *Mail and Telephone Surveys – The Total Design Method*. John Wiley and Sons: Chichester

Edwards, A.M.C., and Winn, P.S.J. (2006) 'The Humber Estuary, Eastern England: Strategic planning of flood defences and habitats'. *Marine Pollution Bulletin* 53: 165–174

English Nature (1991) Cornish Culm Grasslands: Botanical survey and conservation assessment 1989/90. English Nature: Truro, UK. www.wildlifetrust.org.uk/cornwall/wow/Reading/culm.htm

Environment Agency (1997) Broadland flood alleviation strategy: Bank strengthening and erosion protection. Environment Agency: Suffolk

Environment Agency (2000) Planning for Rising Tides: The Humber Estuary Shoreline Management Plan. Environment Agency

French, P.W. (2006) 'Managed realignment – the developing story of a comparatively new approach to soft engineering'. *Estuarine, Coastal and Shelf Science* 67(3): 409–423

Halcrow UK (2000) Humber Estuary Tidal Defences, Urgent Works 1 – Little Humber to Thorngumbald Clough. Engineer's Report prepared for the Environment Agency

HM Treasury (1997) *The Green Book Appraisal and Evaluation in Central Government.* The Stationery Office: London

Jickells, T., Andrews, J., Samways, G., Sanders, R., Malcolm, S., Sivyer, D., Parker, R., Nedwell, D., Trimmer, M. and Ridgway, J. (2000) 'Nutrient Fluxes through the Humber Estuary – Past, Present and Future'. *Ambio* 29(3): 130–135

Langford, I.H. and Bateman, I.J. (1999) 'Multilevel modelling and contingent valuation'. In Bateman, I.J. and Willis, K.G. (eds) *Valuing Environmental Preferences: Theory and Practice of the Contingent Valuation Method in the US, EU, and Developing Countries.* Oxford University Press: Oxford, pp442–459

Langford, I.H., Bateman, I.J. and Langford, H.D. (1996) 'A multilevel modeling approach to triple-bounded dichotomous choice contingent valuation'. *Environmental and Resource Economics* 7(3): 197–211

Ledoux, L., Beaumont, N., Cave, R. and Turner, R.K. (2005) 'Scenarios for integrated river catchment and coastal zone management'. *Regional Environmental Change* 5: 82–96

National Rivers Authority (1992) A flood alleviation strategy for Broadland: Final report annex four – Cost–benefit Studies. NRA, Anglian Region, Peterborough

Pearce, D.W. (2003) 'The social cost of carbon and its policy implications', *Oxford Review of Economic Policy* 19: 362–384

Penning-Rowsell, E.C., Johnson, C., Tunstall, S., Tapsell, S., Morris, J., Chatterton, J. and Green, C. (2005) *The Benefits of Flood and Coastal Risk Management: A Handbook of Assessment Techniques.* Middlesex University Press: London

Pethick, J. (2002) 'Estuarine and tidal wetland restoration in the United Kingdom: Policy versus practice'. *Restoration Ecology* 10(3): 431–437

Sagoff, M. (1988) *The Economy of the Earth.* Cambridge University Press: Cambridge

Saunders, D.A., Hobbs, R.J. and Margules, C.R. (1991) 'Biological consequences of ecosystem fragmentation: A review'. *Conservation Biology* 5: 18–32

Saunders, G. (2003) Culm Grassland: A Review and Vision to the Year 2013. A report on behalf of Devon Wildlife Trust for English Nature

Tol, R.S.J. (2005) 'The marginal damage costs of carbon dioxide emissions: An assessment of the uncertainties'. *Energy Policy* 33: 2064–2074

Turner, R.K. and Brooke, J. 1988. 'Management and valuation of an environmentally sensitive area: Norfolk Broadland, England, case study'. *Environmental Management* 12(2): 203–207

Turner, R.K., Burgess, D., Hadley, D., Coombes, E. and Jackson, N. (2007) 'A cost-benefit appraisal of coastal managed realignment policy'. *Global Environmental Change* 17: 397–407

Turner, R.K., Doktor, P. and Adger, W.N. (1995) 'Assessing the costs and benefits of sea level rise'. *Environment and Planning A* 27: 1777–1796

UK Census (2001) Office of National Statistics, HM Government, www.statistics.gov.uk/census/default.asp

Weitzman, M. L. (2001). 'Gamma discounting'. *American Economic Review* 91: 260–271

West, J.J. and Dowlatabadi, H. (1999) 'Assessing economic impacts of sea level rise'. In Downing, T.E., Olsthoorn, A.A. and Tol, R. (eds) *Climate Change and Risk*. Routledge: London, pp205–220

Wigley, T.M.L. and Raper, S.C.B. (1993) 'Future changes in global mean temperature and sea level'. In Warrick, R.A., Barrow, E.M. and Wigley, T.M.L. (eds) *Climate and Sea Level Change: Observations, Projections and Implications*. Cambridge University Press: Cambridge

Woodward, R.T. and Wui, Y-S. (2001) 'The economic value of wetland services: A meta–analysis'. *Ecological Economics* 37: 257–270

Yohe, G. and Neumann, J. (1997) 'Planning for sea level rise and shore protection under climate uncertainty'. *Climatic Change* 37(1): 243–270

Yohe, G., Neumann, J. and Ameden, H. (1995) 'Assessing the economic cost of greenhouse-induced sea level rise – methods and application in support of a national survey'. *Journal of Environmental Economics and Management* 29(3): S78–S97 Part 2 Suppl. S

7

Conclusions and Future Prospects

In earlier chapters we set out the reasons why we believe that the economic (monetary) valuation of a range of wetland goods/services is a practicable and meaningful exercise. There are, however, limits to this set of procedures and particular care needs to be taken to avoid double counting errors (given ecosystem complexities) and whenever value data transfers (over time and space) are being considered. A typology of values based on the total economic value concept is an appropriate way to represent the long-run and multifaceted characteristics of the benefits associated with wetlands. Further, despite some ambiguities around the precise demarcation of use and non-use value categories, the total economic value calculation is a practical and policy relevant method. Taking wetland management decisions on the basis of the ecosystem service and extended cost–benefit analysis approach is both necessary and sufficient to meet the initial requirements of a sustainable development policy strategy.

But wetlands are only one particular ecosystem and the ESApp has been conceived as a generic approach. While precise details will vary across different ecosystems, the ESApp principles and practice illustrated via wetland examples do provide generic guidance. Ecosystem services research is still in a relatively early stage of development and so one important question to ask is: What are the prospects for its meaningful adoption by the policy process? According to some (Carpenter et al, 2006) further theoretical work and empirical studies on the connection between ecosystem services and human welfare will be critical for guiding society towards sustainability goals. Societal preferences and changing public attitudes will also be a key aspect, but must in the end be anchored to sound science. So where do matters stand currently?

Fisher et al (2008) have sought to shed some light on the extent to which ecosystem services research is infiltrating the policy formulation and decision making process around the world. They have conducted a literature search for peer-reviewed articles that analysed ecosystem services with either an explicit or a potential policy interaction. This search was then followed up by a questionnaire survey of the authors of the identified papers. The literature search encompassed three types of policy contexts:

1   contexts where ecosystem service analysis helped to clarify existing policy decisions (*ex post*);

2   contexts where ecosystem service analysis has been a integral part of the policy process (*ex ante*);

3   contexts where an ecosystem service analysis has the potential to inform future policy.

In the first context the idea was to pick up studies where good management has followed legislative requirements. This serves as an important heuristic for future policy, highlighting examples where a detailed valuation exercise followed the management/policy intervention, and where unforeseen service benefits (e.g. tourism) were subsequently realized. The second context requires that a monitoring exercise has been undertaken on policy implementation and only a few studies were identified within this category. The final context sought to capture studies with the potential to inform policy makers.

Some 34 cases were identified and were categorized according to their location in developed or developing countries and whether the ecosystems under investigation were susceptible to abrupt or relatively smooth disturbance profiles (Turner et al, 2003); see Appendix C. This typology is not definitive, meaning that an ecosystem service analysis may fit in more than one box, but it can serve to illuminate several issues simultaneously (i.e. the nature of the ecosystem state change and whether it qualifies as a 'marginal' change suitable for economic valuation; what benefits capture or compensation possibilities might be feasible, etc.). Fisher et al's review showed that almost all of the studies considered multiple rather than single ecosystem services, with water regulation figuring prominently. Most studies also only provided a snapshot in time rather than changes in service delivery across disturbance states. It is the latter context that provides the most policy relevant information (Balmford et al, 2002). There were a few cases where service valuations were compared across alternative land uses, which can be considered a second-best situation for research findings, given that true marginal changes are not always easy to define in dynamic and complex ecosystems (Turner et al, 1998). Finally, the problem of double counting of benefits was rarely acknowledged and direct links to the policy process from ecosystem analysis were not numerous.

The questionnaire survey of authors revealed some further insights (Fisher et al, 2008). Most of the research was initiated or commissioned by agents within the policy process. The degree to which the research penetrated the policy process ranged from minimal impact through to a direct effect on policy decision. Post-policy or post-research appraisals are also not commonplace. Fisher et al (2008) concluded that ecosystem service research can be designed to have strong policy foresight, to facilitate cooperation between policy agents and scientists, and possibly to provide robust implementation effects. Keys to success include the act of making an economic argument (as a buttress for scientific and or moral argumentation); delivering results in common language; elucidating tangible benefits to livelihoods in the short run; and multiple and sustained points of contact with those involved in the policy process.

Understanding the role that ecosystems play in supplying human welfare and linking this understanding to public policy has underlain tax reliefs for conservation easements, public subsidies for environment-friendly agricultural production, and now the increasingly popular *payments for ecosystem services* (PES). All these represent ways in which society is trying to create incentives for managing ecosystems for the public services they provide.

One small point to keep in mind is that the development and implementation of these mechanisms generally assumes that ecosystem service provision needs the help of markets and macroregulation to overcome problems associated with externalities, public goods and imperfect information. While this might be generally true at large spatial scales, humankind has organized sustainable governance of public and common pool goods for thousands of years (Ostrom et al, 1999). However, these successes typically occur on a small scale where resource governance can be handled face-to-face. While our continually more interconnected world might preclude local sustainable governance, in many cases successful provision of ecosystem services, and therefore ecosystem services research, needs to consider a variety of management options for effective and equitable outcomes and not focus simply on market-based interventions.

The research approach described here and the case study work shows that there are several keys to initiating robust and policy relevant ecosystem service research. To summarize these again:

- The distribution of the costs and benefits of ecosystem services will be heterogeneous across the space and time. Waste assimilated in wetlands is likely to have been produced in other parts of the watershed, and the service benefits people across the landscape into the future.
- Stakeholders will have different priorities and perceptions of ecosystem services. This is likely to result in trade-offs: for example, one person's perception that managing a wetland for maximum biodiversity will probably conflict with another's need to manage the system for sustainable reed cutting for building materials. These trade-offs will have to be managed through social systems, and may perhaps require monetary valuation for finding the optimal solution for society.
- Governance and property rights will determine what practical solutions exists for compensating people who 'lose' welfare under some conservation or conversion scheme by those who receive welfare 'gains'. If benefits flow from private lands to society writ large, then perhaps payments systems will be required to sustain that flow of services. However, if the state owns the land from where benefits flow, perhaps monetary compensation will not be necessary and simply statutes can suffice.
- Some level of ecosystem structure and process will be required in order to ensure ecosystem service flows. For most ecosystem services we are unaware of the minimum levels needed and so a safe-minimum-standards approach

will be required. This should be based on the best available ecological information and should be considered apart from any trade-off analysis.

Overall, while ecosystem service research is relatively new, its future prospects are bright. There is an emerging theoretical base, a growing understanding of how human and ecological systems are linked and increasing public and governance awareness of the importance of well-functioning ecosystems to sustainable livelihoods and poverty alleviation.

REFERENCES

Balmford, A., Bruner, A., Cooper, P., Costanza, R., Farber, S., Green, R.E., Jenkins, M., Jefferiss, P., Jessamy, V., Madden, J., Munro, K., Myers, N., Naeem, S., Paavola, J., Rayment, M., Rosendo, S., Roughgarden, J., Trumper, K., Turner, R.K. (2002) 'Economic reasons for conserving wild nature'. *Science* 297: 950–953

Carpenter, S.R., Defries, R., Dietz, T., Mooney, H.A., Polasky, S., Reid, W.V. and Scholes, R.J. (2006) 'Millennium Ecosystem Assessment: Research needs'. *Science* 31, 4(5797): 257–258

Fisher, B. et al (2008) 'Integrating ecosystem services and economic theory'. *Ecological Applications* (in press)

Ostrom, E., Burger, J., Field, C.B., Norgaard, R.B. and Policansky, D. (1999) 'Sustainability: Revisiting the commons: Local lessons, global challenges'. *Science* 284(5412): 278–282

Turner, R.K. (1993) *Sustainable Environmental Economics and Management: Principles and Practice*. Belhaven Press: London and New York

Turner, R.K., Adger, W.N. and Brouwer, R. (1998) 'Ecosystem services value, research needs and policy relevance: A commentary'. *Ecological Economics* 25(1): 61–65

Turner, R.K., Van den Bergh, J.C.J.M. and Brouwer, R. (eds) (2003) *Managing Wetlands: An Ecological Economics Approach*, The Royal Swedish Academy of Sciences, Stockholm, Sweden, 16–17 November

Economic Valuation Techniques

Valuation method	Market analysis (derived demand and market-based transactions)
Description and basis of approach	These approaches make use of a household's or firm's inverse demand function to estimate the user's willingness to pay for the environmental good, or look at transactions between suppliers and users. The former is based on observations of use behaviour. The approach combines concepts from consumer theory with observed usage and makes use of econometric procedures to derive a demand curve for the good. Market-based transactions concerning water are often observed between water utility suppliers and individual water users, usually involving a 'take it or leave it' price schedule. Despite the usual monopolistic nature of supply, because the buyer can buy as much as desired at the price scheduled it is possible to derive inferences on willingness to pay and demand, as long as sufficient observations are observed across variations in real price.
Applicability	Applicable to all areas where market data is available; applicable to other areas where marketed product data is available, e.g. timber, fish. To value wetlands, one could look at what organizations such as nature conservation organizations have paid to purchase wetlands. Includes transactions in water rights.
Data requirements and implementation issues	The data are obtained preferably from observations on water use behaviour of individual households, though this can be costly so aggregate data from suppliers is often used. Statistical regression analysis is employed to estimate the parameters of the demand equation. For market transactions valuation, the key requirement for accurate valuation with this approach is finding market sales of resources with comparable characteristics to the publicly owned resource. Market data may be collected from secondary sources, or by primary collation.
Advantages (strengths)	Can use readily available data on price. Market data is often readily available. Robust.
Disadvantages (weaknesses)	Limited to cases for which there is market data. Estimates lower bound of value. Estimates highly sensitive to functional form assumed for demand curve.

Valuation method	Market analysis (derived demand and market-based transactions)
Validity	Theoretically sound technique. High level of validity since based on actual market relationships.
Value concept compatibility with TEV (incl. non-use)	Direct and indirect use value only; lower bound estimate of TEV.
Value measure	Depending on study: marginal value based on price; not max WTP; sometimes net average value and gross average value depending on purpose of study; sometimes consumer and producer surpluses.
References	Young (2005) and Renzetti (2002); studies of transactions have been conducted in the south-western US states (Saliba and Bush, 1987), and elsewhere in the world (Easter and Hearne, 1995)

Valuation method	Production functions and variants
Description and basis of approach	The production function approach focuses on the indirect relationships that exist between a non-market environmental good or service and the production of a marketed good. By considering changes in production of market goods that arise as a result of changes in the provision of the environmental good or service, one can infer the value of the environmental good or service. The approach considers environmental goods and services as factor inputs into production processes, alongside land, labour and capital, which lead to the output of marketed goods and services. Changes in environmental inputs will lead to changes in a firm's production costs, which in turn will affect the quantity of output and price of the final market good. The change may also affect returns to factor inputs (e.g. rent to land and capital, wages to labour). Ultimately, changes in market output and price and factor returns will result in changes in consumer and producer surpluses. The change in these surpluses gives an estimate of the value of the environmental good or service in its function as a factor input.
	The approach focuses on the production function, which relates the output of a given good to its factor inputs. In addition, the same effect can be analysed by considering the cost function, which relates the cost of production of a given good to the cost of factor inputs (e.g. the quantity of the input multiplied by the price of the factor).

Valuation method	Market analysis (derived demand and market-based transactions)
	There are two channels through which a change in the provision of an environmental input can lead to changes in surpluses. First, the change in the input can affect the production costs of all firms. Hence an improvement in environmental quality lowers production costs, enabling more output to be produced and also reducing market price. Consumers thus benefit from increased consumer surplus. Second, a single producer can experience a change in the input such that the firm's marginal costs change; Lower marginal costs along with unchanged overall market price will mean that the firm benefits from increased producer surplus.
	Related approaches include the *Residual imputation approach*, *Yield comparison approach*, *Value added approach*, *Changes in Revenue/Productivity approach*.
Applicability	Limited to uses of environmental good or service in production process, e.g. effects of air or water quality on agricultural production and forestry output; it is most suitable for use in cases where the input contributes significantly to output.
Data requirements and implementation issues	Typically uses data on input use, capacity and output. Implementation of the approach requires a considerable amount of data concerning the final goods market and factor inputs. It is also necessary that the production function and market structure be specified.
	The key assumptions here are that all other inputs are priced and that total value of output can be apportioned according to the marginal product of the inputs. Data are derived from either extensive surveys of production and inputs, or from secondary data that is used to derive average output and production costs. Secondary data may differ considerably from actual inputs and outputs being assessed. Assuming model specification is accurate, the prices for all inputs and products must be reviewed because some inputs may not be paid and the prices of others may be distorted due to taxes, subsidies, trade protection, etc. A great deal of judgement is thus required in order to determine and estimate the shadow prices.
	Calculation of values requires considerable information and accuracy in allocating contributions among the range of resource inputs.
Advantages (strengths)	Data are often readily available; robust and conceptually straightforward.

Valuation method	Production functions and variants
Disadvantages (weaknesses)	In practice it may be difficult to assess the response of production to changes in environmental factor inputs. The approach requires the assumption that producers (and consumers) act to optimize their behaviour in order to allow estimates of change in producer and consumer surplus to be arrived at. Also, a number of considerations underline the complexity of analysis, including the nature of production (single- or multi-product firms), the market structure (e.g. vertically linked markets) and the presence of market distortions (e.g. monopoly power, price subsidies, etc.).
	Imposes rigorous conditions. Market distortions need to be accounted for. Difficult to implement when the input being considered has a small cost share. Due to confidentiality reasons, data on cost structures and functions may be difficult to obtain for certain goods.
Validity	Validity of the approach requires, first, that profit maximizing producers employ productive inputs up to the point at which marginal product is equal to the opportunity cost; second, that the total value of the product can be divided, so each input can be 'paid' according to its marginal productivity, and the total value of product is thereby exhausted.
Value concept compatibility with TEV (incl. non-use)	Indirect use value only; only lower bound estimate of TEV.
Value measure	Estimates producers' surplus which can be converted to net average value; marginal value also from residual value, change in revenue/productivity approaches.
References	Young (2005); and Renzetti (2002)

Valuation method	Hedonic Price Method (HPM)
Description and basis of approach	Hedonic pricing employs differences in the prices of marketed goods to derive the value of environmental characteristics. Marketed goods can be viewed as comprising a bundle of characteristics; for some goods these include environmental characteristics. Individuals' preferences for environmental quality are reflected in the differential prices that they pay for such goods. Statistical analysis of the prices and characteristics of the goods is employed to derive an implicit value for the environmental characteristic.

In the case of housing, hedonic pricing assumes that the expected stream of benefits of living in a property is capitalized into the market value of the property. In this way, two properties in areas popular for water-based recreation that differ only in respect of water quality may have different market values, due to people's preferences for the difference in water quality. Hedonic pricing uses this difference in value as the implicit price of the difference in water quality. With adequate data and analytical skills, it is possible to determine the implicit price for environmental quality for properties that differ in not just one, but many factors.

To obtain a value for changes in the environmental characteristic of interest, its implicit price (as indicated by the hedonic price function) is regressed against physical and socio-economic variables that are thought to influence demand for housing. The supply of housing is assumed to be fixed in the short run to enable identification of the demand or bid function, which is required for benefit estimation. A functional form for the hedonic price function is identified that best fits the data. This determines the functional form of the marginal implicit price function: the price is not necessarily constant; it might fall with increases in the characteristic, or it might be dependent on the level of another property characteristic.

Hedonic pricing rests on a number of stringent assumptions. It assumes a freely functioning and efficient property market and that individuals have perfect information and mobility. In reality, a large part of the housing stock may be in the public sector, the market may be segmented resulting in restrictions in mobility between areas, and individuals may not be fully informed about the environmental characteristics of properties prior to purchase. A further assumption is that the measure used for the environmental characteristic in hedonic pricing reflects individuals' perceptions. Though an objective quantitative measure is required for the analysis, it may be that people perceive the environmental characteristic qualitatively. A further complication arises in the statistical analysis: if correlation occurs between variables, a trade-off has to be made between multicollinearity and bias due to the omission of significant explanatory variables.

Valuation method	Hedonic Price Method (HPM)
Applicability	Applicable only to environmental attributes likely to be capitalized into the price of housing and/or land. Has been applied to air and water quality, visual amenity, landscape, quiet, as well as flooding.
Data requirements and implementation issues	Implementation is dependent on the quality of data, the specification of an appropriate functional form (e.g. linear, etc.), the inclusion or omission of explanatory variables in the initial analysis, etc.
	Hedonic pricing requires data that can be used to relate house prices to relevant characteristics of individual properties (characteristics of the house e.g. number of rooms, type of neighbourhood, and environmental characteristics, e.g. noise, water quality). Data on sale prices for actual market transactions are preferred over individuals' own valuations of their property. Practical applications require large amounts of data, particularly on property prices and property characteristics. Compilation of data on determinants of house prices may be difficult to measure and obtain. Data may be expert opinion of property values, self-reporting or related to actual sales, although the latter is the most accurate. If data are collected from secondary sources (e.g. Land Registry, census data, etc.), it is generally not possible to link a particular individual buyer to the purchase price and other characteristics of a given property. Instead, the socio-economic characteristics of the neighbourhoods are used as these are assumed to be sufficiently similar to the individual buyers who live in or move into these neighbourhoods.
	One solution to data collection and sorting difficulties is through the application of geographical information systems (GIS) to measure and compile data. If house price data are sufficiently disaggregated (e.g. to the level of an individual property) GIS can be useful in determining accessibility variables for individual properties (e.g. travel time, distance to amenities) as well as linking socio-economic and demographic census data to neighbourhood quality variables.
	Aside from data issues, practical implementation of the HPM requires statistical (econometric) expertise.
Advantages (strengths)	A distinct advantage of revealed preference techniques such as HPM is the use of readily available market data from actual behaviour and choices. Hedonic pricing is grounded firmly in the principles of economic theory, relying on the derivation of demand curves and elasticity estimates. Moreover, the theoretical expectations of HPM have typically been borne out by empirical studies.

Valuation method	Market analysis (derived demand and market-based transactions)
Disadvantages (weaknesses)	Disadvantages of HPM lie in the requirement for copious amounts of data and specialist econometric expertise. In terms of undertaking hedonic analysis, other weaknesses arise from issues of identification and complementarity. HPM is not suited for use where environmental impacts are not perceived (or observed) in property purchasing decisions, or where environmental impacts are yet to occur, since environmental values are revealed from situations with precedents.
Validity	Hedonic pricing is founded on a sound theoretical basis and is capable of producing valid estimates of benefits as long as individuals can perceive the environmental change of interest. Market failures may mean that prices distorted, that is markets may not behave as required by the approach. Data on prices and factors are determining prices are often difficult to come by. Hedonic pricing has been employed to produce reliable estimates of the values of actual environmental changes.
Value concept compatibility with TEV (incl. non-use)	Direct and indirect use value.
Value measure	Marginal value if second stage of analysis undertaken, otherwise average value of water derived.
Reference	Bockstael and McConnell (2007)
Valuation method	Travel Cost Method (TCM)
Description and basis of approach	The travel cost approach takes the costs of travel that are incurred by individuals in visits made to recreational sites as a proxy for the value of recreation. The costs of travel (the costs of transport plus the value of time) are used as implicit prices to value the service provided. Expenses will differ between sites (or for the same site over time) with different environmental attributes. Travel costs measure only the use value of sites and are usually limited to recreational use values.

There are two variants of the simple travel cost visitation model. The first can be used to estimate individuals' recreational demand functions. The visitation rate of individuals who make trips to a recreational site are observed as a function of the travel cost. This 'individual' travel cost model (ITCM) requires that there is variation in the number of trips that individuals make to the recreational site, in order to estimate their demand functions. |

Valuation method	Travel Cost Method (TCM)
	The second variant, known as the 'zonal' travel cost model (ZTCM), estimates aggregate or market demand for a site. The unit of observation is the 'zone' as opposed to the individual. Zones are specified as areas with similar travel costs; the region surrounding a site is divided into zones of increasing travel cost. The method entails observation of the number of visits to the recreational site per capita of population for each zone. Data are again collected through a survey of visitors to the site.
	For both variants, the demand curve is estimated by the regression of the visit rate against socio-economic factors (such as income), the travel cost of visiting the site and some indicator of site quality. The data requirements are, therefore, considerable. For the individual model, data is required on each individual's socio-economic characteristics; in the case of the zonal model, these data are required for the population of each zone. Data are also required on the nature of each trip to the site, the distance travelled, time taken and cost of travel. The data are usually gained from existing or specially commissioned surveys. The method also requires a measure of site quality, which can be an intangible variable. A measure of site quality can range from angling catch rates to biochemical indicators such as concentrations of dissolved oxygen. The measures of site quality must be in accordance with measures that individuals perceive as relevant.
	Unless the site that is being valued is unique, individuals have access to substitute sites that they can use for the same or similar recreational activities. Omission of substitute sites from the analysis creates a source of bias in the analysis. There is, however, no simple means of incorporating substitute sites into the individual and zonal travel cost models presented here. Multi-site models can be used. These vary in their complexity and their ability to explain substitute behaviour.
Applicability	Generally limited to recreational activities.
Data requirements and implementation issues	The TCM survey is required to collect data on place of residence of visitors, demographic and attitudinal information, frequency of visit to the site and other similar sites and trip information (e.g. purposefulness, length, associated costs, etc.). Practical application of the ZTCM requires data concerning population of each of the travel cost zones that are identified. Data on explanatory variables that are also likely to influence visit rates, e.g. income, preference and availability of alternative sites is also important, as is the mode of travel (car, rail, etc.) to the site. Limited availability of data is likely to mean that only reduced forms of the trip-generating function can be estimated.

Valuation method	Travel Cost Method (TCM)
	A particular problem associated with the ITCM model is that variation in trips is not always observed, especially as not all individuals make a positive number of trips to a recreational site; some individuals do not make any. Non-participants can thus be excluded from the data set under certain statistical techniques (e.g. Ordinary Least Squares (OLS)). This exaggerates participation rates and results in the loss of potentially useful information about the participation decision. However, inclusion of data on individuals in the sampling area requires use of more complex statistical methods, such as discrete choice models.
	Use of geographical information systems (GIS), particularly in applications of the ZTCM, can help define travel costs zones to account for areas with similar travel costs, availability of substitute sites and socio-economic characteristics (Bateman et al, 2005).
	In addition to collecting appropriate data, the TCM also requires econometric expertise. For certain sites it may be necessary to sample at different times of the year in order to provide an accurate account of seasonal variations in visitor patterns and number.
Advantages (strengths)	Estimated values are revealed from actual behaviour of individuals and the formulation of demand curves.
Disadvantages (weaknesses)	The technical and data requirements should not be underestimated; travel cost is unlikely to be a low-cost approach to valuation of non-marketed services. Practical applications of the approach may be limited by data availability. More methodological concerns may disadvantage the use of TCM results, particularly with regard to different estimates of consumer surplus that may arise as a result of adopting either the ITCM or ZTCM approach, as well as the treatment of substitute sites, the choice of appropriate functional form and the calculation of the value of time. Finally, the TCM is not able to account for environmental goods (or evils) that are imperceptible to short-term visitors.
Validity	The travel cost method is a technically well-developed valuation approach that has been extensively employed over the past two decades. It is theoretically correct, but complicated when there are multi-purpose trips and competing sites.
	The individual travel cost model is generally preferred to the zonal variant. The latter is statistically inefficient, as it aggregates data from a large number of observations into a few zonal observations. Also, it assumes that the cost of travel to the site for all individuals within each zone is equal, which is often not the case.

Valuation method	Travel Cost Method (TCM)
Value concept compatibility with TEV (incl. non-use)	Direct and indirect use.
Value measure	Usually consumer surplus-based and hence average value of water; sometimes marginal value.
Reference	Bockstael and McConnell (2007)

Valuation method	Contingent Valuation Method (CVM)
Description and basis of approach	In contingent valuation (CV) studies, people are asked directly to state, or are asked a question that will reveal, what they are willing to pay to gain an improvement in the provision of a good or service, or to avoid a detrimental change in the provision of a good or service. Alternatively (or additionally) they may be asked what they are willing to accept to forgo an improvement or tolerate a detrimental change. The situation the respondent is asked to value is hypothetical (hence 'contingent'), although respondents are assumed to behave as if they were in a real market. Structured questions can be devised involving 'yes/no' answers to questions regarding the acceptability of a proposal at a specified price. Econometric techniques are then used on the survey results to find the mean value of WTP.
	There are three basic parts to most CV survey instruments. First, a hypothetical description (scenario) of the terms under which the good or service is to be offered is presented to the respondent. Information is provided on the quality and reliability of provision, its timing and logistics, and the method of payment. Often the good needs to be described in the overall context of the general class of environmental goods under consideration.
	Second, the respondent is asked questions to determine how much he or she would value a good or service if confronted with the opportunity to obtain it under the specified terms and conditions. These questions take the form of asking how much an individual is willing to pay or accept for some change in provision. Respondents are often reminded of the need to make compensating adjustments in other types of expenditure to accommodate this additional financial transaction.

Valuation method	Contingent Valuation Method (CVM)
	Third, questions on socio-economic and demographic characteristics of the respondent are asked in order to relate respondents' answers to the valuation questions to the other characteristics of the respondent, and to those of the policy-relevant population.
	A respondent's choice or preference can be elicited in a number of ways. The simplest is to ask the respondent a direct question about how much he or she would be willing to pay for the good or service – known as continuous or open-ended questions. High rates of non-responses can be a problem with this approach. Alternatively, a respondent can be asked whether or not they would want to purchase the service if it cost a specified amount. These are known as discrete or dichotomous choice questions, and may be favoured because they do not give the respondent any incentive to answer untruthfully; that is, the approach is 'incentive compatible'. A hybrid approach is the 'bidding game', where respondents are asked a series of questions in order to reach the best estimate of their valuation. Alternatively, respondents may be shown a list of possible answers – a 'payment card' – and asked to indicate their choice, though this requires a careful determination of the range of possible answers. Each approach implies particular requirements in terms of statistical methods, and the appropriate choice for a specific problem is a matter of judgement on the part of the analyst.
Applicability	Extensive, since it can be used to derive values for almost any environmental change. This explains its attractiveness to valuers. CVM can be employed to calculate both use and non-use values including option and existence values.
Data requirements and implementation issues	Primarily, the CVM survey instrument will be designed to collate all data required for estimating WTP/WTA values and functions for determining the main influences on respondents' WTP. In addition, a crucial aspect of CVM survey design is ensuring that the survey sample is representative of the population of interest. Generally representativeness will be based on socio-economic characteristics (e.g. sourced from census data).
	Reliable CVM studies are not simple (or inexpensive) to implement. Proper practice in CVM studies requires time to develop the survey instrument and to ensure that the non-market good or service to be valued is clearly explained along with the constructed market and payment method. Overall, from the initial design stages of the survey instrument to aggregating and reporting of results, practical implementation of the CVM could require six months to a year depending particularly on aspects such as complexity of the issue of concern and sample size. Analysis of a CVM dataset, the estimation of WTP/WTA values and functions, as well as validity and reliability testing, require econometric expertise.

Valuation method	Contingent Valuation Method (CVM)
Advantages (strengths)	CVM (along with choice modelling) is the only approach that can estimate non-use value associated with environmental goods and services. Furthermore the CVM approach to valuing environmental goods and services offers a great deal of flexibility; in particular the construction of a hypothetical market can be envisaged for numerous environmental goods and services at differing degrees of quality. In addition the CVM enables a great deal of information to be collated and analysed from the target population concerning their attitudes towards, use and experience of environmental goods and service in addition to eliciting WTP/WTA amounts and WTP functions concerning the determinants of WTP.
Disadvantages (weaknesses)	Economic analysis has typically favoured evidence based on actual market behaviour over hypothetical approaches. However, it would appear that is necessary to trade-off these 'real' market data with data from hypothetical markets in order to account for non-use values. Much emphasis should also be placed on ensuring that practical applications of the CVM are guided by current best practice. This may imply that the approach is relatively expensive to undertake, although the cost of undertaking a CVM study should be viewed in comparison to the actions which are the concern of the decision making context.
Validity	The literature has identified various forms of potential bias. 'Strategic bias' arises if respondents intentionally give responses that do not reflect their 'true' values. They may do this if they think there is potential to 'free ride'. However, there is limited evidence of strategic bias. 'Hypothetical bias' arises because respondents are not making 'real' transactions. Costs of studies usually limit the number of experiments involving real money (criterion validity), but some studies exist. Convergent validity is good. Construct validity – relating value estimates to expectations of values estimated using other measures – is debated, especially the marked divergence in many studies between WTP and WTA compensation.
Value concept compatibility with TEV (incl. non-use)	Use and non-use; together with choice experiments this is the only method for eliciting non-use values.
Value measure	Average, marginal or total value can be estimated depending on purpose of study.
References	Bateman et al (2002) and Mitchell and Carson (1989)

Valuation method	Description and basis of approach
Choice modelling	Choice modelling approaches are based around the notion that a good can be described in terms of its characteristics (or 'attributes') and the levels that these characteristics take. For example, a lake may be described in terms of its ecological quality, chemical quality, etc. Likewise, woodland can be described in terms of its species diversity, age and recreational facilities. The following briefly summarizes the different choice modelling approaches:

- Choice experiments – in this approach respondents are presented with a series of alternatives and are asked to choose their most preferred. In order for estimates of economic value to be derived, a baseline option corresponding to the status quo or a 'do nothing' option is included in the choice set presented to respondents. With choice experiments, respondents are required to trade-off changes in attribute level against the cost of these changes. In addition, though, the baseline option implies that respondents can opt for the status quo at no additional cost. Data from choice experiments are typically analysed by econometric techniques based on the theory of rational probabilistic choice, enabling estimates of willingness to pay to be derived for different attributes of environmental goods and services.

- Contingent ranking – in this approach respondents are required to rank a set of alternative options. Each alternative option is characterized by a number of attributes which vary in level across different options. In order for results from contingent ranking exercises to be consistent with economic theory, one of the options presented to respondents must represent the status quo. If the status quo is not included, then respondents are effectively 'forced' to choose one of the alternative options (neither of which they may actually prefer).

- Contingent rating – with this approach respondents are presented with a number of scenarios and are asked to rate each one on a numeric or semantic scale. Notably contingent rating does not involve the direct comparison of alternative options.

- Paired comparisons – in this approach respondents are required to choose their preferred alternative out of a set of two choices and to indicate their strength of preference on a numeric or semantic scale. Effectively a paired comparison exercise combines elements of choice experiments (selecting the most preferred alternative) and rating exercises (rating strength of preference).

Valuation method	Choice modelling
Applicability	Extensive, since it can be used to derive values for almost any environmental change. An important advantage compared to CVM is the valuation of environmental attributes, making it possible to derive marginal economic values for a range of environmental changes. This explains its attractiveness to 'valuers'. It requires substantial knowledge of econometric analysis. Together with CVM it is the only method for eliciting non-use values.
Data requirements and implementation issues	As for CVM.
Advantages (strengths)	One distinct advantage of choice modelling is that it can be seen as a generalized form of a discrete choice CVM study (e.g. a change or no-change scenario). However, in the CVM approach it is not possible to analyse the attributes of the change in question without designing different valuation scenarios for each level of the attribute, which would be a costly undertaking. However, since choice experiments can incorporate more than two alternatives, they are more suited to this form of analysis. In addition, choice experiments are more suited to measuring the marginal value of changes in the characteristics of environmental goods, which may be useful from a management of resources perspective, rather than focusing on either the gain or loss of the good and more discrete changes in attributes. Choice experiments may also avoid some of the response difficulties which are encountered in CVM studies. For instance, CVM studies using a dichotomous choice format may be subject to 'yea-saying' where respondents see a positive answer as a socially desirable response or as a strategic response. However, in a choice experiment setting, respondents get many chances to express a positive preference for a good over a range of payment amounts; hence such behaviour will probably be avoided.
Disadvantages (weaknesses)	Disadvantages of choice modelling include the fact that more complex choice modelling designs may cause problems for respondents leading to an increased degree of random error in responses. Therefore it should be expected that as the number of attributes (or rankings) increases the likelihood of inconsistent responses will also increase due to limits in cognitive ability. Additionally, contingent rating and paired comparisons will not yield values consistent with economic theory due to the absence of a status quo option for respondents.

Valuation method	*Choice modelling*
Validity	Use and applicability has increased in the literature over the past five years. From a welfare-theoretical point of view, superior to contingent ranking. Important methodological issues include the independency between attributes and the orthogonal design of the experiment.
Value concept compatibility with TEV (incl. non-use)	Use and non-use; together with contingent valuation it is the only method for eliciting non-use values.
Value measure	Marginal, average and total value can be estimated depending on purpose of study.
References	Kanninen (2007), Bateman et al (2002) and Louviere et al (2000)

Valuation method	*Avertive behaviour and defensive expenditures/Avoidance costs*
Description and basis of approach	This approach considers the costs and expenditures incurred in mitigating the effects/avoiding damages of reduced environmental functionality. Adverse impacts can be avoided by buying durable foods, non-durable goods, changing daily routines, etc. to avoid exposure to pollutants etc.

Perfect substitutability provides the basis for the averting behaviour and defensive expenditures technique, which focuses on averting inputs as substitutes for changes in environmental characteristics. For instance, expenditures on sound insulation can be used to indicate householders' valuations of noise reduction; and expenditure on liming might reflect the value of reduced water acidification. Fairly crude approximations can be found by looking directly at changes in expenditure on a substitute good that arise as a result of some environmental change. Alternatively, the value per unit change in an environmental characteristic can be determined. This involves determining the marginal rate of substitution between the environmental characteristic and the substitute good, using known or observed technical consumption data. The marginal rate of substitution is multiplied by the price of the substitute good to give the value per unit change in the environmental characteristic. |
| Applicability | Limited to cases where households spend money to offset environmental hazards, for example water filters. |
| Data requirements and implementation issues | The approach requires data on change in an environmental characteristic of interest and its associated substitution effects. Econometric analysis on panel and survey data is sometimes needed. |

Valuation method	*Avertive behaviour and defensive expenditures/Avoidance costs*
Advantages (strengths)	It is a potentially important source of valuation estimates since it gives theoretically correct estimates which are gained from actual expenditures and which thus have high criterion validity.
Disadvantages (weaknesses)	If observed averting behaviour is not between two perfect substitutes, the value of the environmental characteristic is underestimated. For example, if there is an increase in environmental quality, the benefit of this change is given by the reduction in spending on the substitute market good required to keep the individual at their original level of welfare. However, when the change in quality takes place the individual does not reduce spending (in order to stay at the original level of welfare). Income effects cause reallocation of expenditure between all goods with a positive income elasticity of demand and consequently the reduction in spending on the substitute for environmental quality does not capture all the benefits of the increase in quality.
	Further problems with the approach are that individuals may undertake more than one form of averting behaviour in response to an environmental change, and that the averting behaviour may have joint costs and multiple outputs/other beneficial effects that are not considered explicitly (e.g. air conditioner cools and cleans air at the same time; the purchase of bottled water to avoid the risk of consuming polluted supplies may also provide added taste benefits). Furthermore, averting behaviour is often not a continuous decision but a discrete one – a water filter is either purchased or not, for instance. In this case the technique again gives an underestimate of benefits unless discrete choice models for averting behaviour are used.
	Simple avertive behaviour models can, therefore, give incorrect estimates of value if they fail to incorporate the technical and behavioural alternatives to individuals' responses to change in environmental quality.
Validity	Theoretically correct. Insufficient studies to comment on convergent validity. Uses actual expenditures so criterion validity is generally met.
Value concept compatibility with TEV (incl. non-use)	Direct and indirect use.
Value measure	Lower bound estimate of WTP; marginal or average value depending on nature of study.
References	Dickie et al (1991) and Champ et al (2003)

Valuation method	Replacement/restoration cost and cost savings (opportunity cost)
Description and basis of approach	Potential expenditures are incurred in replacing/restoring the function that is lost; for instance by the use of substitute facilities or 'shadow projects'. The replacement cost estimates the benefits of an environmental asset based on the costs of replacement or restoration. The replaced or restored asset is assumed to provide a direct substitute for the original. The technique is widely used because the data that are required are usually readily available from actual expenditures or estimated costings. The underlying assumption is that the costs of replacement equal the benefits that society derives from the asset. However, the benefits derived from the asset could substantially outweigh the costs of renovation or restoration, in which case the technique will underestimate the value of the asset. The replacement cost is thus a valid measure of economic value only in situations where the remedial work is required to comply with an economically determined environmental standard. Use of the replacement cost assumes that complete replacement or restoration is feasible. In the case of environmental assets this is often not the case. There are also temporal issues as replacement or restoration of an alternative water resource, e.g. a wetland, may not coincide directly with the damage or loss of the original resource. The cost savings method is similar to the replacement cost, but determines the savings in costs made through use of a good or service versus the next best (cheapest) alternative source of the good or service. The method is fairly commonly employed in a number of contexts. For example, the value of using water as a means of transporting goods is measured in terms of the cost savings that result from not transporting the same goods via an alternative means, typically by train. The approach does not allow for the large differences in time costs between different transport modes. The method has also been used to value hydroelectric power generation by estimating the difference between the cost of generating hydroelectric power and the next cheapest alternative method of power generation (e.g. coal-fired). As with replacement costs, the approach equates cost savings with value, and hence can be criticized on the grounds that it implicitly assumes demand will be unresponsive to changes in costs.
Applicability	Replacement cost approaches can be used in situations where there is an alternative relevant market for the good in question, e.g. man-made defences used to replace wetland storm protection.
Data requirements and implementation issues	Replacement cost: ascertain environmental damage and then estimate cost of restoring environment to its original state. Information on replacement costs can be obtained from direct observation of actual spending on restoring damaged assets or from engineering estimates of restoration costs.

Valuation method	Replacement/restoration cost and cost savings (opportunity cost)
Advantages (strengths)	The approach is widely used because it is often easy to find estimates of such costs; robust.
Disadvantages (weaknesses)	Can under/overestimate benefits since cost relates to achieving some agreed environmental standard, or other overall constraint requiring that a certain level of environmental quality is achieved. Data limitations on production cost and alternative production processes. The technique implies various assumptions, for instance, that complete replacement is, in fact, feasible. In general, because of the highlighted potential for confusion between costs and benefits, the replacement cost technique should be used with some care.
Validity	Replacement cost: validity limited to contexts where agreed standards must be met. The approach is valid when it is possible to argue that the remedial work must take place because of some other constraint such as an environmental standard. Replacement will only be economically efficient, however, if the environmental standard was itself economically determined. Otherwise, the approach estimates only the costs of replacement; it is not a technique for benefit estimation.
Value concept compatibility with TEV (incl. non-use)	Does not measure non-use values.
Value measure	Net average value based on market price of replacement; can be used as proxy for marginal value.
Reference	Champ et al (2003)

BENEFITS TRANSFER

It is not always possible for valuation studies to be conducted for all the benefits accruing to wetland values. To get around this benefits transfer is used; in valuation, it is inevitable that not all data will be readily available and budgetary constraints are likely to prohibit extensive collection of primary data. Thus, if a similar project has previously been undertaken elsewhere, estimates of its economic consequences might be usable as an indicator of the appropriate values for the impacts of the new project.

Such an approach has been termed 'benefits transfer' because the estimates of economic benefits are 'transferred' from a site where a study has already been completed to a site of policy interest. Using a benefits transfer approach appropriately will yield significant time and cost savings as compared to the time and resource-intensive process of designing, testing and implementing a new valuation study. The benefits transferred from the study site could have been measured using any of the direct or indirect valuation techniques.

Environmental value transfer is commonly defined as the transposition of monetary environmental values estimated at one site (study site) through market-based or non-market-based economic valuation techniques to another site (policy site). The most important reason for using previous research results in new policy contexts is cost-effectiveness. Applying previous research findings to similar decision situations is a very attractive alternative to expensive and time-consuming original research to quickly inform decision making. However, this technique of 'benefits transfer' is fraught with difficulties and subject to a number of caveats, where any results and recommendations that transpire should explicitly be made conditional on these limitations.

Several necessary conditions should be met to perform effective and efficient benefit transfers (Desvousges et al, 1992).

First, the policy context should be thoroughly defined, including:

- Identifying the extent, magnitude and quantification of expected site or resource impacts from the proposed action.
- Identifying the extent and magnitude of the population that will be affected by the expected site or resource impacts.
- Identifying the data needs of an assessment or analysis, including the type of measure (unit, average, marginal value), the kind of value (use, non-use, total value), and the degree of certainty surrounding the transferred data (i.e. the accuracy and precision of the transferred data).

Second, the study site data should meet certain conditions for critical benefit transfers:

- Studies transferred are based on adequate data, sound economic method, and correct empirical technique (Freeman, 2003).
- The study contains information on the statistical relationship between benefits (costs) and socio-economic characteristics of the affected population.
- The study contains information on the statistical relationship between the benefits (costs) and physical/environmental characteristics of the study site.
- An adequate number of individual studies on a recreation activity for similar sites have been conducted in order to enable credible statistical inferences concerning the applicability of the transferred value(s) to the policy site.

And third, the correspondence between the study site and the policy site should exhibit the following characteristics:

- The environmental resource and the change in the quality (quantity) of the resource at the study site, and the resource and expected change in the resource at the policy site should be similar. This similarity includes the quantifiability of the change and possibly the source of that change.
- The markets for the study site and the policy site are similar, unless there is enough usable information provided by the study on own and substitute prices. Other characteristics should be considered, including similarity of demographic profiles between the two populations and their cultural aspects.
- The conditions and quality of the recreation activity experiences (e.g., intensity, duration and skill requirements) are similar between the study site and the policy site.

Study quality is an important criterion, which can be assessed in a number of ways. Above all, one can look at the internal validity of the study results, that is, the extent to which findings correspond to what is theoretically expected. This internal validity has been extensively researched over the past three decades in valuation studies. Studies should contain sufficient information to assess the validity and reliability of their results. This refers, among others, to the adequate reporting of the estimated WTP function, including the applied statistical techniques and the definition of variables. Desvousges et al (1998) suggest the following criteria for assessing the quality of study site values for use in benefits transfer:

- *scientific soundness* – data collection procedures, empirical methodology, consistency with scientific or economic theory, statistical techniques;
- *relevance* – change in environmental quality, baseline environmental quality, affected services and commodities, site characteristics of affected commodity, duration and timing of effects, exposure path and nature of health risks, socio-economic characteristics of the affected population, property rights;

- *richness in detail* – definition of variables and means, treatment of substitutes, cost of time (in travel cost studies), participation rates ('Extent of market' i.e. number of affected people).

Thus, while benefit transfer provides a quick and cheap alternative to original valuation research, some conditions must be met if it is to provide reliable results. Above all, the local circumstances and conditions in the new decision making context need to be close enough to the ones prevailing in the original research. The risk of obtaining misleading results may be controlled and reduced by integrating more explanatory variables into the transfer. However this also increases the data requirements and the complexity of the analysis. Furthermore, the possibilities of conducting a sound and reliable benefits transfer hinge on the number, quality and diversity of valuation studies available – the larger the better, and the more diverse the existing set of studies is the more likely it is that there will be a primary study close enough to the policy site for results to be transferable.

Meta-analysis enables researchers to identify criteria for valid environmental value transfer or to test the convergent validity of value estimates (for further details on meta-analysis, see Brouwer et al, 1999). In the first case the data set is entirely used to determine the factors which help to significantly explain variances in valuation outcomes. In the second case the data set can be split, for example in two parts, one of which is used for the first purpose and another to test whether the value estimates based on the significant factors fall within the confidence interval of the other half's estimates.

As more information about factors influencing environmental valuation outcomes becomes available, for instance through meta-analysis, transfers across populations and sites seem to become more practicable, using either existing (secondary) information only or supplementing this information with new original (primary) data. The decision on whether to undertake an original study or to use existing value estimates can be considered in terms of the acceptability of errors produced by benefits transfer and the level of precision sought, i.e. the purpose of the study and when transfer errors may be too big for this purpose. It is difficult to say how large the errors can be expected to be when using existing economic value estimates in new decision making contexts. Very little published evidence exists of studies that test the validity of environmental value transfer. In some cases the errors can be very low, in other cases they can be as high as almost five times the value that would have been found if original valuation research was carried out. No distinct differences can be found when comparing transfer errors for contingent valuation and travel cost studies. The acceptability of the error will depend on subjective judgement by the user, the purpose and nature of the evaluation, and the phase of the policy cycle in which the evaluation is carried out.

Problems common to all methods of benefits transfer, in addition to the requirement for good quality studies of similar situations, are the considerable potential for changes in characteristics between different time periods and the inability to value novel changes. As Green et al (1994) point out, the quality of a cost–benefit analysis carried out using transferred benefits estimates will be no better than the quality of the transferred data itself, in the context of the study area to which it is applied. And Garrod and Willis (1994, p23) suggest that, for the UK at least, even careful modification of available benefits estimates would not 'yield transfer estimates which were reliable and robust enough to be used with confidence in policy applications'. Benefits transfer might be more robust if essential scientific variables at different sites, based on ecosystem characteristics and processes as well as socio-economic variables, were considered.

REFERENCES

Bateman, I.J., Carson, R.T., Day, B., Hanemann, W.M., Hanley, N., Hett, T., Jones-Lee, M., Loomes, G., Mourato, S., Ozdemiroglu, E., Pearce, D.W., Sugden, R. and Swanson, J. (2002) *Economic Valuation with Stated Preferences Techniques: A Manual.* Edward Elgar: Cheltenham

Bockstael, N.E. and McConnell, K.E. (2007) *Environmental and Resource Valuation with Revealed Preferences: A Theoretical Guide to Empirical Models.* Springer: Dordrecht, The Netherlands

Brouwer, R., Powe, N.A., Turner, R.K., Bateman, I.J. and Langford, I.H. (1999) 'Public attitudes to contingent valuation and public consultation'. *Environmental Values* 8(3): 325–347

Champ, P., Boyle, K.J. and Brown, T.C. (eds) (2003) *A Primer on Nonmarket Valuation.* Kluwer Academic Publishers: Dordrecht, The Netherlands

Desvousges, W.H., Johnson, F.R., Dunford, R.W., Boyles, K.J., Hudson, S.P. and Wilson, K.N. (1992) *Measuring Non-use Damages Using Contingent Valuation: An Experimental Evaluation of Accuracy.* Research Triangle Institute Monograph 92–1, Research Triangle Park, NC: Research Triangle Institute

Desvousges, W.H., Johnson, F.R. and Banzhaf, H.S. (1998) 'Environmental policy analysis with limited information. Principles and applications of the transfer method'. In Oates, W.E. and Folner, H. (eds) *New Horizons in Environmental Economics.* Edward Elgar: Cheltenham

Dickie, M., Gerking, S. and Agee, M. (1991) 'Health benefits of persistent micropollutant control: The case of stratospheric ozone depletion and skin damage risks'. In Opschoor, J.B. and Pearce, D.W. (eds) *Persistent Pollutants: Economics and Policy.* Kluwer: Dordrecht, The Netherlands

Easter, K.W. and Hearne, R. (1995) 'Water markets and decentralized water resources management: International problems and opportunities'. *Water Resources Bulletin* 31(1): 9–20

Freeman, A.M. III (2003) *The Measurement of Environmental and Resource Values: Theory and Methods.* Resources for the Future: Washington DC

Garrod, G.D. and Willis, K.G. (1994). 'Valuing biodiversity and nature conservation at a local level'. *Biodiversity and Conservation* 3: 555–565

Green, C., Tunstall, S., Garner, J. and Ketteridge, A.M. (1994) 'Benefits transfer: Rivers and coasts'. Paper presented for the CEBG meeting on benefits transfer, HM Treasury. Publication No 231, Flood Hazard Research Centre, Middlesex University

Kanninen, B.J. (2007) *Valuing Environmental Amenities using Stated Choice Studies.* Springer: Dordrecht, The Netherlands

Louviere, J.J., Hensher, D.A. and Swait, J.D. (2000) *Stated Choice Methods, Analysis and Application.* Cambridge University Press: Cambridge

Mitchell, R.C. and Carson, R.T. (1989) *Using Surveys to Value Public Goods: The Contingent Valuation Method.* Resources for the Future, Washington DC

Renzetti, S. (2002) *The Economics of Water Demands.* Kluwer Academic Press: Norwell, MA

Saliba, B.C. and Bush, D.B. (1987) *Water Markets in Theory and Practice: Market Transfers and Public Policy.* Westview Press: Boulder, CO

Young, R. (2005) *Determining the Economic Value of Water: Concepts and Methods.* Resources for the Future, Washington DC

Appendix B

Wetland Ecosystem Services: Overview of Empirical Studies

We now present an overview of empirical studies related to wetland service valuation. The overview is wide-ranging but not comprehensive, and does indicate that valuation techniques have been extensively applied to a large range of wetland ecosystem services. It also indicates that although the economic values are significant, there is nevertheless wide variation across wetland valuation studies. The wide variation found in studies will mean that 'benefits transfer' is fraught with difficulties and subject to a number of caveats, where any results and recommendations that transpire should explicitly be made conditional on these limitations. If a benefits transfer approach is chosen as part of an economic valuation then the main challenge faced is in finding the most appropriate studies to use in the transfer exercise. Further details on the problems and recommendations for undertaking benefits transfer are found in Appendix A.

The overview of studies presented classifies the studies in terms of the service use provided by the wetland wherever possible. Due to the multi-purpose nature of many studies, in many cases it is not possible to specify this precisely, if at all. Hence many of the studies are listed in terms of the more general socio-economic uses and benefits that they consider.

The overview uses the following categories of valuation techniques:

CV = Contingent Valuation

DC = Damage Cost Approach

HP = Hedonic Pricing

MV = Market-based

OM = Optimization Models (Residual imputation or variant)

RC = Replacement Cost Method

TC = Travel Cost

Bibliographic study characteristics

Author(s)	Title	Bibliographical details	Year	Issue addressed in study/general Service-use identification	Valuation
Bateman, I. et al	Recreation and environmental preservation value of the Norfolk Broads: A contingent valuation study	Report to the National Rivers Authority	1992	Average WTP to preserve present landscape.Service-use: habitat, non-use value	CV
Bateman, I.J., I.H. Langford, R.K. Turner, K.G. Willis and G.D. Garrod	Elicitation and truncation effects in Contingent Valuation studies	*Ecological Economics* 2: 161–179	1995	Analysis of methods of eliciting WTP in a CV study of flood protection of a UK wetland	CV
Bergstrom, J.C., J.R. Stoll, J.P. Titre and V.L. Wright	Economic value of wetlands-based recreation	*Ecological Economics* 2: 129–147	1990	Wetlands loss and recreational value Service-use: recreation	CV
Breaux, A., S. Faber and J. Day	Using natural coastal wetlands systems for wastewater treatment: An economic benefit analysis	*Journal of Environmental Management* 44: 285–291	1995	Wetland value for waste treatment use. Service-use: industrial supply	RC

Year of data collection	Measurement unit	Estimated value characteristics: mean/total	Water system: ground water/ surface water	Spatial scale	Country
	UK£ per person per year	Use values: 78–105. Non use values of local - population: 14.7. Non-use values of the rest of UK: 4.8	Broads	Regional	United Kingdom
1991 August, September	UK£/pa		Wetland	Local	United Kingdom
1986– 1987	US$ per user	360	Wetlands	Regional	USA
	US$ per year per firm	a. Value represents annualized cost saving to the firm to the firm a more extensive discharge dispersion system on a 6.2 acre wetlands site: 26700; b. Estimate is wetland's treatment value per acre, including all plants' capitalized cost savings and based on treatment systems with a 25-year lifetime (low estimate): 6231	Wetlands	Local	USA

Bibliographic study characteristics (Cont'd)

Author(s)	Title	Bibliographical details	Year	Issue addressed in study/general Service-use identification	Valuatic
Broadhead, C., J.P. Amigues, B. Desaigues and J. Keith	Riparian Zone Protection: The Use of the Willingness to Accept Format (WTA) in a Contingent Valuation Study	Paper presented at the World Congress of Environmental and Resource Economists in Venice, Italy	1998	In 1997, a study was financed by the French Ministry of Environment to evaluate the costs of preserving riparian habitat on the banks of the Garonne River. The CVM was used to study households that currently own land on the banks of the river. More precisely, a WTA was used to estimate the loss to owners for no longer being able to farm riverbank areas actively. Results of this study are reported and analysed in this paper.	CV
Brouwer, R. and L.H.G. Slangen.	Contingent Valuation of the public benefits of agricultural wildlife management: the case of dutch peat meadow land.	*European Review of Agricultural Economics* 25: 53–72.	1998	To provide a conservative estimate of the public benefits of agricultural wildlife management on Dutch peat meadow land and to provide a monetary estimate of the public benefits of management agreements. Service-use: habitat, rare or endangered species	CV
Cooper, J. and J.B. Loomis	Testing whether waterfowl hunting benefits increase with greater water deliveries to wetlands	*Environmental and Resource Economics* 3(6): 545–561	1993	Impact on recreational waterfowl hunting benefits of an increase in refuge water supplies to levels necessary for biologically optimal refuge management	TC

Year of data collection	Measurement unit	Estimated value characteristics: mean/total	Water system: ground water/ surface water	Spatial scale	Country
1997	FF/ha/year	Mean WTA for programme 1373FF/ha	River	Regional	France
1994	Dutch guilders per year	WTP: South Holland/ Friesland/Limburg/ total:131.4/113.6/64.5/124.5	Ditch	Regional	The Netherlands
1990	US$ per acre-foot of additional water supply	0.93–20.40 (OLS), 0.64–14.05 (Poisson)	Wetlands	Regional	USA

Bibliographic study characteristics

Author(s)	Title	Bibliographical details	Year	Issue addressed in study/general Service-use identification	Valuatic
Cooper, J.C.	Using the Travel Cost Method to link waterfowl hunting to agricultural activities	*Cahiers d'Economie et Sociologie Rurales* 35: 5–26	1995	Impact of contaminated irrigation run-off on waterfowl hunting benefits. Service-use: recreation, agricultural supply	TC
Cordell, H.K. and J.C. Bergstrom	Comparison of recreation use values among alternative reservoir water level management scenarios	*Water Resources Research* 29 (2): 249–258	1993	Recreational benefits of three water-level management alternatives in comparison to other use values (hydropower, flood control, etc.) Service-use: flooding, recreation, hydro power generation	CV
Costanza, R., S.C. Farber and J. Maxwell	Valuation and management of wetland ecosystems,	*Ecological Economics* 1: 335–361	1989	Coastal Wetlands in Louisiana Service-use: commercial fishing	MV
Dalecki, M.G., J.C. Whitehead and G.C.	Sample non-response bias and aggregate	*Journal of Environmental Management* 38: 133–143	1993	Wetland preservation Service-use: wetland habitat	CV

Year of data collection	Measurement unit	Estimated value characteristics: mean/total	Water system: ground water/ surface water	Spatial scale	Country
1988	US$ per hunter day and total for Kesterson	55.41	Wetlands	Regional	USA
1988–1989	US$, per individual (>=12 years old) for access to TVA reservoirs per year	41.70–75.05	Lake (reservoir)	Regional	USA
1983	US$ per acre	a present value of the marginal product of an acre of wetland through production of five commercial fishery products (brown and white shrimp, menhaden, oyster, and blue crab)	Wetlands	Regional	USA
	US$ per acre per year	is reported. 3% was used for discounting: 845; b Estimated value of annual average product of an acre of marsh and open water area is reported. This estimate may overvalue the wetland since average product is generally lower than marginal product, the more appropriate.			
1990	US$/ person/ year	a Individual median WTP estimate for wetland preservation of the first wave	Wetlands	Regional	USA

Bibliographic study characteristics

Author(s)	Title	Bibliographical details	Year	Issue addressed in study/general Service-use identification	Valuatic
Blomquist	benefits in Contingent Valuation: An examination of early, late, and non-respondents.				
Foster, V., I.J. Bateman and D. Harley	Real and hypothetical willingness to pay for environmental preservation: A non-experimental comparison	In *Environmental Valuation, Economic Policy and Sustainability: Recent Advances in Environmental Economics.* Melinda Acutt and Pamela Mason (eds) Northampton, MA: Edward Elgar, pp35–49	1998	Land purchases, species preservation and habitat conservation Service-use: habitat, rare or endangered species	MV
Gren, I.M.	Alternative nitrogen reduction policies in the Malar Region, Sweden	*Ecological Economics* 7(2): 159–172	1993	Denitrification services of wetlands Service-use: habitat	RC

ear of ata ollection	Measurement unit	Estimated value characteristics: mean/total	Water system: ground water/ surface water	Spatial scale	Country
		(response rate = 24%): 24.4; b. Individual median WTP estimate for wetland preservation of the fourth wave (response rate = 67%): 6.54.			
995	UK£ per mailing	a Reported value is the mean donation per mailing to the RSPB fund raiser. The fund raising appeal was for the land purchase of maritime heath habitat on Ramsey Island in 1992. This is the average donation (includes returned and not returned): £1.73/mailing;	Wetlands	National	UK
	UK£	b Reported value is the total value of donations for the RSPB fund raiser. The fund raising appeal was for the protection of reedbed habitat for bittern in 1993: £268,430.			
991	SEK millions (1US$ = SEK 5.8)	a Value is the total cost of restoring wetlands that reduce the load of nitrogen by 1194 tons. Significant cost reduction for nitrogen abatement can be attained through restoring wetlands: 49;	Wetland	Regional	Sweden
	SEK/kg N	b Value is the high-end estimate for the marginal cost of abating 1kg of nitrogen through restoring wetlands. Significant cost reduction for nitrogen abatement can be attained through restoring wetlands.			

Bibliographic study characteristics

Author(s)	Title	Bibliographical details	Year	Issue addressed in study/general Service-use identification	Valuati
Gupta, T.R. and J.H. Foster	Economic criteria for freshwater wetland policy in Massachusetts.	*American Journal of Agricultural Economics* 57(1): 40–45	1975	Service-use: recreation Multiple uses/benefits associated with wetlands (value of wildlife, visual-cultural benefits, water supply, and flood control benefits of wetlands)	DC
Heimlich, R.E.	Costs of an agricultural wetland reserve	*Land Economics* 70(2): 234–46	1994	Wetlands converted from cropland	RC
Klein, R.J.T. and I.J. Bateman	The recreation value of Cley Marshes Nature Reserve: An argument against managed retreat?	*Water and Environmental Management* 12: 280–285	1998	The main aim of this study is to provide an estimate of the recreational value of the Cley Reserve Service-use: recreation, habitat	CV
Kooten, G.C. van	Bioeconomic evaluation of government agricultural programmes on wetland conversion.	*Land Economics* 9(1): 27–38	1993	Wetlands providing migratory waterfowl habitat and recreation opportunities Service-use: agricultural supply	OM
Kosz, M.	Valuing riverside wetlands: The case of the Donau-Auen National Park	*Ecological Economics* 16: 109–127	1996	The aim of this paper is briefly to review the main results of the cost–benefit analysis concerning all the variables that depend	CV

Year of data collection	Measurement unit	Estimated value characteristics: mean/total	Water system: ground water/ surface water	Spatial scale	Country
1972	US$ per acre per year acres: 10;	a Value represents average benefits from flood control flood control b Value represents average benefits from flood control for high quality acres: 80>	Wetlands	Regional	Jordan
1982	US$ per acre	a Value is the high estimate of the marginal costs of 5 million acres of wetland reserve: 1184; b Value is the high estimate of the total average cost (in US$/acre) that minimizes reserve costs for wetland reserve of 1 million acres: 286.	Wetlands	National	USA
1996	A: In UK£ per household per year or per visit. B: In UK£ per party per annum	A: WTP fee (incl. zero-bids, in UK£): 1.58; WTP fee (excl.): 2.22; B: WTP tax (incl.): 48.15; WTP tax (excl.): 62.08	Reserve	Regional	UK
1988	US$ per acre per year	Marginal value of waterfowl habitat as cropland per acre year is reported. Government subsidy of $4.50 per bushel of grain and an average yield of 30 bushels/acre were assumed (land has no livestock value): 37.97.	Wetland	Regional	USA
1993 (June and July)	Austrian Schillings 1993/pa	2a) 919.80; 2b) 329.25; 3a) 694.9; 3b) 122.21; 4a) 689.85; 4b) 69.63	River	Regional	Austria

Bibliographic study characteristics

Author(s)	Title	Bibliographical details	Year	Issue addressed in study/general Service-use identification	Valuati
				on direct anthropocentric use, including energy production with hydroelectric power stations, shipping, groundwater protection, stabilization of the river bed to stop channel erosion, visitors' benefits, forestry, farming, fishing, hunting and the costs of establishing a national park. This was done because there was a plan to build one or more hydroelectric power stations in the area under study, the Donau-Auen. This was operationalized by 4 different development projects: (1) Establishing a national park in all easily available areas (not included in the WTP value (2) Founding a national park in all available areas including private property; concept of hydraulic engineering including extensive measures artificially changing the waterway to avoid further river bed erosion. (3) Construction of a hydroelectric power station near Wolfsthal. (4) Construction of a hydroelectric	

ear of ata ollection	Measurement unit	Estimated value characteristics: mean/total		Water system: ground water/ surface water	Spatial scale	Country

Bibliographic study characteristics

Author(s)	Title	Bibliographical details	Year	Issue addressed in study/general Service-use identification	Valuati
				power station near Wildungsmauer. (The last project is bigger than the third).	
Mannesto, G. and J.B. Loomis	Evaluation of mail and in-person Contingent Value surveys: Results of a study of recreational boaters.	Journal of Environmental Management 32: 177–190	1991	Wetland loss Service-use: recreation	CV
Miyata, Y. and H. Abe	Measuring the effects of flood control project: Hedonic land price approach	Journal of Environmental Management 42: 389–401	1994	Aim is to measure the effects of a flood control project planned for the Chitose River Basin in Japan by evaluating the reduction in expected physical flood damage derived by construction and improvement of flood control facilities Service-use: flooding	HP

Year of data collection	Measurement unit	Estimated value characteristics: mean/total	Water system: ground water/ surface water	Spatial scale	Country
interview data from 9 August to 9 October 1987; mailing data also in this same period	US$ 25% increase or 50% increase of total delta wetlands	1a) 69.80; 1b) 37.12; 1c) 37.85; 2a) 59.27; 2b) 39.47; 2c) 33.14.	Delta Lake Bay	Regional	USA
1990	Yen per km², cm and unit area	The total annual average cost of the flood control project for the Chitose River (in million yen): case 1: project cost/ annual average cost: 0/0; case 2: 96787/4898; case 3: 143225/7247; case 4: 201848/10214; case 5: 267405/13531; case 6: 310366/15705. Total benefit: Ebvetsu: 5032.0/146.3; Chitose: 12499.2/336.0; Eniwa: 24460.3/497.2; Hiroshima: 8191.5/615.9; Nanporo: 7479.2/138.2; Naganuma: 26390.2/288.4; Total: 84052.4/300.5. The corresponding total cost is estimated as 310.4 billion yen and the total estimated benefit computed from the land price variations is 84 billion yen, thus the flood control project under this study may be deemed as a less cost-efficient project.	River basin; catchment	Regional	Japan

Bibliographic study characteristics

Author(s)	Title	Bibliographical details	Year	Issue addressed in study/general Service-use identification	Valuatic
Roberts. L.A. and J.A. Leitch	Economic Valuation of Some Wetland Outputs of Mud Lade, Minnesota, South Dakota	Agricultural Economics Report No 381, Department of Agricultural Economics, North Dakota State University, USA	1997	The purpose of this study was to approximate some economic values of Mud Lake, a managed wetland on the border between Minnesota and South Dakota, to provide information to promote more efficient and effective management of Mud Lake and its wetlands. This is done by evaluating some selected outputs: flood control, water supply, fish and wildlife habitat, recreation and aesthetics, and disamenities to water quality. The DVM was used to evaluate fish and wildlife habitat, recreation, and aesthetics.Water quality was valued by estimating the extra costs of water treatment, flood control by damage prevented, and water supply by estimating a residual return to public wear utilities. Service-use: recreation, flooding	CV
Steever, W.J., M. Callaghan-Perry, A. Searles, T. Stevens and P. Svoboda	Public attitudes and values for wetland conservation in New South Wales, Australia	*Journal of Environmental Management* 54(1): 14	1998	Wetland conservation Service-use: habitat	CV

Year of data collection	Measurement unit	Estimated value characteristics: mean/total	Water system: ground water/ surface water	Spatial scale	Country
1995	US$ per year per acre	Flood control: total: $440; water supply/conservation: $94; WTP regarding fish/wildlife habitat recreation, and aesthetics: 1) $7; 2) $8; 3) $6;	Lake	Regional	USA
1996	Aus$/ person/ year for 5 years	a Value represents median WTP for the pooled sample. Value from the pooled sample omits those respondents who did not express WTP: 100; b Value represents aggregate value for	Wetlands	Regional	Australia

Bibliographic study characteristics

Author(s)	Title	Bibliographical details	Year	Issue addressed in study/general Service-use identification	Valuatic
Stevens, T.H., S. Benin and J.S. Larson	Public attitudes and economic values for wetland preservation in New England	*Wetlands* 15(3): 226–231	1995	Wetlands in New England Service-use: flooding	CV
Whitehead, J.C.	Measuring willingness to pay for wetlands preservation with the Contingent Valuation Method	*Wetlands* 10(2): 187–201	1990	Preservation of a bottomland hardwood forest wetland Service-use: habitat	CV
Whitehead, J.C.	Environment interest group behaviour and self-selection bias in Contingent Valuation mail surveys	*Growth and Change* 22(1): 10–21	1991	Wetland preservation Service-use: habitat	CV

Year of data collection	Measurement unit	Estimated value characteristics: mean/total	Water system: ground water/ surface water	Spatial scale	Country
		wetlands in New South Wales, Australia, assuming a WTP per household of AUS$17.10 and 2.23 million households in the state: 38.			
993	US$ per respondent	a Value is the high end estimate of respondents' yearly WTP to protect New England wetlands that provide flood protection, water supply and pollution control: 80.41; b Value is the low end estimate of respondents' yearly WTP to protect New England wetlands that provide flood protection, water supply and pollution control: 73.89.	Wetlands	Regional	USA
989	US$/ household/ year	Value measures mean WTP for wetland preservation estimated from log-linear form of model: 6.31.	Wetland	Local	USA
989	US$/ person/ year	a Value is the average WTP per person/year in the general sample for the preservation of the Clear Creek wetland area assuming 15% of the general population belongs to an environmental interest group): 4.12; b Value is the average WTP per person/year in the environmental	Wetland	Local	USA

Bibliographic study characteristics

Author(s)	Title	Bibliographical details	Year	Issue addressed in study/general Service-use identification	Valuatic
Willis, K.G.	Valuing non-market wildlife commodities: An evaluation and comparison of benefits and costs	*Applied Economics* 22: 13–30	1990	WTP for the preservation of the current state of the wetlands Service-use: recreation, habitat	CV

ear of ata ollection	Measurement unit	Estimated value characteristics: mean/total	Water system: ground water/ surface water	Spatial scale	Country
		interest group sample for the preservation of the Clear Creek wetland area: 42.83.			
	UK£/ha	a Total use value: 44; b Total non-use value: 807.	Wetlands	Regional	UK

Appendix C

Case Studies Used for Policy Review and Survey

Case study	Country	Region	Ecosystem	Turner et al, 2003 typology	Ecosystem services	Policy relevance	References
1 Ex post							
Working for water/ invasive species removal[1]	South Africa	Africa	Fynbos, thicket, forest, grassland and semi-arid savannah (rangelands) biomes	Type 2: smooth, restoration, (ex post of restoration and ex ante for future conservation)	Water regulation and supply (availability), provision of habitat (invasive species removal)	Dual goals of natural capital restoration and poverty alleviation; linking ecological, economic and social aims; clash of socio-political and ecological priorities? Lack of data and monitoring and valuation. Ecosystem services approach not always explicitly stated but implied.	Van Wilgen et al (2001); (2004); Milton et al (2003); Binns et al (2001); Le Maitre (2002)
UK reforestation programme and forest services	UK	Europe	Temperate forest	Type 1: reforestation	Timber, recreational services, aesthetic values	Designed to help the UK Forest Commission decision making process. Before this, the reforestation programme was based solely on private benefits from timber	Garrod and Willis (1992)

Case study	Country	Region	Ecosystem	Turner et al, 2003 typology	Ecosystem services	Policy relevance	References
						production and so the reforestation was mainly through coniferous trees. The study showed that this was the optimum decision from the private point of view. When social benefits related to recreational services and aesthetic values (measured by the hedonic price method) were taken into account, however, broadleaf trees were the most beneficial option.	
Ecosystem services and green national accounting	Brazil	South America	Tropical forest	Type 2: ex post (for past deforestation costs)/ex ante (for future conservation benefits)	Timber, NTFPs, recreational, global climate regulation, flood control, water regulation, erosion control, option benefits, existence benefits	The work combines green accounting methodology and TEV concept to estimate the economic costs of past deforestation in the Brazilian Amazon. The Net Present Value of the ecosystem services lost exceeds the joint value income of the nine Amazonian states for every year of the study. Even Brazilian national GDP per capita growth of 0.7% pa falls in the Amazon forest 'stock' are included	Torras (2000)

Case study	Country	Region	Ecosystem	Turner et al, 2003 typology	Ecosystem services	Policy relevance	References
Surat Thani (economic value of mangroves and role of community conservation)	Thailand	Asia	Wetlands (mangroves)	Type 4: conversion	Storm protection, shore stabilization, control of soil erosion and flooding, nursery habitat; timber, charcoal, offshore fisheries; eco-tourism; non-use values.	Market and non-market valuation illustrating policy failure in converting mangroves to shrimp aquaculture. Conversion for aquaculture delivered greatest private gains (neglecting external costs). Global benefits (e.g. carbon sequestration) similar for intact and degraded systems. Social benefits almost zero after conversion. TEV of intact mangroves exceeded aquaculture by approx. 70% (Balmford et al, 2002). Consideration of the role of international compensatory transfer to support local conservation strategy.	Sathirathai (1998);(2003); Sathirathai and Barbier (2001); Balmford et al (2002); Turner et al (2003)
Florida Everglades	USA	North America	Wetlands	Type 1 and Type 3: restoration and continued degradation	Water quality and supply, flood protection, provision of habitat and biodiversity, disease control	One of largest natural capital restoration projects in world ($8 billion over 30 years). Illustrates key ecosystem losses in terms of species, discharges, diseases, purification ability. Influence of ES paradigm?	Milon and Scrogin (2006); Schuyt and Brander (2004)

Case study	Country	Region	Ecosystem	Turner et al, 2003 typology	Ecosystem services	Policy relevance	References
Ecosystem service values and land use change	China	Asia	Various: lakes/rivers; cropland; forest; urban; estuaries	Type 1 and Type 2: smooth ex post over developed and developing contexts	Biomes identified in Costanza et al's (1997) ecosystem services valuation model. Most representative biome used as proxy for each land cover category	Multiple services considered and tracking site changes over time; using LANDSAT™ and/or ETM data sets to estimate changes in size of five land-cover/land use categories; used previously published value coefficients (Costanza et al, 1997) to value changes in ecosystem services delivered by each land cover category.	Zhao et al (2003)
Ecosystem service values and land use change (San Antonio)	USA	North America	Rangelands (14,000ha in TX)	Type 1: ex post	Three watersheds looking at relevant biomes identified in Costanza et al (2007)	Land use change 1976–1991 and effect on delivery of ES (using Costanza et al, 1997 coefficients) as well as services values per hectare. Loss in ES due to urbanization over 15 years: $6.49/ha/yr. TEV not estimated as economic benefits from residential and commercial capacity from land use change not valued.	Kreuter et al (2001); Turner et al (2003)
Nordic forests under different	Scandinavia and Finland	Europe	Temperate (boreal) forest	Type 1: ex post	Timber; agriculture; food; raw materials; carbon sequestration;	Comparison of private value of forestland (according to value of timber production)	Hoffren (1997); Holgen et al

Case study	Country	Region	Ecosystem	Turner et al, 2003 typology	Ecosystem services	Policy relevance	References
management regimes					recreation; existence values	to agricultural land (market price); distortion by agricultural subsidies. Contingent valuation showed WTP of $4500–$6500/ha. Question of type of institutional arrangements needed to ensure broad set of forest benefits; preservation possible of highest values use of marginal units of forest.	(2000); Hoen and Winther (1993); Bateman et al (1996); Turner et al (2003)
Converted and conserved wetlands	Canada	North America	Temperate wetlands	Type 3: ex ante/ ex post	Agricultural/production; recreation; nitrogen fixation; water supply; habitat	Economic case in favour of conservation is clear once subsidies have been removed even without inclusion of the full set of environmental services.	Van Vuuren and Roy (1993); Turner et al (2003)
2 Ex ante							
Ream National Park	Cambodia	Asia	Coastal wetlands (mangroves)	Type 2: smooth conservation	Fisheries, firewood, food, medicinal plants, construction materials, carbon sink, prevent saltwater intrusion and coastal erosion, storms and flood protection	Total value, net value and average value/household estimated Justify economic benefits associated with declaring the area a national park. Aimed to show reliance of community livelihoods on park resources and to quantify local opportunity costs of switching from activities that degrade wetland biodiversity.	Emerton (ed) (2005); Emerton et al (2002)

Case study	Country	Region	Ecosystem	Turner et al, 2003 typology	Ecosystem services	Policy relevance	References
Portland Bight Protected Area (PBPA)	Jamaica	North America (Caribbean)	Various: wetlands, forests and marine (integ. terrestrial and marine PA)	Type 2: smooth conservation	Fish/fisheries, wood/(mangrove) forestry, tourism and recreation, coastal protection, carbon fixation, biodiversity/habitat provision	CBA (using NPV, incremental costs and benefits) for establishing PBPA. To illustrate benefits over costs of managing such an area. Results to feed into management plan.	Cesar et al (2000)
Masoala National Park	Madagascar	Africa	Tropical forest	Type 2: smooth conservation	Timber, ecotourism, NTFPs, biodiversity products, watershed protection, carbon conservation	Compares the benefits of conservation with those of alternative uses (logging and agriculture) at local, national and global scales. Conservation offered superior benefits on both local and global scales, but conversion is the most beneficial option from the national point of view. As the country's decisions about national parks are made at this last level, the study calls for the creation of a market for the protection of tropical forests (specifically for mitigating climate change).	Kremen et al (2000)
Ecosystem services vs economic	Brazil	South America	Tropical forest	Type 2: smooth conservation	Timber, NTFPs, water cycling, nutrient cycling, fire protection,	Compares the costs of deforestation (i.e. conservation benefits) with its benefits.	Andersen et al (2002)

Case study	Country	Region	Ecosystem	Turner et al, 2003 typology	Ecosystem services	Policy relevance	References
benefits of conversion (Brazilian Amazon)					watershed protection, tourism, carbon storage, biodiversity protection, recreational value, existence value	Deforestation costs are divided into private, local public and global values. Special attention to double counting leads to discarding nutrient cycling benefits. Deforestation benefits are measured by the impact each deforested hectare has on the rural GDP. Concludes that at the present point deforestation benefits are equivalent to global costs. Suggests that as deforestation advances its global costs are going to rise.	
Kakadu Conservation Zone vs mining profits	Australia	Oceania	Mixed (mostly tropical forest)	Type 1: smooth	Existence values	Was part of a decision making process by the Australian Government about whether to allow the opening of a new mine in Kakadu Conservation Zone or to integrate it into Kakadu National Park. The study was based on contingent valuation surveys and concludes that the conservation benefits to the Australian people were greater than the potential gains from the mining activity.	Carson et al (1994)

Case study	Country	Region	Ecosystem	Turner et al, 2003 typology	Ecosystem services	Policy relevance	References
						The Australian government opted for the conservation of the area (but publicly stated that this decision was based on concerns for aboriginal people).	
Kenyan parks	Kenya	Africa	Savannah	Type 2: smooth	Timber, ecotourism	Compares the conservation benefits from ecotourism and sustainable forestry to the potential returns of agriculture and livestock production. Concludes that on a national level the benefits of alternative activities are higher than those of conservation. Suggests that including global values in the analysis would show that conservation is the global optimum choice. States that this situation is not sustainable in the long run and that the international community should bear part of the costs of conservation.	Norton-Griffiths and Southey (2005)
TEV and opportunity costs in the	Brazil	South America	Tropical forest	Type 2: smooth	Timber, NTFPs, ecotourism, carbon storage, option value	Compares unit TEV of the standing Amazon forest with the rental value of the land.	Seroa da Motta (2005)

Case study	Country	Region	Ecosystem	Turner et al, 2003 typology	Ecosystem services	Policy relevance	References
Brazilian Amazon					(biodiversity), existence value	Argues that this is a better measure of opportunity costs in the region than the land's selling value because of medium-/long-term property rights uncertainties. Concludes that national ecosystem services benefits are usually below opportunity costs and that it is necessary to internalize part of the forest's global external benefits.	
Kala Oya River Basin	Sri Lanka	Asia	Wetlands; traditional 'tank systems' in dry zone landscape	Type 2: smooth, conservation; ex ante:	Water (crops, livestock, domestic); food (plants, fish); plants (ornamental/ ceremonial use); habitat (breeding areas); regulating: (flood mitigation, water purification, nutrient retention)	Economic values articulated supported their inclusion in regional land and water use decision making. Valuation also played an important role in the development of different scenarios for various tank management options which fed into a cost–benefit analysis using both quantitative and qualitative indicators. Value of wetlands in livelihood and biodiversity terms to aid conservation.	Emerton (2005) (author contacted); Vidanage et al (2005)
Dutch Wadden Sea	The Netherlands	Europe	Coastal wetlands, marine	Type 1: debated Type 3	Issue of impacts of gas extraction; multiple services studies	CBA which undermined assumptions of original industry study. Social	Wetten et. al (1999); Schuijt (2003)

Case study	Country	Region	Ecosystem	Turner et al, 2003 typology	Ecosystem services	Policy relevance	References
						cost–benefits and economic arguments fuelled political debate at the time.	
Pantanal	Brazil	South America	Wetlands	Type 2 (local cases of Type 4)	Multiple: regulating; provisioning…	Costanza et al 1997 study re-estimated with more detailed and accurate data at a local level; better understanding of the potential for the people of Pantanal to benefit from environmental stewardship.	Seidl and Moraes (2000); Schuyt and Brander (2004)
Leuser ecosystem and National Park, Northern Sumatra	Indonesia	Asia	Tropical forest	Type 4: potential stepped as under severe threat of deforestation	Water supply, fisheries, flood and drought prevention, agriculture and plantations, hydro-electricity, tourism, biodiversity, carbon sequestration, fire prevention, non-timber forest products and timber	Rainforest decline causing loss of ecosystem services. Study assessed economic consequences of deforestation vs conservation vs selective use. TEV for ecosystem over 30 years calculated under different scenarios. Despite economic benefits of conservation, deforestation continues; largely due to political power of the logging and plantation industries as well as wide dispersion of the main beneficiaries of conservation.	Van Beukering et al (2003)

Case study	Country	Region	Ecosystem	Turner et al, 2003 typology	Ecosystem services	Policy relevance	References
Value of Zambezi wetlands	Southern Africa (Zambia, Zimbabwe, Botswana)	Africa	Wetlands	Type 2	An inventory of production and information services is made for each wetland; study has been limited to the quantification of use values	Wetland values derived from each service are estimated based on market prices. Results show that flood recession agriculture is the main contributor to the TEV of wetlands in the Zambezi basin. Conservative estimate of the total value of the wetlands.	Seyam et al (2001); Emerton and Bos (2004)
Natural assets: boreal forests	Canada	North America	Temperate (boreal) forests	Type 1	Included timber from forests, oil and gas, and hydroelectricity and ecosystem services provided by wetlands and forests such as purifying water, regulating climate and oxygen	Study aimed to begin to identify, inventory and measure the full economic value of the ecological goods and services provided by Canada's boreal region; aimed to give Canadian decision makers a boreal natural capital 'balance sheet' for assessing the sustainability, integrity and full economic value of the boreal region.	Anielski and Wilson (2005)
Value of timber and NTFPs, Selangor	Malaysia	Asia	Tropical forest	Type 2: ex ante	Timber and NTFPs; water supply and regulation; recreation; maintenance of carbon stocks, endangered species	Quantified net marginal benefits of human uses under various management regimes, e.g. comparison of reduced impact and high-intensity logging whereby the latter drew greater private	Kumari (1994); Balmford et al (2002)

Case study	Country	Region	Ecosystem	Turner et al, 2003 typology	Ecosystem services	Policy relevance	References
						benefits but reduced social and global benefits. TEV of sustainable forestry 14% greater than otherwise.	
Mount Cameroon; comparison low-impact logging and stepped land use change	Cameroon	Africa	Tropical forest	Type 2/Type 4	Timber and NFTPs; social benefits such as sedimentation control, flood prevention, carbon storage	Forest conversion delivers higher private benefits. Conversion to palm oil and rubber plantations yielded negative private benefits; Sustainable forestry yielded highest social and global benefits. TEV of sustainable forestry 18% greater than small-scale farming; plantations had a negative TEV.	Yaron (2001); Balmford et al (2002)
Mulanje Mountain valuation study: current and projected use	Malawi	Africa	Tropical forest	Type 2/Type 4	Water regulation; water provision; timber and non-timber products	Effort at identifying and developing ways for conservation of natural resources to pay its own way through natural products industry development. In particular an exploration of whether water could become a 'saleable' product in the Malawi context, through	Hecht (2006)

Case study	Country	Region	Ecosystem	Turner et al, 2003 typology	Ecosystem services	Policy relevance	References
Marshes on the east shore of Lake St. Clair in south-western Ontario	Canada	North America	Wetlands (freshwater marshes)	Type 3: ex ante (possible ex post)	Agricultural yields; hunting; angling; trapping; nursery and habitat	Private and social returns from wetland preservation vs conversion (draining for agricultural purposes). For three marsh types considered, conversion yielded net private benefits, but TEV was 60% greater when wetlands remained intact. PES, and provided information for watershed management.	Van Vuuren and Roy (1993); Balmford et al (2002)
Philippine coral reef destruction	Philippines	Asia	Coral reefs	Type 4: ex ante (after initial ex post)	Tourism and recreation (diving); coastal fishing; habitat; coastal protection	Destructive reef exploitation (e.g. blast fishing) gave high initial benefits but followed by a far lower NPV of sustainable fishing. Social benefits from sustainable use gave TEV 75% greater than destructive fishing.	White and Vogt (2000); Balmford et al (2002)
TEV over alternative land uses	Cameroon, Sri Lanka and Malaysia	Africa and Asia	Tropical forests	Type 2: ex ante	Goods and services location specific; affected by ecosystem attributes, cultural values and extraction and intensity of use	In all studies forest conversion benefits short-term private gains but conservation makes economic sense when social and global	Yaron (2001); Batagoda (2000); Kumari (1994); Turner et al (2003)

Case study	Country	Region	Ecosystem	Turner et al, 2003 typology	Ecosystem services	Policy relevance	References
						benefits accounted for. Conservation strategy requires global community to provide incentives to local communities.	
Changes in TEV under different management scenarios	El Salvador	North America (Central)	Wetlands (mangroves)	Type 4: ex ante	Timber; fuelwood; food/fisheries (artisanal and industrial shrimp and fish); erosion prevention; carbon sequestration benefit	Sustainable Management Option (i.e. felling only mature mangrove trees) delivers estimated NPV of $2344/ha/yr. Actual distribution of local benefits (through mangrove conversion) skewed away from poorest in society.	Gammage (1997); Turner et al (2003)

3 Informing

Case study	Country	Region	Ecosystem	Turner et al, 2003 typology	Ecosystem services	Policy relevance	References
Bhitarkanika mangroves	India	Asia	Wetlands (mangroves)	Type 4: stepped/discrete conversion (ex post)	Storm and coastal protection, cyclone mitigation, flood control, erosion prevention	Economic valuation of cyclone damage to houses, livestock, fisheries. Damage compared across three villages with different levels of protection and ES intact.	Badola and Hussain (2005); (2003)
New Orleans and Hurricane	USA	North America	Wetlands	Type 3; stepped/discrete; conversion	Storm and coastal protection, hurricane mitigation,	Cost of reinstating natural infrastructure, ecosystem restoration – wetlands	Kunreuther and Pauly (2006);

Case study	Country	Region	Ecosystem	Turner et al, 2003 typology	Ecosystem services	Policy relevance	References
Katrina				ex post	flood control, erosion prevention	and coastal systems – to reduce vulnerability. Lessons learned in economic terms to feed into policy/management plans and rebuilding process.	Barbier and Heal (2006); Costanza et al (2006)
Mangroves as tsunami defence	Sri Lanka	Asia	Wetlands (mangroves)	Type 4: stepped/ conversion; ex post	Storm and coastal protection, tsunami defence, flood control, erosion prevention	Effect of degraded/ converted wetlands and mangrove forests in contributing to damage inflicted by tsunami. Implications for rebuilding/ restoring natural defences.	Guebas et al (2005)
Rewarding upland poor for environmental services (RUPES)	Indonesia, Nepal, Philippines	Asia	Tropical and agroforests	Type 2: smooth, conservation, restoration, conversion forming part of policy process	Watershed services (regulation, erosion control), carbon sequestration	Dual goals of environmental/ policy goals of biodiversity conservation and poverty alleviation; payment mechanisms in place to reward upland poor for land management practices; attempts at institutionalization with mixed results. Environmental services approach adopted. Economic valuation only really featured (varying 'success' in 3 of 6 sites).	Kallesioe and Iftikhar (2005); Van Noordwijk (2005); Beria (2005) (contacted)

Case study	Country	Region	Ecosystem	Turner et al, 2003 typology	Ecosystem services	Policy relevance	References
MBI approaches	Australia	Oceania	Various (mainly agricultural landscapes)	Type 1: ex post and ex ante	Biodiversity, carbon, salinity mitigation; water quality and NRM issues	Various case studies piloting MBIs in conservation and land management (NRM); trading mechanisms, auctions and price signals to change behaviour	Coggan et al (2005); Whitten et al (2004)

Notes:
1 Case studies in bold indicate cases where researcher responded to our survey.

Source: B. Fisher et al, 2008.

Bibliography

Abdalla, C. (1994) 'Groundwater values from avoidance cost studies: implications for policy and future research'. *American Journal of Agricultural Economics* 76: 1062–1067

Abdalla, C.W., Roach, B.A. and Epp, D.J. (1992) 'Valuing environmental-quality changes using averting expenditures: An application to groundwater contamination'. *Land Economics* 68(2): 163–169

Adams, W.M., Brockington, D., Dyson, J. and Vira, B. (2003) 'Managing tragedies: Understanding conflict over common pool resources'. *Science* 302(5652): 1915–1916

Aitchson, J. and Ashby, M. (2000) The common lands of Devon: A biological survey, report. Rural Surveys Research Unit, Department for the Environment, Transport and the Regions. www.defra.gov.uk/wildlifecountryside/issues/Common/biosurvey/county reports/devon.pdf

Allen, T. and Starr, T.B. (1982) *Hierarchy: Perspectives for Ecological Complexity*. University of Chicago Press: Chicago

Andrews, J.E., Samways, G., Dennis, P.F. and Maher, B.A. (2000) 'Origin, abundance and storage of organic carbon and sulphur in the Holocene Humber Estuary: Emphasising human impact on storage changes'. In Shennan, I. and Andrews, J. (eds) *Holocene Land–Ocean Interaction and Environmental Change around the North Sea*. Geological Society: London, Special Publications 166: pp145–170

Arrow, K., Solow, R., Schuman, H., Ragner, R. and Portney, P.P. (1994) 'Report to the NOAA Panel on Contingent Valuation'. *US Federal Register* 58(10): 4602–4614

Badola, R. and Hussain, S.A. (2003) 'Valuation of the Bhitarkanika Mangrove ecosystem for ecological security and sustainable resource use'. Study Report. Wildlife Institute of India: Dehra Dun, 101pp

Badola, R. and Hussain, S.A. (2005) 'Valuing ecosystem functions: An empirical study on the storm protection function of Bhitarkanika mangrove ecosystem, India'. *Environmental Conservation* 32 (1): 85–92

Balmford, A., Bruner, A., Cooper, P., Costanza, R., Farber, S., Green, R.E., Jenkins, M., Jefferiss, P., Jessamy, V., Madden, J., Munro, K., Myers, N., Naeem, S., Paavola, J., Rayment, M., Rosendo, S., Roughgarden, J., Trumper, K., Turner, R.K. (2002) 'Economic reasons for conserving wild nature'. *Science* 297: 950–953

Balmford, A., Gaston, K.J., Blyth, S., James, A. and Kapos, V. (2003) 'Global variation in terrestrial conservation costs, conservation benefits, and unmet conservation needs'. *Proceedings of the National Academy of Sciences of the United States of America* 100(3): 1046–1050

Barbier, E.B. (1994) 'Valuing environmental functions: Tropical wetlands'. *Land Economics* 70(2): 155–173

Barbier, E.B. and Sathirathai, S. (2001) 'Valuing mangrove conservation in southern Thailand'. *Contemporary Economic Policy* 19: 109–122

Barbier, E.B., Markandya, A.A. and Pearce, D.W. (1990) 'Environmental sustainability and cost–benefit analysis'. *Environmental Planning* 22(9): 1259–1266

Bateman, I.J., Carson, R.T., Day, B., Hanemann, W.M., Hanley, N., Hett, T., Jones-Lee, M., Loomes, G., Mourato, S., Ozdemiroglu, E., Pearce, D.W., Sugden, R. and Swanson, J. (2002) *Economic Valuation with Stated Preferences Techniques: A Manual*. Edward Elgar: Cheltenham

Bateman, I.J., Day, B.H., Georgiou, S. and Lake, I. (2006) 'The aggregation of environmental benefit values: Welfare measures, distance decay and total WTP'. *Ecological Economics* 60(2): 450–460

Bateman, I.J. and Langford, I. H. (1997) 'Non-users' willingness to pay for a national park: An application and critique of the contingent valuation method'. *Regional Studies* 31(6): 571–582

Bateman, I.J., Langford, I.H. and Rasbash, J. (1999) 'Elicitation effects in contingent valuation studies'. In Bateman, I.J. and Willis, K.G. (eds) *Valuing Environmental Preferences: Theory and Practice of the Contingent Valuation Method in the US, EU, and Developing Countries*. Oxford University Press: Oxford, pp511–539

Bateman, I.J., Langford, I.H., Turner, R.K., Willis, K.G. and Garrod, G.D. (1995) 'Elicitation and truncation effects in Contingent Valuation Studies'. *Ecological Economics* 2: 161–179

Bateman, I.J., Langford, I.H., Willis, K.G., Turner, R.K. and Garrod, G.D. (1993) 'The impacts of changing willingness to pay question format in contingent valuation studies: An analysis of open-ended, iterative bidding and dichotomous choice formats'. GEC Working Paper 93–05, Centre for Social and Economic Research on the Global Environment (CSERGE), University of East Anglia and University College London

Bateman, I.J., Willis, K.G., and Garrod, G.D. (1994) 'Consistency between Contingent Valuation estimates – a comparison of 2 studies of UK National Parks'. *Regional Studies* 28(5): 457–474

Bateman, I.J., Willis, K.G., Garrod, G.D., Doktor, P.P., Langford, I.H. and Turner, R.K. (1992) Recreation and environmental preservation value of the Norfolk Broads: A contingent valuation study. Report to the National Rivers Authority, Environmental Appraisal Group, University of East Anglia, p403

Becker, C.D. (2003) 'Grassroots to grassroots: Why forest preservation was rapid at Loma Alta, Ecuador'. *World Development* 31(1): 163–176

Begon, M., Townsend, C.R. and Harper, J.L. (2005) *Ecology*. Blackwell Publishing: Oxford

Binns, J.A., Illgner, P.M. and Nel, E.L. (2001) 'Water shortage, deforestation and development: South Africa's working for water programme'. *Land Degradation and Development* 12(4): 341–355

Bishop, R.C. (1978) 'Endangered species and uncertainty: The economics of a safe minimum standard'. *American Journal of Agricultural Economics* 60: 10–18

Black and Veatch/Halcrow, (2005) Humber Estuary Flood Defence Strategy: Strategy Development Study Technical Report. Report to the Environment Agency, Leeds

Boadway, R.W. and Bruce, N. (1984) *Welfare Economics*. Basil Blackwell: Oxford

Bockstael, N.E. and McConnell, K.E. (2007) *Environmental and Resource Valuation with Revealed Preferences: A Theoretical Guide to Empirical Models*. Springer: Dordrecht, The Netherlands

Boddington, M.A.B. (1993) 'Financial and economic measurement of environmental factors'. *Journal of the Institute of Water and Environmental Management* 7: 125–133

Boyd, J. (2007) 'Nonmarket benefits of nature: What should be counted in green GDP?' *Ecological Economics* 61(4): 716–723

Boyd, J. and Banzhaf, S. (2007) 'What are ecosystem services? The need for standardized environmental accounting units'. *Ecological Economics* 63(2–3): 616–626

Boyle, K.J. and Bergstrom, J.C. (1992) 'Benefits transfer studies: Myths, pragmatism, and idealism'. *Water Resources Research* 28(3): 657–663

Braden, J.B. and Kolstad, C.D. (1991) *Measuring the Demand for Environmental Quality*. North Holland: Amsterdam

Brander, L.M., Raymond, J.G., Florax, M. and Vermaat, J. (2006) 'The empirics of wetland valuation: A comprehensive summary and a meta-analysis of the literature'. *Environmental and Resource Economics* 33: 223–250

Broads Authority (1997) The strategy and management plan for the Norfolk and Suffolk Broads. February

Brooks, T.M., Mittermeier, R.A., da Fonseca, G.A.B., Gerlach, J., Hoffmann, M., Lamoreux, J.F., Mittermeier, C.G., Pilgrim, J.D. and Rodrigues, A.S.L. (2006) 'Global biodiversity conservation priorities'. *Science* 313(5783): 58–61

Brookshire, D.S., d'Arge, R., Schulze, W. and Thayer, M. (1982) 'Valuing public goods: A comparison of the survey and hedonic approaches'. *American Economic Review* 72(1): 478–88

Brouwer, R. (1998) 'Future research priorities for valid and reliable environmental value transfer'. Global Environmental Change Working Paper 98–28, Centre for Social and Economic Research on the Global Environment (CSERGE), University of East Anglia and University College London

Brouwer, R., Langford, I.H., Bateman, I.J., Crowards, T.C. and Turner, R.K. (1997). 'A meta-analysis of wetland contingent valuation studies'. Global Enviromental Change Working Paper GEC 97–20, Centre for Social and Economic Research on the Global Environment (CSERGE), University of East Anglia and University College London

Brouwer, R., Powe, N.A., Turner, R.K., Bateman, I.J. and Langford, I.H. (1999) 'Public attitudes to contingent valuation and public consultation'. *Environmental Values* 8(3): 325–347

Burbridge, P.R. (1994) 'Integrated planning and management of freshwater habitats, including wetlands'. *Hydrobiologia* 285: 311–322

Burgess, D., Jackson, N., Hadley, D., Turner, K. and Georgiou, S. (2004) 'The Tamar Catchment Study'. Centre for Social and Economic Research on the Global Environment, School of Environmental Sciences, University of East Anglia, Norwich

Burgess, D., Jackson, N., Hadley, D., Turner, K., Georgiou, S. and Day, B. (2008) 'Assessing the value of a scientifically important wetland ecosystem: The case of the Culm Grasslands'. CSERGE Working Paper, Centre for Social and Economic Research on the Global Environment, University of East Anglia, Norwich, (forthcoming)

Caddy, J.F. (1993) 'Towards a comparative evaluation of human impacts on fishery ecosystems of enclosed and semi-enclosed seas'. *Reviews in Fisheries Science* 1: 57–95

Carpenter, S.R., Defries, R., Dietz, T, Mooney, H.A., Polasky, S., Reid, W.V. and Scholes, R.J. (2006) 'Millennium ecosystem assessment: Research needs'. *Science* 31, 4(5797): 257–258

Carson, R.T., Wilks, L. and Imber, D. (1994) 'Valuing the preservation of Australia's Kakadu conservation zone'. *Oxford Economic Papers*, New Series, vol. 46, Special Issue on Environmental Economics, pp727–749

Cesar, H.S.J., Öhman, M.C., Espeut, P. and Honkanen, M. (2000) 'An economic valuation of Portland Bight, Jamaica: An integrated terrestrial and marine protected area'. Working Paper, Institute for Environmental Studies, Free University: Amsterdam

Champ, P., Boyle, K.J. and Brown, T.C. (eds) (2003) *A Primer on Nonmarket Valuation*. Kluwer Academic Publishers: Dordrecht, The Netherlands

Chichilnisky, G. and Heal, G. (1998) 'Economic returns from the biosphere'. *Nature* 391: 629–630

Ciriacy-Wantrup, S.V. (1952) *Resource Conservation: Economics and Policies*. University of California Press: Berkeley

Claridge, G.F. (1991) An Overview of Wetland Values: A Necessary Preliminary to Wise Use. PHPA/AWB Sumatra Wetland Project Report No 7. AWB: Bogor, Indonesia

Clark, E.H. (1985) 'The off-site costs of soil erosion'. *Journal of Soil and Water Conservation* Jan–Feb: 19–21

Colby, B. (1989) 'Estimating the value of water in alternate uses'. *Natural Resources Journal* 29(2): 511–527

Conlan, K. and Rudd, T. (2000) 'Sustainable estuarine development? Cumulative impact study of the Humber'. *Journal of the Chartered Institution of Water and Environmental Management* 14(5): 313–317

Coombes, E.G. (2003) *Habitat Creation and Loss within the Humber Estuary, and the Associated Environmental and Economic Costs and Benefits*. MSc research dissertation, University of East Anglia

Cooper, J.C., Hanemann, M. and Signorello, G. (2002) 'One-and-one-half-bound dichotomous choice contingent valuation'. *Review of Economics and Statistics* 84(4): 742–750

Costanza, R. (1994) 'Three general policies to achieve sustainability'. In Jansson, A.-M., Hammer, M., Folke, C. and Costanza, R. (eds) *Investing in Natural Capital: The Ecological Economics Approach to Sustainability*. Island Press: Washington DC

Costanza, R., d'Arge, R., de Groot, R., Farber, S., Grasso, M., Hannon, B., Limburg, K., Naeem, S., O'Neill, R.V., Paruelo, J., Raskin, R.G., Sutton, P. and van den Belt, M. (1997) 'The value of the world's ecosystem services and natural capital'. *Nature* 387: 253–260

Costanza, R., Farber, C.S. and Maxwell, J. (1989) 'Valuation and management of wetland ecosystems'. *Ecological Economics* 1: 335–361

Cowardin, L.M., Carter, V., Golet, F.C. and LaRoe, E.T. (1979) *Classification of Wetlands and Deepwater Habitats of the United States*. US Fish and Wildlife Service: Washington DC

Crocker, T.D. and Tschirhart, J. (1992) 'Ecosystems, externalities and economics'. *Environment and Resource Economics* 2: 551–567

Crooks, S., Turner, R.K., Pethick, J.S. and Parry, M.L. (2001) 'Managing catchment-coastal floodplains: The need for a UK water and wetlands policy'. Policy Analysis (PA) Working Paper 01–01, Centre for Social and Economic Research on the Global Environment (CSERGE), University of East Anglia and University College London

Crowards, T.M. (1996) 'Addressing uncertainty in project evaluation: The costs and benefits of safe minimum standards'. Global Environmental Change Working Paper GEC 96–04, Centre for Social and Economic Research on the Global Environment (CSERGE), University of East Anglia and University College London

Crowards, T.M. (1997) 'Combining economics, ecology and philosophy: Safe minimum standards of environmental protection'. In O'Connor, M. and Spash, C. (eds) *Valuation and Environment: Principles and Practices*. Edward Elgar: Aldershot, UK

Cummings, R.G., Ganderton, P.T. and McGuckin, T. (1994) 'Substitution effects in CVM values'. *American Journal of Agricultural Economics* 76: 205–214

Daily, G.C. (1997) *Nature's Services: Societal Dependence on Natural Ecosystems*. Island Press: Washington DC

Dasgupta, P. (2002) *Economic Development, Environmental Degradation and the Persistence of Deprivation in Poor Countries*. World Summit on Sustainable Development: Johannesburg

Debinski, D.M. and Holt, R.D. (2000) 'A survey and overview of habitat fragmentation experiments'. *Conservation Biology* 14(2): 342–355

DeBusk, W.F. (1999) *Nitrogen Cycling in Wetlands*. A fact sheet of the Soil and Water Science Department, Florida Co-operative Extension Service, Institute of Food and Agricultural Sciences, University of Florida

DEFRA (Department for Environment, Food and Rural Affairs) (2000) *Flood and Coastal Defence Project Appraisal Guidance: Economic Appraisal*. FCDPAG3

DEFRA (2001) FCDPAG3 Flood and Coastal Defence Project Appraisal Guidance: Economic Appraisal. www.defra.gov.uk/environ/fcd/pubs/pagn/fcdpag3/default.htm

Costanza, R., Mitsch, W.J. and Day, J.W. Jr (2006) 'Creating a sustainable and desirable New Orleans'. *Ecological Engineering* 26(4): 317–320

Dahdouh-Guebas, F., Jayatissa, L.P., Di Nitto D., Bosire J.O., Lo Seen D. and Koedam, N. (2005) 'How effective were mangroves as a defense against the recent tsunami?' *Current Biology* 15(12): 443–447

DEFRA (2004) Agricultural land sales and prices in England Quarterly. Online edition (16 June 2004). http://statistics.defra.gov.uk/esg/statnot/alpxls

Desvousges, W.H., Johnson, F.R., Dunford, R.W., Boyles, K.J., Hudson, S.P. and Wilson, K.N. (1992) *Measuring Non-use Damages Using Contingent Valuation: An Experimental Evaluation of Accuracy*. Research Triangle Institute Monograph 92–1. Research Triangle Institute: Research Triangle Park, NC

Devon Biodiversity Partnership (1998) The Nature of Devon: A Biodiversity Action Plan – Rhôs Pasture. www.devon.gov.uk/biodiversity/pasture.shtml

Dewees, C.M. (1998) 'Effects of individual quota systems on New Zealand and British Columbia fisheries'. *Ecological Applications* 8(1): S133–S138

Diamond, J. (2005). *Collapse: How Societies Choose to Fail or Succeed*. Viking: New York, p592

Dickie, M., Gerking, S. and Agee, M. (1991) 'Health benefits of persistent micropollutant control: The case of stratospheric ozone depletion and skin damage risks'. In Opschoor, J.B. and Pearce, D.W. (eds) *Persistent Pollutants: Economics and Policy*. Kluwer: Dordrecht, The Netherlands

Dillman, D.A. (1978) *Mail and Telephone Surveys: The Total Design Method*. John Wiley: Chichester

Dixon, A.M., Leggett, D.J. and Weight, R.C. (1998) 'Habitat creation opportunities for landward coastal re-alignment: Essex case study'. *Journal of the Chartered Institution of Water and Environmental Management* 12: 107–112

Dixon, J.A. (1989) 'Valuation of mangroves'. *Tropical Coastal Area Management Manila* 4(3): 2–6

Dubourg, W.R. (1997) 'Reflections on the meaning of sustainable development in the water sector'. *Natural Resources Forum* 21(3): 191–200

Easter, K.W. and Hearne, R. (1995) 'Water markets and decentralized water resources management: International problems and opportunities'. *Water Resources Bulletin* 31(1): 9–20

Edwards, A.M.C. and Winn, P.S.J. (2006) 'The Humber Estuary, Eastern England: Strategic planning of flood defences and habitats'. *Marine Pollution Bulletin* 53: 165–174

Emerton, L. and Bos, E. (2004) *Value. Counting Ecosystems as an Economic Part of Water Infrastructure*. IUCN: Gland, Switzerland and Cambridge, UK. 88pp

English Nature (1991) Cornish Culm Grasslands: Botanical survey and conservation assessment 1989/90. English Nature: Truro, UK. www.wildlifetrust.org.uk/cornwall/wow/Reading/culm.htm

English Nature (2001) Sustainable Flood Defence: The Case for Washlands. Report Number 406 English Nature: London

Environment Agency (1997) Broadland flood alleviation strategy: Bank strengthening and erosion protection. Environment Agency: Suffolk

Environment Agency (2000) Planning for Rising Tides: The Humber Estuary Shoreline Management Plan. Environment Agency: London

Environment Agency (2003) Project Appraisal Report: Knottingley Flood Alleviation Scheme, Environment Agency: London

Farber, S. and Costanza, R. (1987) 'The economic value of wetland systems'. *Journal of Environmental Management* 24(1): 41–51

Farnworth, E.G., Tidrick, T.H., Jordan, C.F. and Smathers, W.M. (1981) 'The value of ecosystems: An economic and ecological framework'. *Environmental Conservation* 8: 275–282

Faux, J. and Perry, G.M. (1999) 'Estimating irrigation water value using hedonic price analysis: A case study in Malheur County, Oregon'. *Land Economics* 75(3) 40–452

Ferraro, P.J. and Pattanayak, S.K. (2006) 'Money for nothing? A call for empirical evaluation of biodiversity conservation investments'. *PLoS Biology* 4(4): 482–488

Finnoff, D. and Tschirhart, J. (2003) 'Harvesting in an eight-species ecosystem'. *Journal of Environmental Economics and Management* 45: 589–611

Fisher, A.C. and Krutilla, J.V. (1975) 'Resource conservation, environmental preservation, and the rate of discount'. *Quarterly Journal of Economics* 89: 358–370

Fisher, B. and Christopher, T. (2007) 'Poverty and Biodiversity: Measuring the overlap of human poverty and biodiversity hotspots'. *Ecological Economics* 62: 93–101

Fisher, B. et al (2008) Integrating Ecosystem Services and Economic Theory. *Ecological Applications* (in press)

Folke, C. (1991) 'The societal value of wetland life-support'. In Folke, C. and Kaberger, T. (eds) *Linking the Natural Environment and the Economy: Essays from the Eco-Eco Group*. Kluwer: Dordrecht, The Netherlands

Fordham, M. and Tunstall, S. (1990) *The Trade-Off Between Flood Alleviation and Environmental Values*. Publication given at the joint XII/Middlesex Polytechnic Workshop 'Risk and Environmental Management', Flood Hazard Research Centre, Middlesex Polytechnic

Freeman, A.M. (1982) *Air and Water Pollution Control*. John Wiley: New York

Freeman, A.M. III (2003) *The Measurement of Environmental and Resource Values: Theory and Methods*. Resources for the Future: Washington DC

French, P.W. (2006) 'Managed realignment – the developing story of a comparatively new approach to soft engineering'. *Estuarine, Coastal and Shelf Science* 67(3): 409–423

Garrod, G.D. and Willis, K.G. (1994). 'Valuing biodiversity and nature conservation at a local level'. *Biodiversity and Conservation* 3: 555–565

Georgiou, S., Bateman, I.J., Cole, M. and Hadley, D. (2000) 'Contingent ranking and valuation of river water quality improvements: Testing for scope sensitivity, ordering and distance decay effects'. CSERGE Working Paper GEC 2000–18, Centre for Social and Economic Research on the Global Environment. University of East Anglia: Norwich

Gibbons, D.C. (1986) *The Economic Value of Water*. Resources for the Future: Washington DC

Gosselink, J.G., Odum, E.P. and Pope, R.M. (1974) *The Value of the Tidal Marsh*. Center for Wetland Resources Publ. LSU-SG-74–03, Louisiana State University: Baton Rouge

Gowdy, J. and Erickson, J. (2005) 'Ecological economics at a crossroads'. *Ecological Economics* 53(1): 17–20

Green, C.H. and Penning-Rowsell, E.C. (1986) 'Evaluating the intangible benefits and costs of a flood alleviation proposal'. *Journal of Institution of Water Engineers and Scientists* 40(3): 229–248

Green, C.H. and Penning-Rowsell, E.C. (1989) 'Flooding and the quantification of "Intangibles"'. *Journal of the Institute of Water and Environmental Management* 38: 27–30

Green, C., Tunstall, S., Garner, J. and Ketteridge, A.M. (1994) 'Benefits transfer: Rivers and coasts'. Paper presented for the CEBG meeting on benefits transfer, HM Treasury. Publication No 231, Flood Hazard Research Centre, Middlesex University

Gren, I-M., Folke, C., Turner, R.K. and Bateman, I.J. (1994) 'Primary and secondary values of wetland ecosystems'. *Environmental and Resource Economics* 4: 55–74

Grimble, R. and Chan, M.K. (1995) 'Stakeholder analysis for natural resource management in developing countries'. *Natural Resources Forum* 19(2): 113–124

Gammage, S. (1997) 'Estimating the returns to mangrove conversion: Sustainable management or short term gain?' Environmental Economics Programme. Discussion Paper. DP 97-02, June

Garrod, G.D. and Willis, K.G. (1992) 'Valuing goods' characteristics: An application of the hedonic price method to environmental attributes'. *Journal of Environmental Management* 34: 59–61

Groot, R.S. de Wilson, M.A. and Boumans, R.M.J. (2002) 'A typology for the classification, description and valuation of ecosystem functions, goods and services'. *Ecological Economics* 41: 393–408

Gutrich, J.J. and Hitzhusen, F.J. (2004) 'Assessing the substitutability of mitigation wetlands for natural sites: Estimating restoration lag costs of wetland mitigation'. *Ecological Economics* 28(4): 409–424

Halcrow UK (2000) Humber Estuary Tidal Defences, Urgent Works 1 — Little Humber to Thorngumbald Clough. Engineer's Report prepared for the Environment Agency

Hammack, J. and Brown, G.M. (1974) *Water and Wetlands: Towards Bioeconomic Analysis*. Resources for the Future: Washington DC

Hanley, N.D. (1990) Valuation of environmental effects: Final report – Stage One. Industry Department of Scotland and the Scottish Development Agency

Hanley, N.D. and Craig, S. (1991) 'Wilderness development decisions and the Krutilla–Fisher model: The case of Scotland's Flow country'. *Ecological Economics* 4(2): 145–164

Hanley, N.D. and Spash, C.L. (1993) *Cost–benefit Analysis and the Environment*. Edward Elgar: Aldershot

Hecht, J. (2006) 'Valuing the resources of Mulanje mountain current and projected use under alternate management scenarios'. Occasional Paper No. 14. Community Partnerships For Sustainable Resource Management (COMPASS II)

Hein, L., Van Koppen, K., de Groot, R.S. and van Ierland, E.C. (2006) 'Spatial scales, stakeholders and the valuation of ecosystem services'. *Ecological Economics* 57(2): 209–228

Higgs, A.W. (1992) 'Purley on Thames Flood Alleviation Scheme'. Paper to the Economic Appraisal Group, National Rivers Authority

HM Treasury (1997) *The Green Book Appraisal and Evaluation in Central Government*. The Stationery Office: London

Hocking, S. and McCartney, P. (1999) *An Inventory of Culm Grassland in Cornwall*. Vols. 1 and 2. Cornwall Wildlife Trust: Truro, UK

Holmes, T.P. and Adamowicz, W.L. (2003) 'Attribute-based methods'. In Champ, P.A., Boyle, K.J. and Brown, T.C. (eds) *A Primer on Non-market Valuation*. Kluwer Academic Publishing: Dordrecht, The Netherlands

Holmes, T.P., Bergstrom, J.C., Huszar, E., Kask, S.B. and Orr, F. III (2004) 'Contingent valuation, net marginal benefits, and the scale of riparian ecosystem restoration'. *Ecological Economics* 49(1): 19–20

Holway, J.M. and Burby, R.J. (1990) 'The effects of floodplain development controls on residential land values'. *Land Economics* 66(3): 259–271

Hueting, R. (1980) *New Scarcity and Economic Growth*. North Holland Publishing Company: Amsterdam

Jickells, T., Andrews, J., Samways, G., Sanders, R., Malcolm, S., Sivyer, D., Parker, R., Nedwell, D., Trimmer, M. and Ridgway, J. (2000) 'Nutrient fluxes through the Humber Estuary: Past, present and future'. *Ambio* 29(3): 130–135

Jordan, J.L. and Elnagheeb, A.B. (1993) 'Willingness to pay for improvements in drinking water quality'. *Water Resources Research* 29(2): 237–245

Kahneman, D. and Knetsch, J. (1992) 'Valuing public goods: The purchase of moral satisfaction'. *Journal of Environmental Economics and Management* 22(1): 57–70

Kallesoe, M. and Iftikhar, U. (2005) 'Conceptual framework for economic valuation of environmental services in southeast Asia for the RUPES program'. RUPES Online Report

Kanninen, B.J. (2007) *Valuing Environmental Amenities using Stated Choice Studies*. Springer: Dordrecht, The Netherlands

King, A.W. (1993) 'Considerations of scale and hierarchy'. In Woodley, S., Kay, J. and Francis, G. (eds) *Ecological Integrity and the Management of Ecosystems*. St Lucie Press: Ottawa

King, D.M., Wainger, L.A., Bartoldus, C.C. and Wakely, J.S. (2000) Expanding Wetland Assessment Procedures: Linking Indices of Wetland Function with Services and Values. ERDC/EL TR-00–17, US Army Engineer Research and Development Center: Vicksburg, MS

Kosz, M. (1996) 'Valuing riverside wetlands: The case of the "Donau-Auen" National Park'. *Ecological Economics* 16: 109–127

Kremen, C. et al (2000) 'Economic incentives for rain forest conservation across scales'. *Science* 288: 1828–1832

Kreuter, U.P, Harris, H.G., Matlock, M.D., Lacey, R.E. (2001) 'Change in ecosystem service values in the San Antonio area, Texas'. *Ecological Economics* 39: 333–346

Kumari, K. (1994) 'Sustainable forest management in peninsular Malaysia: Towards a total economic valuation approach'. Thesis, University of East Anglia, Norwich

Kunreuther, H. and Pauly, M. (2006) 'Rules rather than discretion: Lessons from Hurricane Katrina'. NBER Working Paper No. 12503. National Bureau of Economic Research: Massachusetts

Krutilla, J.V. and Fisher, A.C. (1985) *The Economics of Natural Environments.* Johns Hopkins University Press: Baltimore

Lahti, D.C. (2001) 'The "edge effect on nest predation" hypothesis after 20 years'. *Biological Conservation* 99: 365–374

Langford, I.H. and Bateman, I.J. (1999) 'Multilevel modelling and contingent valuation'. In Bateman, I.J. and Willis, K.G. (eds) *Valuing Environmental Preferences: Theory and Practice of the Contingent Valuation Method in the US, EU, and Developing Countries.* Oxford University Press: Oxford, pp442–459

Langford, I.H., Bateman, I.J. and Langford, H.D. (1996) 'A multilevel modeling approach to triple-bounded dichotomous choice contingent valuation'. *Environmental and Resource Economics* 7(3): 197–211

Lareau, T.J. and Rae, D.A. (1989) 'Valuing WTP for diesel odor reductions: An application of the contingent ranking technique'. *Southern Economic Journal* 55(3): 728–742

Larson, L.A. (1986) 'Wetland and flooding: Assessing hydrologic functions'. In Kusler, J.A. and Riexinger, P. (eds) *Proceedings of the National Wetland Assessment Symposium,* Association of State Wetland Managers, Portland, ME, 17–20 June 1985

Ledoux, L., Beaumont, N., Cave, R., and Turner, R.K. (2005) 'Scenarios for integrated river catchment and coastal zone management'. *Regional Environmental Change* 5: 82–96

Ledoux, L., Brouwer, R. and Turner, R.K. (2000) Economic Appraisal of the Broads Fen Harvester Project. Final Report of the Life 97 ENV/UK/000511 New Wetland Harvests Final Technical Report

Ledoux, L., Cave, R. and Turner, R.K. (2002) 'The use of scenarios in integrated environmental assessment of coastal-catchment zones: The Humber Estuary, UK'. *Land-Ocean Interactions in the Coastal Zone (LOICZ) Newsletter,* 23

Le Maitre, D.C., van Wilgen, B.W., Gelderblom, C.M., Bailey, C., Chapman, R.A. and Nel, J.A. (2002) 'Invasive alien trees and water resources in South Africa: Case studies of the costs and benefits of management'. *Forest Ecology and Management* 160: 143–159

Limburg, K.E., O'Neill, R.V. and Costanza, R. (2002) 'Complex systems and valuation'. *Ecological Economics* 41(3): 409–420

Loomis, J.B. (1987a) 'The economic value of instream flow: Methodology and benefit estimates for optimum flows'. *Journal of Environmental Management* 24: 169–179

Loomis, J.B. (1987b) 'Balancing public trust resources of Mono Lake and Los Angeles' water right: An economic approach'. *Water Resources Research* 23(8): 1449–1456

Louviere, J.J., Hensher, D.A. and Swait, J.D. (2000) *Stated Choice Methods, Analysis and Application.* Cambridge University Press: Cambridge

Maltby, E., Holdgate, M., Acreman, M. and Weir, A. (1999) *Ecosystem Management: Questions for Science and Society.* Royal Holloway Institute for Environmental Research: Virginia Water, UK

Maltby, E. and Immirzi, C.P. (1993) 'Carbon dynamics in peatlands and other wetland soils: Regional and global perspectives'. *Chemosphere* 27(6): 999–1023

Margat, W., Viscusi, W. and Huber, J. (1987) 'Paired comparisons and contingent valuation approaches to morbidity risk valuation'. *Journal of Environmental Economics and Management* 15

Marin, A. and Psacharopoulos, G. (1982) 'The reward for risk in the labor-market: Evidence from the United Kingdom and a reconciliation with other studies'. *Journal of Political Economy* 90(4): 827–853

Markandya, A. and Pearce, D.W. (1988) 'Environmental considerations and the choice of discount rates in developing countries'. Environment Department Working Paper No 3. World Bank: Washington DC

Milon, J.W. and Scrogin, D. (2006) 'Latent preferences and valuation of wetland ecosystem restoration'. *Ecological Economics* 56: 162–175

Milton, S.J., Dean, W.R.J., Richardson, D.M. (2003) 'Economic incentives for restoring natural capital in southern African rangelands'. *Frontiers in Ecology and the Environment* 1(5): 247–254

Mitchell, B. (1990) *Integrated Water Management: International Experiences and Perspectives*. Belhaven Press: London

Mitchell, R.C. and Carson, R.T. (1989) *Using Surveys to Value Public Goods: The Contingent Valuation Method*. Resources for the Future: Washington DC

Mitsch, W.J. and Gosselink, J.G. (2000) *Wetlands*. 3rd edition. Wiley: New York

Möller, I., Spencer, T., French, J.R., Leggett D.J. and Dixon, M. (2001) 'The sea-defence values of salt marshes: Field evidence from north Norfolk'. *Journal of the Chartered Institution of Water and Environmental Management* 15 (2): 109–116

Morey, E.R. (1984) 'The choice of ski areas: Estimation of a generalised CES preference ordering with characteristics'. *Review of Economics and Statistics* 66: 584–590

Morey, E.R. (1985) 'Characteristics, consumer surplus, and new activities: A proposed ski area'. *Journal of Public Economics* 26(2): 221–236

Morgan, M.G. and Henrion, M. (1990) *Uncertainty: A Guide to Dealing with Uncertainty in Quantitative Risks and Policy Analysis*. Cambridge University Press: Cambridge

Moss, B. (1998) 'The E numbers of eutrophication: Errors, ecosystem effects, economics, eventualities, environment and education'. *Water Science Technology* 37(3): 75–84

Naeser, R.B. and Bennett, L.L. (1998) 'The cost of noncompliance: The economic value of water in the Middle Arkansas river valley'. *Natural Resources Journal* 38(3): 445–463

Naidoo, R. and Ricketts, T.H. (2006) 'Mapping the economic costs and benefits of conservation'. *PloS Biology* 4(11): 2153–2164

National Research Council (1997) *Valuing Groundwater: Economic Concepts and Approaches*. Committee on Valuing Groundwater; Water Science and Technology Board; Commission on Geosciences, Environment and Resources; National Research Council. National Academy Press: Washington DC

National Rivers Authority (1992) A flood alleviation strategy for Broadland: Final report annex four – Cost–Benefit Studies. NRA, Anglian Region: Peterborough

N'Jai, A., Tapsell, S.M., Taylor, D., Thompson, P.M., Witts, R.C., Parker, D.J. and Penning-Rowsell, E.C. (1990) Flood Loss Assessment Information Report. Flood Hazard Research Centre, Middlesex University, UK

Norton, B.G. (1986) *Towards Unity Among Environmentalists*. Oxford University Press: Oxford

Norton-Griffiths, M. and Southey, C. (1995) 'The opportunity costs of biodiversity conservation in Kenya'. *Ecological Economics* 12(2): 125–139

O'Neil, J. (1997) 'Managing without prices: The monetary valuation of biodiversity'. *Ambio* 26: 546–550

O'Riordan, T., Andrews, J.E., Samways, G. and Clayton, K. (2000) 'Coastal processes and management'. In O'Riordan, T. (ed) *Environmental Science for Environmental Management* 2nd edition. Prentice Hall: Harlow, UK, pp243–266

O'Riordan, T. and Ward, R. (1997) 'Building trust in shoreline management: Creating participatory consultation in shoreline management plans'. *Land Use Policy* 14(4): 257–276

Ostrom, E., Burger, J., Field, C.B., Norgaard, R.B. and Policansky, D. (1999) 'Sustainability – Revisiting the commons: Local lessons, global challenges'. *Science*, 284(5412): 278–282

Pagiola, S., Arcenas, A. and Platais, G. (2005) 'Can payments for environmental services help reduce poverty? An exploration of the issues and the evidence to date from Latin America'. *World Development* 33(2): 237–253

Parkes, D. (2003) 'Storage and cycling of organic carbon and nutrients in Holocene coastal sediments'. PhD thesis, UEA, Norwich

Pearce, D.W. (2003) 'The social cost of carbon and its policy implications'. *Oxford Review of Economic Policy* 19: 362–384

Pearce, D.W., Markandya, A. and Barbier, E.B. (1989) *Blueprint for a Green Economy*. Earthscan: London

Pearce, D.W. and Turner, R.K. (1990) *Economics of Natural Resources and the Environment*. Harvester Wheatsheaf: London

Penning-Rowsell, E.C., Johnson, C., Tunstall, S., Tapsell, S., Morris, J., Chatterton, J. and Green, C. (2005) *The Benefits of Flood and Coastal Risk Management: A Handbook of Assessment Techniques*. Middlesex University Press: London

Pethick, J. (2001) 'Coastal management and sea-level rise'. *Catena* 42: 307–322

Pethick, J. (2002) 'Estuarine and tidal wetland restoration in the United Kingdom: Policy versus practice'. *Restoration Ecology* 10(3): 431–437

Pilcher, R., Burston, P. and Davis, R. (2002) *Seas of Change*. RSPB report

Poe, G. (1998) 'Valuation of groundwater quality using a contingent valuation-damage functions approach'. *Water Resources Research* 34(12): 3627–3633

Ponting, C. (1993) *A Green History of the World*. Penguin Books: London

Proctor, W., Cork, S., Langridge, J., Langston, A., Abel, N., Howden, M., Anderies, M., Parry, R. and Shelton, D. (2002) *Assessing Ecosystem Services In Australia*. Sustainable Ecosystems, Commonwealth Scientific and Industrial Research Organisation (CSIRO). 7th Biennial Conference of the International Society for Ecological Economics, Sousse, Tunisia, 6–9 March

Proctor, W., Comerford, E., Hattfield Dodds, S., Stauffacher, M. and Wilkinson S. (2007) *Motivating Change in the Catchment: A Guide to Revegetation Design and Incentives for Catchment Management Bodies*.

Reed, D.J., Spencer, T., Murray, A.L., French, J.R. and Leonard, L. (1999) 'Marsh surface sediment deposition and the role of tidal creeks: implications for created and managed coastal marshes'. *Journal of Coastal Conservation* 5: 81–90

Renwick, A., Bull, A.S. and Petty, J.N. (2002) 'Economic, biological and policy constraints on the adoption of carbon farming in temperate regions'. *Philosophical*

Transactions of the Regional Society of London, Series A – Mathematical, Physical and Engineering Sciences 366(1797): 1721–1740

Renzetti, S. (2002) *The Economics of Water Demands*. Kluwer Academic Press: Norwell, MA

RPA (1998) The Environmental Costs and Benefits of Water Resources. Report prepared for the Environment Agency

Ruttan, V. (1965) *The Economic Demand for Irrigated Acreage: New Methodology and Some Preliminary Projections, 1954–1980*. Resources for the Future: Baltimore

Sagoff, M. (1988) *The Economy of the Earth*. Cambridge University Press: Cambridge

Sagoff, M. (2004) *Price, Principle and the Environment*. Cambridge University Press: Cambridge

Saliba, B.C. and Bush, D.B. (1987) *Water Markets in Theory and Practice: Market Transfers and Public Policy*. Westview Press: Boulder, CO

Salzman, J. and Ruhl, J. (2006) 'No net loss: Instrument choice in wetlands protection'. In Freeman, J. and Kolstad, C. (eds) *Moving to Markets in Environmental Regulation: Twenty Years of Experience*. Oxford University Press: Oxford

Sather, J.H. and Smith, R.D. (1984) An Overview of Major Wetland Functions and Values. FWS/OBS-84/18, Fish and Wildlife Service: US Dept of the Interior

Sathirathai, S. (1998) 'Economic valuation of mangroves and the roles of local communities in the conservation of natural resources: Case study of Surat Thani, south of Thailand'. Unpublished report, Economy and Environment Program for Southeast Asia, Singapore

Saunders, D.A., Hobbs, R.J. and Margules, C.R. (1991) 'Biological consequences of ecosystem fragmentation: A review'. *Conservation Biology* 5: 18–32

Saunders, G. (2003) Culm Grassland: A Review and Vision to the Year 2013. A report on behalf of Devon Wildlife Trust for English Nature

Schuijt, K. (2003) 'Valuation of water: The process of economic valuation of ecosystems in water management'. PhD dissertation, Erasmus University: Rotterdam

Schuyt, K. and Brander, L.M. (2004) *Economic Values of Global Wetlands*. WWF-International: Gland, Switzerland

Seidl, A. and Moraes, A.S. (2000) 'Global valuation of ecosystem services: Application to the Pantanal da Nhecolandia, Brazil'. *Ecological Economics* 33: 1–6

Seroa Da Motta, R. (2005) 'Custos e beneficios do desmatamento na Amazônia'. *Ciencia e Ambiente* 32: 73–84

Seyam, I.M., Hoekstra, A.Y., Ngabirano, G.S. and Savenije, H.H.G. (2001) 'The value of freshwater wetlands in the Zambezi basin'. *Value of Water Research Report Series* No. 7. Delft, The Netherlands

Smith, V.K. (1992) 'Arbitrary values, good causes, and premature verdicts'. *Journal of Environmental and Resource Economics* 22(1): 71–89

Smith, V.K. and Desvousges, W.H. (1986) *Measuring Water Quality Benefits*. Kluwer-Nijhoff Publishing: Boston

Smith, V.K. and Kaoru, Y. (1990) 'Signals or noise? Explaining the variation in recreation benefit estimates'. *American Journal of Agricultural Economics* 72(2): 419–433

Sorg, C.F. and Loomis, J.B. (1984) Empirical Estimates of Amenity Forest Values: A Comparative Review. General Technical Report, RM-107, Rocky Mountain Forest and Range Experiment Station, Forest Service, USDA: Fort Collins, CO

Steele, J.H (1991) 'Marine functional diversity'. *Bioscience* 41: 470–474

Thaler, R. (1984) 'Toward a positive theory of consumer choice'. *Journal of Economic Behaviour and Organisation* 1: 29–60

Tobin, G.A. and Newton, T.G. (1986) 'A theoretical framework of flood induced changes in urban land values'. *Water Resources Bulletin* 22(1): 67–71

Tol, R.S.J. (2005) 'The marginal damage costs of carbon dioxide emissions: An assessment of the uncertainties'. *Energy Policy* 33: 2064–2074

Torras, M. (2000) 'The total economic value of Amazonia deforestation, 1978–1993'. *Ecological Economics* 33: 283–297

Tunstall, S.M., Tapsell, S.M. and Fordham, M. (1994) Public Perception of Rivers and Flood Defence: Final Report. R&D Note 444. National Rivers Authority: Bristol

Turner, R.K. (1993) *Sustainable Environmental Economics and Management: Principles and Practice*. Belhaven Press: London and New York

Turner, R.K. (2000) 'Integrating natural and socioeconomic science in coastal management'. *Journal of Marine Sciences* 25: 447–460

Turner, R.K. (2005) 'Integrated environmental assessment and coastal futures'. In Vermaat, J., Bouwer, L., Turner, R.K. and Salomons W. (eds) *Managing European Coasts: Past, Present and Future*. Springer: Berlin

Turner, R.K., Adger, W.N. and Brouwer, R. (1998) 'Ecosystem services value, research needs and policy relevance: A commentary'. *Ecological Economics* 25(1): 61–65

Turner, R.K. and Brooke, J. (1988) 'Management and valuation of an environmentally sensitive area: Norfolk Broadland, England, case study'. *Environmental Management* 12(2): 203–207

Turner, R.K., Burgess, D., Hadley, D., Coombes, E. and Jackson, N. (2007) 'A cost–benefit appraisal of coastal managed realignment policy'. *Global Environmental Change* 17: 397–407

Turner, R.K., Dent, D. and Hey, R.D. (1983) 'Valuation of the environmental impact of wetland flood protection and drainage schemes'. *Environment and Planning A*, 15: 871–888

Turner, R.K., Doktor, P.P. and Adger, W.N. (1995) 'Assessing the costs and benefits of sea level rise'. *Environment and Planning A* 27: 1777–1796

Turner, R.K., Paavola, J., Cooper, P., Farber, S., Jessamy, V. and Georgiou, S. (2003) 'Valuing nature: Lessons learned and future research directions'. *Ecological Economics* 46(1): 493–510

Turner, R.K. and Pearce, D.W. (1993) 'Sustainable economic development: Economic and ethical principles'. In Barbier, E.B. (ed) *Economics and Ecology: New Frontiers and Sustainable Development*. Chapman and Hall: London

Turner, R.K., van den Bergh, J.C.J.M., Berendregt, A. and Maltby, E. (1997) 'Ecological-economic analysis of wetlands: Science and social science integration'. In Soderquist, T. (ed) *Wetlands: Landscape and Institutional Perspectives*. Proceedings of the Fourth Workshop of the Global Wetlands Economics Network (GWEN). Beijer International Institute of Ecological Economics, The Royal Swedish Academy of Sciences: Stockholm, Sweden, 16–17 November

Turner, R.K., van den Bergh, J.C.J.M. and Brouwer, R. (eds) (2003) *Managing Wetlands: An Ecological Economics Approach*. Edward Elgar: Cheltenham

UK Census (2001) Office of National Statistics, HM Government, www.statistics.gov.uk/census/default.asp

UN (2005) *Millennium Ecosystem Assessment*. Island Press: Washington DC

US Environmental Protection Agency (1985) *Costs and Benefits of Reducing Lead in Gasoline: Final Regulatory Impact Analysis*. EPA-230-05-85-006: Washington DC

van Beukering, P.J.H., Herman Cesar, S.J., Janssen, M.A. (2003) 'Economic valuation of the Leuser National Park on Sumatra, Indonesia'. *Ecological Economics* 44: 43–62

van Noordwijk, M. (2005) *RUPES Typology of Environmental Service Worthy of Reward*. World Agroforestry Centre (ICRAF): Bogor, Indonesia

van Vuuren, W. and Roy, P. (1993) 'Private and social returns from wetland preservation versus those from wetland conversion to agriculture'. *Ecological Economics* 8: 289

van Wilgen, B.W., de Wit, M.P., Anderson, H.J., Le Maitre, D.C., Kotze, I.M., Ndala, S., Brown, B. and Rapholo, M.B. (2004) 'Costs and benefits of biological control of invasive alien plants: Case studies from South Africa'. *South African Journal of Science* 100: 113–122

van Wilgen, B.W., Le Maitre, D.C. et al (1998) 'Ecosystem services, efficiency, sustainability and equity: South Africa's Working for Water Programme'. *Trends in Ecology and Evolution* 13(9): 378

Wallace, K.J. (2007) 'Classification of ecosystem services: Problems and solutions'. *Biological Conservation* 139: 235–246

Weatherhead, E.K. and Knox, J.W. (2000) 'Predicting and mapping the future demand for irrigation water in England and Wales'. *Agricultural Water Management* 43(2) 203–218

Weitzman, M. L. (2001) 'Gamma discounting'. *American Economic Review* 91: 260–271

Wetten, J. van, Joordens, J., Dorp, M. van and Bijvoet, L. (1999) *De Schaduwkant van Waddengas*. AIDEnvironment: Amsterdam

West, J.J. and Dowlatabadi, H. (1999) 'Assessing economic impacts of sea level rise'. In Downing, T.E., Olsthoorn, A.A. and Tol, R. (eds) *Climate Change and Risk*. Routledge: London, pp205–220

Whigham, D.F. (1999) 'Ecological issues related to wetland preservation, restoration, creation and assessment'. *Science of the Total Environment* 240(1–3): 31–40

White, A and Vogt, H.P. (2000) 'Philippine coral reefs under threat: Lessons learned after 25 years of community-based reef conservation'. *Marine Pollution Bulletin* 40: 537–550

Whitten, S., Bennett, J., Moss, W., Handley, M. and Phillips, W. (2002) 'Incentive measures for conserving freshwater ecosystems. Review and recommendations for Australian policy makers'. Environment Australia

Whitten, S.M., Coggan, A., Reeson, A. and Gorddard, R. (2007) 'Putting theory into practice: Market failure and market based instruments (MBIs)'. Working Paper 2 in the Socio-Economics and the Environment in Discussion CSIRO Working Paper Series Number 2007-02, May

Wigley, T.M.L. and Raper, S.C.B. (1993) 'Future changes in global mean temperature and sea level'. In Warrick, R.A., Barrow, E.M. and Wigley, T.M.L. (eds) *Climate and Sea Level Change: Observations, Projections and Implications*. Cambridge University Press: Cambridge

Willis, K.G. and Benson, J.F. (1988) 'A comparison of user benefits and costs of nature conservation at three nature reserves'. *Regional Studies* 22: 417–28

Winn, P.J.S., Young, R.M. and Edwards, A.M.C. (2003). 'Planning for the rising tides: The Humber Estuary Shoreline Management Plan'. *The Science of the Total Environment* 314–316: 13–30

Woodward, R.T. and Wui, Y-S. (2001) 'The economic value of wetland services: A meta-analysis'. *Ecological Economics* 37: 257–270

Yaron G. (1999) 'Forest, plantation crops or small-scale agriculture? An economic analysis of alternative land use options in the Mount Cameroon area'. CSERGE Working Paper GEC 99-16. GY Associates: Herts, UK

Yaron, G., (2001) 'Forest plantation crops or small-scale agriculture? An economic analysis of alternative land use options in the Mount Cameroon area'. *Journal of Environmental Planning and Management* 44(1): 85

Yohe, G. and Neumann, J. (1997) 'Planning for sea level rise and shore protection under climate uncertainty'. *Climatic Change* 37(1): 243–270

Yohe, G., Neumann, J. and Ameden, H. (1995) 'Assessing the economic cost of greenhouse-induced sea level rise: Methods and application in support of a national survey'. *Journal of Environmental Economics and Management* 29(3): S78-S97 Part 2 Suppl. S

Young, R. (2005) *Determining the Economic Value of Water: Concepts and Methods.* Resources for the Future: Washington DC

Young, R.A. (1996) 'Measuring economic benefits for water investments and policies'. World Bank Technical Paper No 338

Young, R.A. and Gray, S.L. (1972) Economic Value of Water: Concepts and Empirical Estimates. Technical Report to the National Water Commission. NTIS no. PB210356. National Technical Information Service: Springfield, VA, March

Zhao, B., Kreuter, U., Lia, B., Ma, Z., Chena, J. and Nakagoshi, N. (2004) 'An ecosystem service value assessment of land-use change on Chongming Island, China'. *Land Use Policy* 21: 139–148

Index